Russian Flag
Over Hawaii

**The young American suffered for weeks in
the dungeon of the fort in the Kingdom of
"Atooie," as Captain Cook had named
the island of Kaua'i.**

RUSSIAN FLAG
OVER HAWAII

The Mission of Jeffery Tolamy

a novel by

DARWIN TEILHET

MUTUAL PUBLISHING PAPERBACK SERIES
TALES OF THE PACIFIC
HONOLULU · HAWAII

Printed in Australia by
The Dominion Press-Hedges & Bell, Victoria, 1986.

Cover design by Bill Fong, The Art Directors.

Cover painting by Guy Buffet, courtesy of Hawaii State
     Foundation on Culture and the Arts.
     "Russian Fort on the Waimea River, Kaua'i, 1816."

     ISBN 0-935180- 28-1

**THIS BOOK CONTAINS THE COMPLETE TEXT
OF THE ORIGINAL HARDBOUND EDITION**

To W. S., and M. S., with gratitude

1. Early on the morning of April 22, 1816, one hundred and sixty-five days out of Baltimore, Jeffery first heard the cry from the deck in his sleep. He was out of the bunk and groping for his clothes before he was fully awake. The cry came again, "Land to starboard!"

When he ran on deck the schooner, *Clymestre*, was swathed in the pale mist of early morning. Captain Sam Crowell said there was land somewhere beyond; twice they had caught glimpses of it; they would sight it again as soon as the wind thinned off the mist. For an hour the ship slid through green swells, the sun edging higher. Suddenly, within the space of a few minutes, the mist lifted like a curtain, and there was the land, less than half a league away.

Jeffery stared at the sight of the huge tumbled mass of cliff lifting in the distance, mountains rolling away behind it. He could not quite believe the voyage was finally ending.

From behind him Sam Crowell's big hand gripped Jeffery's shoulder. "That's Diamond Hill, over there. Could you ask for any better arrival? A clear view of the harbor, with mist hiding us till we got here, and no British frigate in sight."

As the schooner rounded the point of Diamond Hill, the whole southern half of the island of Woahoo slowly spread before Jeffery—the curving Bay of Whyteetee, a village there with its multitude of peaked huts under palm trees like tattered green umbrellas. At a distance of two or three miles from the ship, the huts under the trees reminded him of sunburnt haystacks. Extending north from white sandy shores was a broad meadow country sloping up toward a series of densely green hills. Behind the hills were serrated ridges and behind the ridges rose a lofty range of mountains which seemed to divide the island parallel to the coast line. Although it was early morning, the air was warm and drenched with a flood of yellow light. Jeffery could feel his heart pounding.

"My God," he said to Sam, "it's beautiful, isn't it?"

"It ain't going to be so beautiful to us," Sam said, "if that king what's-his-name learns we're arriving with a cargo of contraband weapons for Ben Partridge."

While the Clymestre shortened sail, coasting in closer to where she would wait for a pilot and canoes to take her into the harbor, Jeffery examined every detail of the island he could see. Already the pagans, far away, were industriously working the fields exactly as farmers would be working in Pennsylvania fields by this time of morning. No British ships were visible. Jeffery hoped the Yankee trader, Ben Partridge, was somewhere along that coast line, watching the approach of the Clymestre and preparing to board her as soon as possible to say how the contraband cargo was to be got ashore. Everything now depended upon what Partridge had arranged.

Jeffery no longer had to remind himself that it took almost half a year for a ship to sail from the Sandwich Islands to the other side of the world. But he could not help remembering it hadn't been until last November that Mr. Monroe, in Washington, D.C., had finally received the dispatch which Ben Partridge had forwarded from Honoruru giving warning that the old heathen king of the islands planned to place his kingdom under the British crown. It was now nearly a year since Partridge had forwarded his desperate appeal to the American Secretary of State through the services of a Yankee captain of an American trading vessel. Jeffery was afraid to think of what might have become of Ben Partridge in all this time. The old heathen king of the Sandwich Islands might have discovered Partridge's scheme to incite a rebellion. By now, Partridge might be captured or killed.

"What's your guess?" Jeffery asked Sam Crowell. "Will Partridge meet us?"

Sam gave Jeffery a reflective look. He passed one of his pistols to Jeffery, saying, "We ain't going to worry till we got reason to. But just keep that pistol handy if you have to go into Honoruru village to hunt Partridge up." He asked, "Scared?"

After a pause, Jeffery disgustedly admitted, "Yes."

Often during the voyage he had asked himself if anyone with his limited qualifications ever before had been so hastily brevetted captain in the United States Army, or if anyone with less training had ever been given special orders making him neither more nor less than one of Mr. Monroe's secret agents. With the voyage now almost at an end, he found his doubts about himself increasing. He became aware of Sam's broad red face grinning sympathetically down at him.

"Jeff, if you'd said you wasn't scared I'd known you was lying. It's nat'ral for anybody to be scared when waiting for what's going to happen."

"You're going to tell me," Jeffery said skeptically, "you're scared, too?"

"Why, prob'ly I'm as nervy as you are, sure. It's because I got too much beef on my face to show it. That's all. You got to learn to let your mind think on something else when you're waiting it out." Sam took the glass, raised it to sight toward shore.

Jeffery had never met anyone whom he had liked so well, from the first day of sailing, as he liked Sam. Although Sam was fifteen years older, he hadn't tried to come over Jeffery because of the extra years. And if Jeffery hadn't previously known who Captain Samuel Crowell was, along with almost everyone else along the east coast of the American continent, from Sam's old-shoe manners Jeffery would never have suspected this was the same man who had made such a great name for himself as a privateer's captain during the war against the British.

Jeffery heard Sam mutter, "Damn if them dugouts putting from shore ain't loaded with pretty wenches! What'd I tell you?"

Jeffery looked suspiciously at Sam. Usually, Sam was much more subtle. Although Sam had the innocent and deceptive solidness of a Pennsylvania farmer, Jeffery had learned during the voyage that Sam was about as slow-witted as a fox. However, Jeffery had managed not to be taken in by Sam's yarns. During the long months it had helped to pass away the time to prove logically and reasonably to Sam why his stories of tall beautiful girls with curly black hair who went around without a stitch on them and wanted only to get in bed with you when you arrived at the Sandwich Islands were fabrications made up by sailors too long away from women. It seemed to Jeffery that the subject of island women had worn thin by now. But if Sam was trying to help distract his mind, Jeffery was prepared to have a try at being distracted.

"Let me have a look, Sam. I'll certify if they're pretty or not."

Sam offered the glass to Jeffery but withdrew it after a shrewd glance at him. "No, sir," Sam said. "You wait till you can see the wenches close up and I can watch you when you see 'em. No diddling with 'em, either, this morning. We won't have time."

Sam pushed the glass shut and called to Mr. Foster, the first mate, repeating his warning against any diddling this morning with the wenches in a voice loud enough to carry over the entire ship.

By seven in the morning the anchor was lowered with a splash, and the ship moored beyond the reefs to wait for the pilot. Toward it from the harbor a swarm of canoes flashed through the water. Almost as a solid mass the crew ran and stumbled along the lee rails, waving and bellowing over the side. A dozen dugouts, Jeffery counted, no, by God, thirteen, were paddling toward the ship. He had never known the sight of girls floating toward you could give you a feeling like this. He tried to contain himself and stand there, near Sam, who was wary and quiet and a little aloof from the uproar. After its long voyage the whole ship seemed to steam under the yellow flood of morning light, the green waves gently lapping at its sides.

Jeffery stared at the dugouts, forgetful even of Sam. They were from thirty to forty feet long, of single hollowed logs, with slender outriggers fore and aft. They rode easily over the breakers which crashed heavily over the coral reefs a dozen ships' lengths away. Every dugout, he saw, now held from five to ten brown-skinned men and older women, twice that many girls, and piles of sugar cane, sweet potatoes, yellow bananas, watermelons, strangely shaped fruits, and odd brownish lumps which he thought looked something like small parboiled dogs. That was exactly what the small brownish lumps were, too, he very soon discovered.

Lines had been dropped to the dugouts. First the girls climbed aboard, followed by the older women and men who had fetched along their produce in woven baskets as if everything was in the nature of a morning's business.

The older women and men squatted on the ship's planks and traded their produce for iron ship's nails and broken pieces of looking glass and combs and pipes and whatever odds and ends the crew could offer. The men of the crew, ravenous for both fresh food and girls after five months at sea, lost precious little time in getting at both. Jeffery gazed at the girls with astonishment because they were everything that Sam had claimed for them and more.

Sam grinned at Jeffery. "How do you like them girls? Ain't they ugly, though? See their snaggle teeth and potbellies."

Three of them had run up the companionway, stopping before Sam and Jeffery. In comparison with Philadelphia girls, all three were tall but two were no more than a finger's width above Jeffery and the third stood even with Sam, an inch possibly over six feet. One had skin of deep coral, one of amber, and one of gold. Their dark curly hair streamed in the breeze. They were naked to the waist, but around their shoulders they wore necklaces of flowers and ferns which, with the prettiest and most beguiling of gestures, they placed over Sam and Jeffery's heads; and when they had finished, they stepped back, smiling.

Around their hips they wore a single garment which wasn't of cloth, Jeffery had learned from his reading, but of a thick supple paperish material made of beaten mulberry fibers. As Jeffery found himself staring at the girl with skin like polished coral, the dark cloud of hair, the smiling face, the smiling body, all of her calling urgently to all his nerves and senses, he felt more than the hotness of the morning sun upon his face.

"Let me hear how much of the language you picked up from that heathen who got himself into the Philadelphy hospital same time you did. Go on. Talk to her, Jeff."

He decided to ask her in her language what her name was. But he let himself gaze at the strong young breasts and at her laughing face and again at her breasts and at her long slim legs, the drops of sea water sparkling like diamonds on the coral flesh. Next, she took his hand and clasped it to her—and of a sudden he could not recall a single word of her language.

Then he became aware of cries and yells, an increasing clamor. The coral-skinned girl released his hand and whirled, her hair like a cloud. Sam stepped over to the companionway, all dallying forgotten.

"Mr. Foster!" Sam's hoarse, solid voice never sounded overwhelming but you could hear it from one end of the ship to the other. "Mr. Foster, will you give the pilot a hand? Git the men to their stations!"

Hastily Jeffery looked around. A sturdy white man with gray whiskers that reached his chest was coming up the rope ladder.

He was followed by a very large native who wore a nearly new frock coat split down the back; behind came two more, all three evidently chiefs.

Jeffery wanted to rub his eyes. He was convinced he heard planks creak under the weight of the three huge heathens. The third must weigh almost four hundred pounds. He stared. He recalled reading in Captain Cook's account of discovering the islands how the common natives had the fear of death of their chiefs and instantly gave way before these great men or fled from them. Within three minutes the ship was cleared of the crowd of natives who had paddled out from the village of Whyteetee. The three chiefs stayed where they were. They were planted like trees on the deck, observing the ship and the white men, speaking quietly among themselves, puffing at their stone and Chinese brass pipes. They were lords, Jeffery thought, half amused, half awed. They hadn't even flicked an eye at the nearly naked girls running about them in panic a few minutes ago. Evidently these three pagan nobles were above such common trash. Jeffery found himself wondering how beguiling a princess of these islands might be, when the common trash of girls were like young angels.

He realized his mind was straying badly. What of Partridge? For a few minutes Jeffery had almost forgotten about Partridge. The sight of those bold smiling girls knocked everything else out of your mind! He watched Sam come up the steps with the white man. He was John Harbottle, he said, the king's pilot. He appeared to be fifty or so, an Englishman still in his prime, in a patched sea jacket.

At once Sam asked, "How about going into the harbor, Mr. Harbottle? How safe is it now for an American vessel?"

"Safe?" Harbottle was obviously perplexed by the question. "Certain, it's safe."

Jeffery saw Sam looking pointedly at him. It seemed to be all right. Evidently they had arrived in time. "What's the gen'ral practice now, Mr. Harbottle? Is a ship's captain supposed to call on King Tommy-hommy-ha . . ." The king's name gave Sam trouble. ". . . soon's a ship gits anchored in the harbor?"

"You won't call on King Tamehameha at this port, cap'n. He don't keep residence here any more. He lives on the island of

Owhyee, to the south. You'll see Gov'nor Young here. John Young's gov'nor of Woahoo."

Jeffery was startled. John Young alive? He had read Captain Cook's *A Voyage to the Pacific Ocean* and Captain Vancouver's *Voyage of Discovery* during the months outward bound from Baltimore. Although it was now nearly forty years since Captain Cook had first discovered these islands, Cook's account and Vancouver's record, made twenty years later, still remained the best sources of information on these islands. And, Jeffery remembered, John Young was the English boatswain who had arrived here a quarter of a century ago and who, along with King Tamehameha, had been praised highly in Vancouver's chronicles.

Harbottle spat into the wind. "Cap'n, if you'll send a man fo'rard to take soundings, we'll have a go at the passage—"

"One thing more. Is there any means of signaling Ben Partridge for him to meet us at the wharf?"

"Ben Partridge?"

"Ain't he a trader here?" asked Sam, very easy, the sun shining on his broad red face. "We got a cargo for him."

"Sure, Partridge's a trader here, one of the biggest. He's not here now, though. Partridge sailed a couple of weeks ago to Atooie."

"Don't that contrary everything, though! What's to be done with the cargo we've brung him?"

"His partner ought to know. If the partner don't, you can ask Partridge's daughter, Susan, at her pa's compound. She banged her head a day or so ago against a canoe but she ought to be up enough by now to talk to you."

Jeffery held silent. Sam rubbed his bristly chin. Jeffery didn't know anything about a partner or a daughter. In Washington last November, Mr. Monroe hadn't mentioned either of them. Sam had been here ten years ago but that was a year or so before Partridge had established himself.

"Let me see," Sam was saying now, still very easy. "I knew Partridge when I was here before the war. He never had a daughter or a partner then, did he? I don't rec'lect he did."

"Cap'n, you must have met his daughter. Susan got in just before the war. Ben Partridge meant to send her on to Australy with kin of his there and never did—the war came on. He was afraid for her to risk the voyage. She's been staying ever since."

"What about this partner?"

"Scheffer? Scheffer bought in with Partridge last year. He's a German doctor by trade, though he spends most of his time c'lecting flowers around here. Scheffer's a good man—don't need to worry 'bout him, cap'n. If you got a cargo for Partridge, Scheffer'll tend to you till Partridge gets here. Now . . . if we're to make the passage before the tide changes?"

"Maybe we won't go in today. Wait a minute."

Sam took Jeffery's arm, leading him aft. Sam got his voice down to a rumble. "It looks safe enough. What do you think?"

"Suppose I get ashore and try to talk to the partner?"

"You fish with him. We won't give our business away, less we're satisfied the partner's in it with Partridge. Damn Partridge. He took a partic'lar unconvenient time to be away."

Jeffery recalled the letter from Partridge which last November Mr. Monroe had read to him. "Sam, Atooie was the island Partridge expected to revolt against the king. Maybe we got here at the right time."

"We'll sail into the harbor and find out."

The ship pitched, tilting until her lee deck was awash, the surf roaring; and then she came through the channel like a horse at full gallop. In smooth water the pilot turned her to the wind until a dozen double-canoes came out from the village of Honoruru, fixed lines, and began towing the Clymestre toward the long wharf.

Anxiously Jeffery watched the village approach. Across the gleaming water came a confused murmur from the tumult of natives collecting along the eastern shores of the harbor. Sam walked aft, stopped near Jeffery, and rested his elbows on the rail. The village was built at the end of a long valley, not far from a limpid stream running into the bay. At the other side of the stream, to the north, were miles of cultivated fields and fishponds. Large groves of coconut palms and breadfruit trees shaded the two or three thousand huts of brown grass and poles erected in disorderly fashion away from the beach.

Now and then among the trees much larger structures than the huts came in view as the Clymestre was towed closer in. The two largest structures had been built upon immense foundations of stone or lava. The harbor pilot, Harbottle, pointed them out to

Jeffery. "See them?" he said. "They're morais—temples, you'd call them—and a white man had best stay clear of them. The people here are peaceful enough, unless a white man's fool enough to get himself into one of their morais. Then they go wild. Last year two white men got drunk and wandered into one. They died quick, too."

Two American whalers were at anchor deep in the harbor. Closer in, near the point, were three ships flying the Russian flag. Sam returned his glass to Jeffery with a grim smile. "There ain't no British ship here, Jeff. There ain't even a British flag to be seen ashore." Even through the glass Jeffery could not decipher the names of the three Russian ships.

"It's the *Ilmen*, the *Kadiak*, and—yes—the *Otkrytie*," Sam explained.

"Well, I'm damned," said Jeffery.

Sam's big red face was unsmiling. "I sailed a Russian whaler out of Rio six rotten months, once, as a boy. I guess at a time like this, anything a man knows comes handy."

Harbottle stepped forward. "Cap'n, there's Dr. Scheffer on the wharf, waiting to come aboard."

For a big man Sam was remarkably quick on his feet. He turned like lightning. "Which one?"

"That big pale smiling fellow. See him? He's next to Nate Winship—I declare, that's Gov'nor Young talking to them now. I guess the gov'nor's planning to come aboard, too."

Sam said, "We don't figure having anyone come aboard, Mr. Harbottle. Jeff'll take the ship's boat back with you to the wharf and have a talk with Partridge's partner first."

"That won't hardly do, cap'n. Even if King Tamehameha moved his residence to Owhyee, the king still likes to have first choice at making offers for a ship's cargo. Gov'nor Young'll be putting out directly. Look there—" Harbottle nodded.

Sam raised his glass. Then, without a word, he gave it to Jeffery. At the end of the wharf four white men had climbed into a long-boat and were waiting while three natives followed. Last came a big man, darker than the others. In a few minutes all eight of them would be asking to come aboard. Here was a contingency which had been impossible to foresee. Sam couldn't refuse permission for the governor of the island to visit the *Clymestre*.

If Governor Young so much as suspected muskets, ball, and barrels of black powder were in the hold— In the warm morning sunshine Jeffery shivered. He dropped his hand to the butt of his pistol and waited. There still might be time for Sam to turn the ship around and have Harbottle steer her back through the passage. If Sam wanted it, Jeffery was ready to put a pistol to Harbottle's head and keep him at the wheel, leaving Sam and the mates free to prepare the crew.

The longboat was pulling away from the wharf. They had ten minutes more, Jeffery decided, perhaps less. He felt Sam's hand as steady as a rock on his shoulder. "Would you kindly inform my mate, sir, to lower the ladder?" he heard Sam ask Harbottle.

When Harbottle had waddled down to the midship's deck and Jeffery had counted off what seemed like sixty agonizing seconds of waiting for Harbottle to go beyond earshot, Sam said, very quick, his mind made up, "Jeff, what we got to do is chew or spit. It all depends what Partridge has told that German partner of his. I'll invite the gov'nor and his crowd to the cabin for noggins of rum. While I keep 'em there, can you git off alone a minute with Scheffer?"

"I'll do what I can."

"You fish what you can from him. Don't make no mistakes because if you do, we could lose cargo and ship, and all be strung higher than kites as filibusterers. After you finish, git back to me quick and say 'No rum for me' if you ain't satisfied with him. Got that?"

Jeffery nodded. He wanted to pinch himself. It was not true. He was not really here. If he shut his eyes, when he opened them he would find himself safely around the other side of the world, back in Philadelphia.

It had been so sudden last November, Jeffery thought violently, all so goddam unexpected. The second week of last November he had been discharged from the Philadelphia City Hospital and driven directly to the three-story brick house on Arch Street. His aunt had had his old room prepared for him, the blinds drawn and hot gruel waiting, as if he still were an invalid. Yes, and an hour later Rebecca Koch had arrived in a new French imported landau so shiny with varnish it put out your eyes to see it down there in the street. Rebecca had brought him flowers from her father's greenhouse. She had been all milk and honey that morning, Jeffery still remembered. He had never seen her so desirable, her hair velvety black, her skin with the whiteness of new pear blossoms.

Jeffery gripped the railing of the ship, watching the longboat approach from the stone wharf. That very afternoon a courier had arrived from Washington, D.C., with an imperative note. It was from Jeffery's uncle, who was one of the congressmen on the newly established committee which dealt with foreign affairs. Jeffery still remembered one line in that note which he had had to read three times, "Mr. Monroe wants to see you as soon as possible, so don't lose a minute getting here, will you?", because he had not been able to conceive of any reason why Mr. Monroe would want to see him. Until that moment he had never even known that Mr. Monroe was aware of him. By evening, Jeffery had been well on his way toward Washington. A week later he had sailed from Baltimore on the *Clymestre*. All of it, Jeffery told himself, had happened too quickly. It was still happening too quickly. He was here. And whatever he did, he must do very quickly and do dead right. He was quite certain he did not want to be strung higher than a kite as a filibusterer.

He heard Sam's hoarse voice announce, "Here they come. We'll git down to meet 'em as they climb aboard."

Up to the ship's deck climbed an old scrawny man, a tattered hat of palm leaves on his head and a black pipe in his mouth. He had a red sea coat tied by the sleeves about his shoulders and the rest of him was bare except for the loincloth of kapa fabric about his middle and the leather sandals on his feet. He paused there and mildly contemplated Sam and Jeffery.

With something of a flourish Harbottle said, "Gentlemen, His Ex'lency, Gov'nor John Young . . . Sir, presenting Cap'n Sam'l Crowell, Mr. Tol'my, supercargo of the schooner *Clymestre*, out of Balt'more, five months last."

John Young puffed at his black pipe and silently acknowledged the bows. Behind him came the three white men and the tall Negro—Dr. Scheffer, Mr. Winship, Mr. Davis, and Mr. Allan, all traders at Honoruru, Harbottle said.

Jeffery shaded his eyes with one hand, sighting against the glare at Dr. Scheffer. The German, who had a pistol stuck carelessly in his sash, was broad as an ox and about fifty years of age. He had a blunt-featured, pale, and cheerful face in which were set wonderfully quick eyes of a gray so light as to be silvery.

Sam broke the silence. "Dr. Scheffer, we've brung a cargo here for Mr. Partridge. I hear you're his partner."

"Nothing so great as that. You might say I'm a surgeon out to grass with a passion for botanical collecting. Mr. Partridge permits me to earn my keep by helping him the best I can." Scheffer had a round, unaccented voice. There was no trace of German in it that Jeffery could detect.

"It's unconvenient for us for Mr. Partridge to be off the island," Sam went on.

"Mr. Partridge will be most chagrined, sir. Two weeks ago he received unexpectedly good news. The vassal king of Atooie agreed to negotiate with him for the sandalwood concession on that island."

With a Yankee drawl, Mr. Winship remarked enviously, "I tell you, Cap'n Crowell, I wish I had Partridge's luck but I'm not so highly regarded as he is on the leeward island."

Governor Young continued to puff his pipe in silence. Jeffery watched him, wondering what Captain Vancouver had seen in him to praise twenty-two years ago. Governor Young looked back at Jeffery, looked him up, looked him down, dismissed him, turning his misty old eyes again to Sam.

Sam was staving them off, counting upon him to fish information one way or the other from Partridge's big, smooth-faced partner. Dr. Scheffer had tucked his thumbs in his sash, assuring Sam, "Mr. Partridge asked me to keep watch for the ship bringing goods to him, and when yours was signaled off the reefs this morning I hoped it might be the one. Rum and tobacco wasn't it, captain?"

"And bar iron." Sam looked hard at Jeffery.

It had to be plausible. Harbottle had said Partridge's partner liked to collect flowers. Dr. Scheffer had mentioned he had a passion for botanical collecting. Botanist? Flowers? Jeffery remembered the roses his aunt grew in Philadelphia.

"Dr. Scheffer, if you collect botanical specimens you might be interested in the rose cuttings I've brought—in moss from Philadelphia."

"Rose cuttings? Indeed I would be, sir. Roses do remarkably well in these latitudes. For a good specimen I might be induced to trade you five piculs of sandalwood."

You couldn't have asked for any response quicker than that.

Sam immediately told his first mate, "Mr. Foster, will you kindly have a bar'l of our best rum brought up from the for'ard hold?" and waved his hand toward the main cabin's door. "Gentlemen, will you step inside?"

Jeffery was about to suggest to Dr. Scheffer that they go on through the cabin to his berth to have a look at the rose cuttings when from behind him an amazingly deep voice uttered a single word, "Rum?" Jeffery looked around, startled.

Again Governor Young opened his mouth. From the frail chest and throat issued, not a thin treble, but a thunderous discharge of sound. "Cap'n, thankee. I'll accept a noggin o' rum before we 'ave a look at your ship's list."

"The rose cuttings, Mr. Tolamy?" Dr. Scheffer quietly reminded Jeffery.

Jeffery made an effort. He told Sam, "I'll fetch in the ship's list after I've shown Dr. Scheffer the rose cuttings I stowed away in my berth."

"Why, sure," Sam said. "It'll give us time for a couple of noggins of rum all around."

It was a tight fit for a man of Dr. Scheffer's bulk but the man got himself between the bunks and opposite bulkhead like a big agile monkey. Jeffery closed the door and bolted it. Dr. Scheffer stuck his thick thumbs in his sash, waiting.

Jeffery lowered his voice. "I don't believe I can show you those rose cuttings after all, Dr. Scheffer."

"They died, did they? That often happens to cuttings. Did you water them?"

"Too much, perhaps."

"Mr. Partridge's daughter will be disappointed when she hears of it. Poor Susan! She struck her head by falling against a canoe a few days ago. She was still somewhat delirious yesterday evening. However, I hope to have Susan up in time to be hostess for you and Captain Crowell. You must tell her, yourself, of your rose cuttings . . ." The gray, silvery eyes twinkled. "I trust, sir, you will not permit Mr. Partridge's temporary absence to disaccommodate any arrangements concerning your cargo?"

It was a small opening, if it was one; but Jeffery had to chance it. "Did Mr. Partridge happen to mention to you the cargo he ordered?"

"He did, sir."

"Could you name the goods we've brought?"

"Three thousand muskets, and a quantity of ball and black powder, along with whatever else you've used to fill the hold. Is that right?"

"It is," Jeffery said.

Dr. Scheffer was smiling. "Mr. Partridge showed me the copy of the letter he wrote to Mr. Monroe almost a year ago."

Jeffery felt as if he could breathe more easily. He smiled back. "How do we stand now? Has Mr. Partridge gone to Atooie to prepare them for the rebellion—"

"Good God, sir!" Dr. Scheffer whispered hastily. "No talk of that here, if you please, Mr. Tolamy. Wait until we can be by ourselves at the compound."

Jeffery felt himself reddening. It was a mistake to have asked. "But what about the muskets, sir? Captain Crowell has to know. How'll we manage with Governor Young aboard?"

"I propose quite simply to inform the governor that the arms are aboard."

Jeffery moved so fast he surprised himself. He reached under his jacket, whipped out his pistol, cocked it with his thumb, and thrust the muzzle into Dr. Scheffer's belly. With his other hand, he plucked Dr. Scheffer's pistol from the sash and tossed it on the bunk.

"Young man—"

Dr. Scheffer had taken a second look at Jeffery's face. Slowly, his hands lifted. He sucked in his breath. "Gently, Mr. Tolamy—"

"Now, listen. I'm going to step to the door and ask Sam to come here a minute."

"I beg of you! You saw the three Russian ships in the harbor? Why do you think they have been waiting here for the past three weeks? How do you believe Mr. Partridge planned to get the arms off your ship? Mr. Partridge proposed explaining to the governor the muskets were destined for the Russians to carry to New Archangel."

Jeffery lowered his pistol. Possibly he had jumped too fast. It was a hell of a lie, though, to expect Governor Young to swallow. "If that's true," he said, "you can't possibly get away with it."

"Mr. Partridge believed we could, sir. He arranged with the Russians to back him up."

"The Russian shipmasters'll say they're taking our guns and ammunition?"

"They'll swear to it. If necessary, they'll send men to help your crew unload the cargo. Well, sir?" The silvery eyes looked down at Jeffery's pistol. The big arms lowered.

Jeffery thrust his pistol into his jacket. "You'll explain to Governor Young," he ordered. "And I'll be in back of you. To speak plainly, I shouldn't much mind shooting you from the rear or any place else if I find you've taken me in."

"Accept my word on it: if you shoot a man from behind, aim for his kidneys. He's certain to die. Moreover, he'll die in mortal pain. Now, let me have your ship's cargo list and you can place yourself behind me or wherever you like. I promise you, everything will be perfectly accommodated with Governor Young."

---

2. In the main cabin Dr. Scheffer spread the ship's list for the governor and whoever else would like to read. There it was, rum, tobacco, yellow as well as bright, bar iron, cotton goods, muskets, ball, barrels of powder, in both kind and quantity.

Scheffer's toneless voice asked the governor, "Now, sir, has King Tamehameha any law prohibiting the bringing of arms to these islands to be placed on Russian ships bound for New Archangel? Were Mr. Partridge here, sir, he would explain that months ago he arranged with Governor Baranov to supply the Russians in New Archangel with all necessities required . . ." As if exhausted, Governor Young closed his eyes.

"If you doubt me, governor, why not call in the masters of the Russian ships? Let *them* assure you, sir."

Dr. Scheffer sounded most convincing. Even though Jeffery knew he was lying, he was so earnest and cheerful that you wanted to believe him.

"Gov'nor, can I lay down my farthing's worth?" Nathan Winship asked. "Why don't you wait till Partridge gets here afore you stir up the Roossians with any questions? When he gets here he might be willing to let the king hev a bid on the muskets. He'd sell to the king if the bid was higher. Is that true, Scheffer?"

"You know how we come by our living, Mr. Winship."

"There you are, governor. You can send a fast-sailing canoe to the king and receive word from him in four days' time or less if he wants the muskets. He could send you a price he's prepared to pay. Ben Partridge will be here tomorrow or next day—"

"Certainly by Thursday," Dr. Scheffer said.

"Cap'n Crowell don't hev to unload his cargo. Let it wait in the ship for Partridge."

Dr. Scheffer agreed with Mr. Winship. The Russians wouldn't sail off. There was no good reason why everyone concerned couldn't wait until Mr. Partridge returned and settled the matter to the governor and the king's satisfaction. The old man slowly got out of his chair. He nodded in agreement. He gathered up his sea cloak. With a sort of trot and shamble he passed into the flood of light on deck.

Sam looked pleased; Jeffery was pleased, himself. Back home, Jeffery thought someday when he heard about it Mr. Monroe ought to be very pleased with this morning's work.

On the deck the traders shook hands with Sam and Jeffery. The tall Negro, Mr. Allan, grave and courteous, thanked Captain Crowell and Mr. Tolamy for their hospitality. After the chiefs had lowered themselves into the longboat, he descended nimbly, followed by Mr. Davis and Mr. Winship. For a moment, Governor Young remained on deck.

"Will I give you a hand with the ladder, sir?" Jeffery asked.

Governor Young shook off Jeffery's hand. He peered up at Jeffery. Again the amazingly deep voice went off like a sixteen-pounder. "The rose cuttings, Mr. Tolamy? 'Ad they died?"

He laughed in Jeffery's face. All in a flash he scampered down the ladder. He settled himself in the stern, picked up the palm-leaf hat from where it had fallen, and, without once looking upward, nodded for the natives to pull for shore.

Sam said, "Damn if he ain't as agile as an old goat."

"He's an old fox," Dr. Scheffer said, very thoughtfully.

That deep mocking laugh still seemed to echo in Jeffery's ears. He had underestimated John Young even after poring over everything written about him years ago in Vancouver's published chronicles.

"It was my fault as much as anyone's," Dr. Scheffer was saying. "I'll vouch, too, no serious harm has been done. If Governor Young inquires, the Russian shipmasters will swear the cargo is for them. But let us get ourselves to shore and to Partridge's compound, gentlemen, where I can explain in private."

It was not until a few minutes of eleven in the morning that Jeffery climbed from the ship's longboat to the wharf. Walking along the wharf on one side of Dr. Scheffer, Sam on the other, he watched the crowd of natives give way to them as if white men were also counted among the lords and chiefs of the island. After five months and six days Jeffery had at last got his feet upon land.

An open space like a commons separated the wharf from the village under the thick groves of coconut palms, and a lane led away along the upper beach to the south and to a point of land extending into the bay upon which Ben Partridge had located his compound.

The walls of the compound were of clay, sand, and dried grass, and were faced with coral. They were a good fifteen feet high and impressively thick, Jeffery noticed, when they passed through the big gate into the compound. Inside he saw a whole running and going of brown stumpy little men, all very hairy. Dr. Scheffer said they were Kodiaks imported from New Archangel. Ben Partridge had brought in a shipload of them a few months ago, two hundred in all; they were better workers than the Sandwich Island natives and far more reliable.

A row of shacks and sheds, open in front and thatched on the sides and tops, was filled with stores. At the southwest corner of the compound, built into the wall so that it overlooked the bay, was a dwelling of brown and red lava stones, one story, in the shape of a square. Women servants bowed as Dr. Scheffer led Sam and

Jeffery into a pleasant room at the west, with a view of the bay outside through barred windows.

"Now, gentlemen," said Dr. Scheffer, lighting his curved, porcelain pipe, "we can speak as freely as is required." The silvery eyes regarded Sam a moment and then contemplated Jeffery. "As a preliminary, I suggest I explain what I know of the purpose of your voyage as I have heard it from Mr. Partridge. You can decide in your own minds if I warrant your confidence."

"Fair enough," Sam said. "Cards on the table."

Dr. Scheffer puffed thoughtfully at his pipe. "During the war between your nation and the British there was much talk out here of King Tamehameha's request to place his islands under the British crown. When the British navigator, Captain Vancouver, made his last visit to the islands some twenty-two years ago he promised King Tamehameha that a man-of-war armed with brass guns would be sent to him by the British government. For twenty-two years King Tamehameha has been waiting for that man-of-war. Last year, Mr. Partridge learned from the king's advisers that the king had heard the British government was at last building him the man-of-war. The ship's arrival was anticipated within half a year. It was the king's intention to announce formally, after the ship arrived, that the Sandwich Islands were being ceded to the British crown. This would place all ports under the British. Without these ports midway in the Pacific, no vessel can continue trade profitably between the west coast of the American continent and China. Consequently, almost a year ago, gentlemen, my partner, Mr. Partridge, sent a dispatch to your American Secretary of State, Mr. Monroe. He warned of King Tamehameha's plans. He wrote that the leeward isle, Atooie, was restless under King Tamehameha. If he could be supplied with arms, he believed he could engage with the chiefs and the king of this island to revolt, to cease paying tribute to King Tamehameha—in short, gentlemen, to maintain Atooie at least independent, with ports open to American vessels."

"That's about it," Sam said.

"Although Mr. Partridge did not say as much in his dispatch, gentlemen, he recognized if he were supplied with arms it would have to be done in the nature of a private expedition." The gray eyes briefly twinkled. "Otherwise, the American nation might find itself again engaged with the British." Dr. Scheffer pushed down the burning tobacco in his pipe with a broad thumb. He looked inquiringly at Sam, with a quick glance toward Jeffery. "Well, gentlemen?"

"That's putting down your cards fair enough," Sam said. "Far's I go, I used to be in the Atlantic trade. I owned my own ship. During the war, you might say I come off lucky 'gainst the British. The cargo I brung with me was paid for by me and—" He stroked his big chin for a moment. "Jeff, here, bought a small share in our venture. The rest of the money was supplied by his uncle. It's a private expedition, no question of that. The British nor anybody else can't say it ain't."

"And Mr. Tolamy's uncle, sir?"

Jeffery said, "My uncle's Jonathan Perkins of Philadelphia."

"I see," said Dr. Scheffer as if he did not quite see.

Sam added, "Jeff's uncle is a congressman. It might be Mr. Monroe happened to show Jeff's uncle that letter what came in from Mr. Partridge. But if later me and Jeff's uncle decided to buy up a spare lot of muskets and powder from the war, nobody can say it wasn't our own idea. Mr. Monroe nor anybody else in the nation's government don't have any official knowledge of this voyage."

"And why shouldn't you purchase a few guns and barrels of powder, captain?" said Dr. Scheffer. "And Mr. Tolamy came along as supercargo? Why not indeed?" said Dr. Scheffer promptly. "But you see, sir, the situation has materially changed since Mr. Partridge first addressed himself to Mr. Monroe nearly a year ago. I have now got to inform you, seven or eight months ago the traders on the islands, along with Governor Young, succeeded in persuading King Tamehameha it would better serve these islands to remain independent."

"They—talked with the king against ceding to the British?" Sam said.

"They not only talked with him. They succeeded in persuading King Tamehameha not to cede the islands. Last fall the king announced his eldest son would inherit the crown. As far as we know, sir, the British have never had any intention of taking these islands by force. Consequently, last fall, as soon as we heard King Tamehameha had officially announced his decision, Mr. Partridge forwarded a second letter to request Mr. Monroe to refrain from taking either official or—or private action, gentlemen, to impose any changes in the Pacific. The reason Mr. Partridge is in Atooie this week, between us privately, gentlemen, is to discourage any talk of revolting against King Tamehameha. American interests— all our interests will now be best served by maintaining a status quo."

After a silence, Jeffery heard Sam say heavily, "Don't that beat everything! It means we've come out here for nothing, then?"

Jeffery's mouth felt dry. He asked, "All danger of British dominion over these islands has ended?"

"I cannot conceive of such a danger now, Mr. Tolamy. However, I won't take it the wrong way for you to want to wait until Mr. Partridge returns to have the facts from him."

Sam growled, "You and Partridge actually mean to sell our arms to the Roossians?"

"It's the best means of escaping a very awkward situation, sir."

"But how did you learn them Roossians needed muskets and ammunition?"

"Fortunately for Mr. Partridge, I knew Governor Baranov of New Archangel was in want of arms because for two years I was his personal physician. That was before I departed last October for a botanical study of my own on these islands, engaging to earn my keep while here by assisting Mr. Partridge. When Mr. Partridge finally told me of his predicament early this year, I was able to suggest if his second letter arrived too late and you had already sailed that we could dispose of the muskets and ammunition to the Russians."

"Jeff," Sam said, "that settles it. We've come out here for nothing!"

"For nothing, Captain Crowell?" Dr. Scheffer asked. "Why, sir, do you consider a handsome profit to be nothing? You can count on specie payment from the Russians for your muskets, ball, and powder. There are four thousand piculs of sandalwood in Mr. Partridge's yard which I hope you will agree to carry for us to China, at another profit to us all. How much better it is to voyage to these islands and to receive a fine profit than to find yourselves risking your lives in a dubious venture? Do you not agree, Mr. Tolamy?"

A dubious venture? Jeffery was prepared to admit it might have seemed as such. Even he had had doubts. But he had never thought of Mr. Partridge, who had believed a revolt possible, thinking it a dubious venture. Nor would he have anticipated hearing Mr. Partridge's partner so condemning it. Suddenly he could not help recalling how convincingly Dr. Scheffer had lied to old Governor Young.

"I hadn't much thought if it was a dubious venture or not," he answered. "If the ports are to remain open, the news will greatly please Mr. Monroe. It's true, is it? You anticipate no future trouble from the British? The ports are to remain open?"

"Open? They will be free to the coming and going of all the ships of the world! Believe me, Mr. Tolamy, you are fortunate, very fortunate! When you have become my age you will have learned that fighting and shedding of blood are to be avoided as you avoid the pest. Please believe me. You are a most fortunate young man; how fortunate you cannot realize."

Dr. Scheffer nodded reassuringly at Jeffery. In his round, unaccented voice he repeated, "So very very fortunate, sir, that almost I could envy you."

———————

3. Dr. Scheffer pushed himself up from his chair and put down his curving porcelain pipe. Mr. Partridge would arrive tomorrow or next day, the German reminded them, and could satisfy Captain Crowell and Mr. Tolamy upon any points remaining to be cleared. He knew he spoke for Mr. Partridge when he asked them to consider this establishment as theirs while on shore. Lunch would be late, in an hour, for he had previously invited a Captain Quorn who was recently in with a cargo of sandalwood from Ranai.

He called in a servant no more than five feet tall, with shoulders, it seemed to Jeffery, as wide as the creature was tall, and a skin that was covered with grayish hair. The man had a nose like a water rat's snout and his eyes were like yellow glass. It was Gebbo, Scheffer explained, chief of the Kodiaks whom Mr. Partridge had brought down from New Archangel. Jeffery looked at him curiously.

Dr. Scheffer's eyes twinkled. The Kodiaks were devoted to their masters, he said, and they believed all white men were gods. He would have Gebbo guide them to the beach where they could wash, and provide them with clean garments suitable to this climate. He spoke to Gebbo briefly in what sounded to Jeffery like nothing more than a clacking of his tongue and a series of barks. Gebbo groveled, jumped up, and darted to the doorway.

"You speak Kodiak too, sir?" asked Jeffery.

"Only enough to accommodate myself with them. Gebbo has no knowledge of English but he'll read your gestures and obey you. In an hour, then, gentlemen . . ."

Sam and Jeffery were led by Gebbo and a small cavalcade of other house servants to a curve of white beach where they washed in the surf, had fresh water poured over them, and were dressed in clean silk jackets and trousers. The air quivered with light. The radiance was blinding. The enormous slope, checkerboarded by cultivated fields, lifted for miles beyond the thick groves of palms and bread-fruit trees. Little figures like beetles and ants were working in their patches of taro; beyond were the blue ridges, and above the ridges was the purple roundness of a mountain shaped like a vast bowl.

The British were not here, Dr. Scheffer had said, and they were not intending to take over the islands. These ports in the Pacific would remain free. It was great and surprising news.

"Sam," said Jeffery slowly, "what do you make of it? It's almost too good to be true, isn't it?"

"Scheffer's a fool if he ain't telling us the truth. We can have a talk with Gov'nor Young and we can sit tight till Partridge gits here and gives us all the facts from his side. It's wonderful good news and I reckon Scheffer's telling it to us straight."

It made Jeffery realize he had been jumping at shadows. He was satisfied if Sam was.

The stone chamber into which Jeffery was shown after returning from the beach was furnished with a bed and two chairs made in China and a rude wooden cabinet of native wood. Servants already had brought his sea trunk from the ship, along with all his books.

Sam's chamber was next door and he looked in at Jeffery. "I'll git shaved," he said. "You'd better, too, if Partridge's daughter expects to eat with us. What do you figger she'll be like?"

THE MISSION OF JEFFERY TOLAMY   29

Jeffery didn't know or greatly care. He would see as little of her as possible. He had not come halfway around the world to have his time taken by a trader's daughter eager to hear gossip about the latest clothes and fashions.

Sam closed Jeffery's door which, Jeffery noticed, had no hinges at all. It swiveled on two points of hard wood set top and bottom in stone holes. Jeffery opened his sea trunk, taking out razor, a last slim sliver of his aunt's soap, and a badger-hair brush. As he shaved before the Chinese looking glass he tried to think how quickly he could complete a fully documented report for Mr. Monroe and get back around the world with it.

He'd talk with Partridge. He'd see Governor Young and hope to speak to local chiefs here and try the language out on them, and he wanted to sail to Owhyee long enough to have an interview with King Tamehameha if it could be arranged. He gave himself three weeks to a month. With any sort of luck at all he ought to be on his way by July and sailing into the nation's capital by late October or early November. While he would not return in the blaze of glory which might have been his, had he been caught up in the fighting of a revolution, at least he would know he had accepted and completed the mission assigned to him.

Jeffery finished shaving. The voyage too, he told himself, ought to be profitable, much more so than anticipated. It was unreasonable to have a faint feeling of uneasiness. He could look forward to finding himself again in Philadelphia by the fall of this year, with a modest fortune and something of a name made for himself.

As he waited for Sam, he glanced at the pile of books along one wall of lava blocks. Neatly to one side of the big leather-bound volumes of Cook and Vancouver's voyages the house servant had arranged all twenty-three, small blue buckram-bound volumes of *Polexandre*, Rebecca's farewell gift to him. It was a romance of a young knight voyaging into the far lands to prove himself worthy of the love and fortune of Alcidiane, the Princess of the Inaccessible Isles. Of all the heroic romances, Jeffery had decided, it probably must be the longest one ever written; but it had helped to beguile him through the months of the voyage.

Sam was taking longer than usual to shave the bristle off his red face. On an impulse, Jeffery reached down to the first volume of *Polexandre*, turning to the flyleaf and again reading the inscription written there in a fine legible hand: "Je t'attendrai, Alcidiane." It was in Rebecca's handwriting. It had been a fancy of hers to sign her promise to wait for him in the name of the heroine of this romance.

Sam opened the door and Jeffery hastily thrust Rebecca from his mind. "It's time to eat," Sam said, "I've been talking with Scheffer while waiting for you. I've agreed to sail Partridge's sandalwood to China. I'll sail as soon as Partridge gits here to have our cargo unloaded and the new cargo put aboard . . ." He closed the door behind him. After a moment, when neither spoke, he said, "Scheffer says a ship's leaving Owhyee in three or four weeks for the Californy coast. He'll git you passage on that."

"I'll miss you," Jeffery said.

"I'd make you go with me if you didn't have to git back home as quick as possible to Mr. Monroe." Then Sam said heartily, "Look here. We don't have to be so glum about breaking up. We'll have a week or so together, won't we? What we need to do is to git drunk and kick off the traces."

"I'm beginning to think we do, at that."

"We can't, though, not around here, so long's there's this Partridge girl in the place. What I say is, we'll do this. We'll have lunch with Scheffer and this Captain Quorn who's come in from one of the islands. Then Scheffer wants me to see the sandalwood he's got stacked up on the beach and you can come with us. After that, we'll git out to the ship. It looks like a storm's blowing up. I'll git the ship towed into deeper water, with storm anchors. I ain't too easy about the men I left aboard, neither. They're all wild to git ashore. Scheffer's offered a dozen of his Kodiaks who'll stay on like they're told. If I'm sailing to China and expect to keep my crew, the men'll want their time here on shore. While you and me finish off with the ship this afternoon, Scheffer's promised to row out and have a talk with the masters of the Russian ships. He'll git the price they'll pay for the muskets. You and me can go to Gov'nor Young tomorrow to clear ourselves with him. If Young or King Tammy can beat the Russian offer, why, I say, we take it."

"Why not?" said Jeffery, smiling a little. It was unimportant now who bought the muskets, ball, and powder. It was merely more cargo to dispose of at the highest price.

"We'll git back about six and meet here with Scheffer and eat with him because he says his food's better than we could git in the village. Afterwards, you and me'll go into the village and stay there the night. How does that suit you?"

In his mind Jeffery suddenly saw the tall beguiling pagan girl who had stood before him on the quarter-deck early this morning with amber breasts, and with flowers in her hair. His heart lifted—and then it dropped as he thought of Rebecca. Next, he remembered she had read through every volume of *Polexandre* before giving it to him to read. Rebecca knew when the time came for the consummation of the knight's love for his princess, in the twenty-third and last volume, that the lovely Alcidiane had only asked her knight if he had been faithful to her in his thoughts. The heroine of *Polexandre*, it seemed to Jeffery, had done it neatly, saving herself distress. Jeffery thought Rebecca would probably do it neatly, too, when he returned to her as a captain in the army with possibly a medal. He would have proved himself. He would marry her and share her fortune, and she would have the old and established name of Tolamy, for whatever satisfaction it brought her.

"You don't have to bother how you look for lunch," Sam said as Jeffery reached for his jacket. "I forgot to tell you. Scheffer said the Partridge girl don't yet feel up to eating with us."

They ate in the big room to the east with the heavy wooden shutters thrown open. Through the windows, which were empty of glass, and beyond the walls of the compound Jeffery could see the bay like blue glass. Quorn was a well-scrubbed man, with a limp to one leg. He said he was engaged in the island trade. When Jeffery asked him if there might not still be danger of the British seizing the island, Captain Quorn stared politely for a second before saying that talk had gone around two or three years ago. Never heard of it any more, he said. King Tamehameha meant to continue his dynasty by giving the islands over to his eldest son.

After lunch, Dr. Scheffer, Sam, and Jeffery went down to the beach north of the compound where sandalwood had been stacked in piles higher than a white man's head. It was sweet and fragrant-smelling, cut in sticks the size and length of Jeffery's arm, and of a brown to golden color. Sam calculated finally, he could store all of it in the *Clymestre* by tearing out the retaining bulkheads between the first and second holds.

Dr. Scheffer said he counted upon Captain Crowell and Mr.

Tolamy having dinner at the compound tonight. Before joining them to have a look at the sandalwood he'd gone to Miss Susan in her quarters on the other side of the stone house. Unfortunately, she was still indisposed, but she had made him promise to entertain her guests; Dr. Scheffer didn't like to have her disappointed.

Sam looked at Jeffery and he looked at the German. Sam said, yes, Jeff and he'd be pleased to have dinner. Afterwards the two of them would go on into the village.

"If you go for the night to the village," Dr. Scheffer said affably, "would you accept a word from me first, sir? A piece of friendly advice?"

"What is it?" asked Sam.

It wasn't, said Dr. Scheffer, the silvery-gray eyes twinkling, that the Sandwich Island women were to be considered immoral. It was merely that they did not have, previous to the begetting of their children, all the attendant rituals and public ceremonies of communities believing in monogamy. In the Sandwich Islands a woman begot children from whosoever pleased her and if she liked a man she thought it reasonable to tell him so and ask him to take her. It was all very natural and sensibly handled.

Furthermore, he said, regarding Sam and Jeffery amiably, it was natural for men who'd had long months at sea to be eager to accept invitations so freely given. Dr. Scheffer had personally nothing against it; but he had, he believed, a responsibility to his guests until Mr. Partridge arrived. He thought they should be informed that most of the young women around the bay had been infected by the French disease. The disease had first been brought to the islands by the sailors in Captain Cook's vessels. Now it had spread among the natives until any man who went with a native woman had a good chance of contracting it.

"The French disease?" said Jeffery, in a very odd tone of voice.

"The French pox, sir; a loathsome dirty infection very often. It is rife around these ports."

Jeffery had never thought of such a horror. You heard or read of men venturing into far places and having gaudy times for themselves but you never were told of them getting themselves infected with the French pox.

Dr. Scheffer explained that the traders who had been here for any time had learned to take very young girls who'd had no chance of being contaminated or they went into the highlands or to the less frequented islands where the women had less opportunity of intercourse with strangers. Then he filled his curving porcelain pipe, said if he was to visit the Russian ships he had better do it before darkness fell; and stepped into the first of the small boats.

Sam rubbed his jaw. "Jeff, I can't believe all them girls have got the French pox."

Jeffery supposed there was only one way you could find out.

After Sam and he had gone aboard the *Clymestre* with the Kodiaks and come away an hour later, with a red dusk pressing down upon the bay, he was still thinking very much the same thing.

It was full night and raining when Sam and Jeffery, both soaked through, arrived at the compound. Dr. Scheffer had not yet returned from the Russian ships.

The rain streamed against the oiled kapa cloth covering the single narrow window in Jeffery's stone room. It was difficult to light the primitive lamp and even more difficult to keep it lit. He stripped and opened his sea trunk to bring out something to wear at dinner tonight. A gust of wind whistled and burst through the wet paper cloth over the window and blew out the lamp. He felt his way across the chamber and paused, thinking he had heard someone outside in the hall. He located the lamp. He tried to find the door again to get to Sam's room for a light when he heard a creaking. Someone came into the chamber and shut the door with a second creaking sound.

"Sam?"

"Shh! Not so loud. I'm Susan Partridge."

Fingers touched his arm. Jeffery jumped back . . . "You're—who?"

"Ben Partridge's daughter. Dr. Scheffer told me the *Clymestre's* captain and supercargo were staying in the house. Which one are you?"

Jeffery's naked foot stepped upon the heap of wet silk clothing he'd discarded a few minutes ago. He reached wildly down in the darkness. "Miss Partridge—would you stay out in the hall for about five minutes?"

"I can't stay out in the hall. Are you Captain Crowell?"

"I'm Jeff Tolamy, supercargo. Either you get in the hall or get to one side so I can—"

"You listen to me, Mr. Tolamy," said her whisper all in one breath, "I need help quick. Scheffer's a swindler. He humbugged my father. He's trying to humbug you and Captain Crowell. Scheffer was sent here by Governor Baranov to help the Russians capture our islands!"

-----

4. Jeffery wanted to lead her back to her room and to the native women who should be there to look after her; but first he wanted to get his pants on. In the darkness the wad of silk did not sort itself out easily. He got his jacket untangled from the pants. It was highly disconcerting to have a girl's hand reach blindly and touch his skin.

"What takes you so long?"

"I've need to get my clothes on."

"Great stars!" she whispered as if it were he who was being irrational. "I've lived long enough on these islands to ignore the common want of dress. If Scheffer returns to the house and finds I've broken free—we're lost!"

Jeffery remembered that Dr. Scheffer had said she had fallen and struck her head against a canoe. He knew you had to deal firmly but gently with anyone whose mind was wandering. He had pulled on his trousers; he now got into his jacket. He was ready to deal with Miss Susan Partridge and her unhappy state of mind.

"Miss Partridge, if you'll permit me to go for one of the women servants—"

"I was afraid you wouldn't believe me. Dr. Scheffer warned me it was no use to try to get away because no one would believe me. Oh, he's smooth as molasses! He humbugged Pa. He'll humbug anyone. As soon as he gets the muskets and powder unloaded from your ship he'll use Pa's compound here as a fort to hold Honoruru for the Russians. I expect he's already talked Captain Crowell into having him place his Kodiaks aboard the ship? That was his plan."

For Jeffery it was like walking briskly in a wide free space, full of confidence and direction, and suddenly colliding with a stone wall he had never seen. Scheffer *had* placed the Kodiaks aboard the *Clymestre*. Sam and Jeffery had gone to the ship in the small boat with them. "You'd better tell me how you learned all this."

"Last week Scheffer was in Pa's counting room and a Yankee trader or seaman was there with him. I heard them talking. Scheffer thought I'd gone to Pearl Island for the day—but I hadn't. I sneaked back into the compound because I wanted to know why he was so eager to get me out of sight. With Pa gone, I had an idea Scheffer was planning something on the sly with one of the other traders—and I listened—and I got caught listening.

"Scheffer caught me and hustled me into that storeroom in the rear. Damn him! He had me there all this week—two makaainana women watching me. Tonight one went for my supper, and, if you want to know, I hit the other on the head with a wooden bowl and came running to find you or Captain Crowell. Where's Captain Crowell? We'd better get him, hadn't we?"

"I think we had," Jeffery said.

Sam listened . . .

Jeffery threw the wooden bar across the heavy slab of koa-wood door and stepped across to the window where the rain was striking against the oiled kapa cloth window covering. He closed the shutters.

Sam's lamp was burning. In that flutter of yellow illumination he saw Susan Partridge very clearly. Her head was thrown back for her to sight up to Sam and her freckled face was all bold forehead and blazing eyes, with a mane of sun-streaked, chestnut hair down her back. She was wearing a garment of heavy green Chinese silk, sleeveless, tied around the waist, falling loosely to bare ankles. She was sixteen or seventeen, he'd have guessed, and had a boy's look to her, very slim and slight. Her father had been ill advised, Jeffery thought, to have kept her out here in times like these.

"Jeff," Sam asked when Susan finished, "what do you think?"

"Captain Crowell—"

"Miss, will you jist give us a second now to git our bearings? Jeff?"

"Let's get to Governor Young—"

"It's no use for you to go to John Young!" she cried. "Locate your crew on shore. Go to your ship before it's too late. The Russians mustn't get those muskets. You've got to do it yourselves; John Young can't lift a hand against the Russians until he receives orders from the king!"

Her alarm was real. The yellow light flickered and the wind was crying outside where rain poured down on the red coral walls. Jeffery blinked sweat from his eyes. "Let's get," he said to Sam.

"That's my opinion, too. Where's your pistol?"

Jeffery had left it in his chamber.

Sam pulled his horse pistol from his belt. "I got two more in my dunnage sack. Take one for yourself and give her the other."

Jeffery knelt on the stone floor, searching through Sam's bag. One thought after another streaked through his head. Scheffer had foxed them. It was Russia who was after the islands, not England. Even Mr. Monroe hadn't suspected. By closing the ports to all commerce not carried in Russian vessels, Russia could control the Pacific. She had New Archangel at the north. She had more, Jeffery remembered. She had Fort Ross somewhere on the Alta California coast. Jeffery pawed through Sam's bag. The pistols weren't in—no, here they were, wrapped in one of Sam's shirts. Susan promptly stuck out a hand to receive one of them.

Even if she used both hands she looked much too small and slight to handle a man's pistol. Jeffery asked, "Can you shoot one of these?"

She gave him a direct look, and nodded, the flame of light reflecting streaks of gold and deep brown in her hair. She took the pistol in her hand and held it up like a man might do, sighting first at the flint to see if it were tight, next at the pan. She pulled back the lock with a flick of her thumb.

Sam explained hoarsely, "The minute I open this door we head straight through the house and down to the gate in the wall for the village. We can decide what next to do there. You ready, miss?"

"When you are, captain."

Sam reached a hand to raise the bar of wood securing the door.

Susan asked Jeffery, "Can you shoot a pistol?"

Her question distracted Jeffery. He turned his head to her but he didn't give her an answer. There was an instant when he noticed she was smiling at him. It made him wonder a little to realize a girl could be saucy, almost making sport of him, when you'd think she'd be ready to jump out of her skin. He decided she had spunk, all right—and then he jumped, the heavy concussion sounding in his ears.

Something from outside in the passageway had struck heavily on the solid slab of koa-wood. In almost a daze of surprise Jeffery saw the wooden door separate into two pieces, splitting down the middle, splinters flying. One segment of door fell with a crash and was followed by the rest. In the passageway a sandalwood log had been used as a battering ram.

Jeffery's next impression was of a whole multitude of hairy creatures caught in the fitful glare of a red torch. Even as he watched, from among the crowd of hairy men emerged the larger bulk of Dr. Scheffer. Calmly, with the air of an old friend, he entered Sam's chamber.

Jeffery looked at the pistol. It was pointed straight at his own chest. Dr. Scheffer observed the room and its contents. He saw Susan, who had stationed herself behind the end piece of the massive Chinese bed. He said mildly, "So there you are, young lady?"

"Yes, I'm here."

The barrel of her pistol rested solidly across the end piece of the bed, aimed directly at Dr. Scheffer. Sam was at the far end of the bed. His pistol covered the doorway, holding the pack of Kodiaks out of the room.

Dr. Scheffer said, still mildly, "It would do none of you the slightest good to shoot me. If you did, the Kodiaks would tear you to pieces. I've taken my precautions. Twelve of them are in the passageway and I've sent a messenger to the Russian ships to send me aid . . ." He gestured with his pistol at Jeffery. "Accommodate yourselves like reasonable people. No harm will come to any of you. Lay down your arms."

It appeared to be a reasonable request. Jeffery lowered his pistol and Dr. Scheffer stepped forward to reach for it. Instead of lowering her pistol, though, and being reasonable, Susan shot Dr. Scheffer. She got him in the right shoulder and not in the heart because she had to shoot past Jeffery.

Dr. Scheffer spun and pitched heavily into Jeffery, knocking him to the floor and cracking his head on the stones. For a moment Jeffery was stunned. Then he pulled himself to his knees, hanging to one of the bedposts. He began to see more distinctly. Sam had an arm around Dr. Scheffer's neck and was using him as a shield. Susan Partridge had snatched Dr. Scheffer's pistol when he had dropped it, throwing her own now useless gun behind her. She aimed at the surge of men in the open door—and fired. For Jeffery the shot was like a rock splashing into his brain.

Now the men in the red torchlight of the passage were shouting and pointing at Sam, who was forcing Dr. Scheffer in front of him. Jeffery saw Sam cuff the man and cuff him again, ordering him to tell the Kodiaks to stay back.

The flat-faced men seemed taken up by a wave of astonishment, being swept back, retreating stiff-leggedly, except for the one on his knees who'd been shot. That one groaned and crawled backward, his musket lying where he had dropped it.

"Jeff, git that musket quick!"

That was Sam telling him what to do. Jeffery shoved himself away from the bed, picked up the musket, and saw Susan's face with its bold forehead and shining eyes floating in space before him. Ever so quietly Susan was saying, "Let me have your pistol."

Jeffery gave up his pistol and got the Kodiak's musket in both his hands. It was a heavy piece, made for short-range firing. Sam had thrust Dr. Scheffer against the wall. There was blood spreading down the German's yellow silk jacket.

Sam stuck the loaded pistol in Dr. Scheffer's ribs. "Walk, when I tell you to. We'll git down to the gate. Jist sing out and order your men not to fire if you want to keep alive."

Dr. Scheffer's big pale face moved around until the silvery eyes could sight back at Sam. "Captain," he said, "this does you no good, you know."

"Walk," Sam ordered.

"Give me one more word. I promise you will be reimbursed for your cargo. I act for Governor Baranov. Now, consider, please, we can reach an accommodation—"

"Damn you, walk," Sam said. "Jeff, keep close behind me with the girl. You hear?"

"Yes," said Jeffery.

Then they were in the dark passage going toward a wide door which framed the light beyond the rain. Scheffer went first, Sam behind him, then Susan, then Jeffery.

The rain beat on the ground and drummed on the roof, its sound like a steady rushing of surf. Through the noise Jeffery heard Sam's voice, hard and solid. "Order them men of yours to fall back!"

And Scheffer spoke up, shouting out in that queer barking speech to the Kodiaks. The moon shone mistily through the rains, streaking light across the enclosure. The expanse of compound melted and wavered in a watery paleness, enough for Jeffery to see the wooden gate down at the western end of the compound. He looked to his right and saw the girl's slight shape directly at his side, pacing along with him.

Sam took his eyes off Dr. Scheffer long enough to look back at Susan and Jeffery. Perhaps it was careless of Sam but it never occurred to Jeffery that it was. After having received a pistol ball in his right shoulder, his right arm gone and dangling uselessly at his side, you'd have assumed Dr. Scheffer knew when his game had ended.

Sam said, "Jeff, you and the girl cut for the village while I—"

Jeffery saw it all and cried a warning and was too late. With Sam in the way, Jeffery couldn't even fire at Dr. Scheffer, whose left hand had plunged inside his silk jacket and was out again, holding one of those little French pieces. The barrel was octagonal and not much longer than a man's finger.

Dr. Scheffer shot point-blank. Sam staggered. He dropped his pistol and slowly bent like a man being pressed down by a great weight. Quickly Jeffery stepped toward Sam. He had thought of Dr. Scheffer as being something like an ox, broad and heavy. There was nothing ox-like about the man as he flung himself for Sam's loaded pistol. In that wet silvery light he was quick and huge as an ape.

Susan had streaked in front of him, kicking aside Sam's pistol. The big man was on her with a bellow, hurling her away with his good arm. Once more he plunged for the pistol. Jeffery got behind him and clubbed him with the musket stock. Scheffer pitched flat, his head flopping, not moving.

Jeffery swung around, wanting to save his single musket charge if he could. Susan grasped the loaded pistol and faced around with him.

"Watch them," said Jeffery to her and bent down. "Sam! Sam!" he said, his voice strange to his own ears.

"Git me up."

"Are you—"

"Do what I say."

Lurching against Jeffery, Sam walked to the gate, Susan coming along sideways, crab fashion, the pistol pointing at the little men who had run as far as Dr. Scheffer. Four or five of them had begun to lift him from the wet ground.

Jeffery tried to shut his mind to his sudden fear for Sam. He wanted to get to the village and find help in a world which had suddenly become altered beyond all recognition.

Susan halted in the wet darkness. "Listen," she said.

They heard the surf now and then they heard a boat grind on the beach and voices. "Scheffer's Russians from the ships have cut us off from the village," she said, "we'll have to strike up into the hills."

———————

5.   Jeffery slung Sam's arm around his shoulder and the two stumbled after Susan. They were in a grove of palms and pandanus trees when she whispered sharply, "Hide quick!" They burrowed into leaves and vines, got down to mud and lay there.

Presently there was a crashing of feet through the brush. Jeffery stiffened and forgot to breathe. He heard a shouting in a language he didn't know—he judged it might be Russian, for it had nothing of that barking clatter of the Kodiaks' tongue. A musket was fired. A few minutes afterwards another musket was fired, farther away.

Jeffery remembered to breathe again and lifted his cheek from the mud. He felt Susan's arm move cautiously and next her hand pressed wetly against his arm. She whispered that if they were quick about it they could get on through the trees and into the taro fields.

The grove of trees rimmed the beach. Next came the taro fields, with now and then a mullet pond. Higher up the slopes were fields of grass, with tall blades strong enough to slice into flesh. Sam and

Jeffery followed behind Susan, sometimes losing her and having to wait until she came thrusting back through the dense grass. Sam began leaning more heavily on Jeffery, his body humping forward. It was hard going now, uphill and across soft ground.

A mile inland and a thousand feet or more above the bay the air lost its murkiness and the rain felt cooler. Sam tried to stand by himself and stumbled heavily. Jeffery knelt beside him, the wet drift of rain in his face. Sam stirred. He swore. He got up on one knee. He began to stand, a blurred dark shape; and then, Susan appeared, like a boy in outline with the wet silk clinging to her.

Jeffery said, "Are we far enough inland to try for the village?"

"If Scheffer's Russians and Kodiaks are searching between us and Honoruru, we wouldn't have a chance. How's Captain Crowell?"

"Jist don't bother 'bout me. I'll keep going."

"If we could climb to Punch Bowl Hill we'd find caves to hide in until morning."

"Git going," said Sam's voice heavily.

They climbed higher and higher over the great slope until they emerged on a shelf of land where hau thickets grew densely, the branches stiff, tearing at Jeffery's arms. There Susan led them into a cave away from the rain. Inside, the lava dust had a gingery smell where Sam lay down, head on his arms, and didn't move.

Jeffery crawled back to the open where Susan was standing watch, with the pistol in her hand. Ragged morning-glory vines, some as big around as a man's arm, covered most of the entrance and straggled down the slope. The rain was thinning, it seemed.

Jeffery held his voice low. "I can't tell how badly he's hurt. Will you stay with him while I get help from the village?"

"I'll go as soon as there's light. You stay with Captain Crowell."

"All I want to know is how to get to the village."

"You can't go down there," she explained impatiently. "You might be stopped by the natives and you don't know the language. When it's light, I'll—"

"I know enough of the language to manage."

"You've been here before?"

"I've never been here before in my life," Jeffery said. "But I was selected to sail with Captain Crowell because I'd learned enough of the language to make myself understood."

"I don't understand."

"I served the last year of the war at Grey's Fort, outside of Philadelphia, and the day peace was announced," said Jeffery, rather
grimly, "we shot off all our cannon. Our fort was equipped with
cannon dating from the Revolution—and mine blew up. I was the
fort's only casualty during the entire war. I was nearly ten months
in the Philadelphia City Hospital. In the cot next to mine was a
native, George Hoomehoome, who'd been kidnaped years ago from
Atooie by a Yankee sea captain, and brought to our country.
George grew up, enlisted in our navy, and got a pike-staff wound in
his side during a sea fight. George and I became friends. For nothing better to do during the months, he taught me something of his
language. I'm afraid I'm not too fluent, but I'll manage to bring
help for you and Sam if you'll tell me how to get to Honoruru."

"You can't go before it's light. If Scheffer's strung his Russians
and Kodiaks along the approaches to the village, you'll risk being
stopped and shot. The only chance of sneaking into the village is
by the north where the Nuuanu stream runs into the bay. But you
can't get through until you have light to see by."

Suddenly Susan was silent, alert, as if listening. He heard her wet
silk rustle against her legs as she whirled around and again held
herself still. Then, with the utmost caution, she began to lift one
of the tangled morning-glory vines she'd pulled over the high narrow cleft that was the entrance into the lava cave. She reached for
Jeffery.

Pressing silently to the vines, he heard her quickened breath,
while he peered beyond the cave's entrance. It was like sighting
upon a new world. All the ragged gigantic landscape below was in
pale shadows now, lava ridges and undulating shrubs like black
mounds revealing themselves under the diffused moonlight. Down
farther, near the darker rectangular patches of the taro fields, he
saw three stubby shadows go scurrying in single file until they had
vanished into a gully. Susan had been right. Scheffer's Kodiaks
were still on the hunt.

Jeffery knelt in the cave and listened to Sam's labored breathing.
He fumbled at Sam's jacket to open it as if by opening it Sam could
breathe more easily. Sam stirred in the darkness. He muttered, "Jist
leave me quiet, Jeff. Where's the girl?"

"Guarding the entrance."

"Git back with her."

"We can't bring help up here until daybreak."

"You take charge, Jeff, till I git more strength in me."

Jeffery returned to the cave entrance and squatted not far from Susan. He set about cleaning the mud and leaves from his musket. He was relieved that she didn't gab. At least it was better being here than a prisoner on board one of Scheffer's Russian ships— providing Sam didn't die. He granted that much. But, by God! she couldn't have calculated that far ahead when she'd blazed away at Scheffer last night with her pistol.

His head still hurt where he'd hit it on the stone floor when Scheffer had fallen on him. He'd been so easily humbugged. Both Sam and he had been humbugged. By now he expected the *Clymestre* was lost, and its cargo with it. Hope of returning to Philadelphia with a profit seemed futile. And deeper still, the core of Jeffery's mind numbly realized the greater catastrophe. For months now, Jeffery realized, the Russians must have quietly prepared to move into the Pacific, after engaging Dr. Scheffer as an advance agent.

As time passed, Jeffery became aware of listening for more than the sound of rain and wind or the approach of men through the thickets beyond the cave. He'd been listening for shots and the firing of cannon to come from the bay as Scheffer and the Russian ships attacked Honoruru. Because there were no sounds of fighting, he had an improbable lifting of hope. Perhaps it wasn't too late for Governor Young to fight back. He spoke to Susan.

She answered in a small whisper, "He won't fight the Russians. He doesn't dare."

"Scheffer can't command more than two or three hundred men in all," Jeffery said, "including everyone aboard those Russian frigates in the bay. Governor Young must have two or three thousand warriors."

"He has more, but it's no use to expect Governor Young or the chiefs to attack. After Captain Cook's murder, forty years or so ago, there was such an outcry that it looked as if the islands might be taken over very quickly. As soon as King Tamehameha got any sort of power he laid down a strict kapu—that's—"

"I know what kapu means. Go on."

"It's much more than a law. It's really a religious commandment," her whisper said earnestly. "King Tamehameha established a kapu protecting all white men. Until now the kapu's staved off trouble. All of us have been safe under the kapu except a few white men who were killed because they were fools or drunk and interfered with the priests and went prowling into the temples. Until Governor Young gets word to King Tamehameha and receives orders, he and the chief'll observe the kapu. They'll do all they can to prevent the common natives from attacking."

"Even if Scheffer raises the Russian flag?"

"I'm afraid so."

Jeffery was stunned. The islanders wouldn't fight. It was a worse catastrophe than he had thought . . . It was beyond all reason. You expected any nation, even a nation of heathen, to resist and make a fight of it. He wiped at his musket, tightening the flint in the clumsy Russian lock. Susan remained silent.

He must have dozed off. When next he lifted his head he could distinguish more clearly the thick tracery of vines across the cave's entrance. He saw the outline of Susan's small head and slim figure where she was huddled beside the cave's opening, a hand holding the pistol in her lap.

"I fell asleep," he said, ashamed. "Is Sam—"

"I looked at him twice. He was resting or asleep."

Jeffery put his head out of the cave. Morning wasn't far off. He took hold of the musket and he tried to sound cool as he said, "It's time for me to go."

"Let me go. I'm smaller and shan't be so apt to be seen as you. Probably I can run much faster, too."

"Probably," said Jeffery, "you can't. You've never seen me run."

"Mr. Tolamy—"

"Jeffery'll do," said Jeffery. "I've got longer legs than you have. They'll go faster. You can see the truth of the first and you'll have to take my word for the last. How do I get to Nuuanu Valley?"

He liked having her promptly answer his question instead of wanting to argue. She said they were on the western slope of Punch Bowl Hill, three miles east of Honoruru and the bay. He was to go north on the slope, staying well above the fields until he saw Nuuanu Valley and the stream. By hiding along the banks of the stream and in the reeds, Susan said, it was possible to approach the village even if Scheffer had posted his men all around the outskirts. In his place, she said, she'd go directly to John Young, who'd know what was best to do in the emergency. You could trust Governor Young. He wouldn't fail Captain Crowell.

She described Governor Young's palace for Jeffery. It resembled a big Connecticut barn of poles and grass instead of wood and was no more than a good stone's throw from the head of the wharf. He'd see it as soon as he got into the village. It was the second biggest structure there and opposite the temple, which was the biggest. He couldn't mistake the one for the other, either, because the temple was nothing at all like a Connecticut barn.

To point out directions she pulled away the vines and stepped a pace or so into the thickets with Jeffery, both of them very wary about showing their heads. It was at least half an hour before sunrise and what light there was came dimly through a greenish haze. Susan tried to point out where the village was but the rainy mist obscured all the bay and village.

Again he was struck by the silence, broken only by faint cries of birds soaring in the dark dim green light over the taro fields so far below. Muskets by now should be rattling from the beach and cannon firing, with three or four thousand heathen warriors massing to fight the Russians and Kodiaks. Susan waited silently until, stirring, he looked down at her and distractedly noticed she'd braided her wet hair while he'd drowsed off; the shining chestnut braids were wrapped tightly around the small erect head.

"Isn't there any means of arousing these natives?" he said, and as he spoke a possible answer came to him. He stared at his legs. He looked back into Susan's face, and continued as if he had not broken off, "Suppose Scheffer's Kodiaks on board our ship drank enough of our rum for them to decide to go into that temple in the village?"

"I wish it might happen but it won't."

"If it did, would Governor Young's kapu hold back the natives?"

"It's the king's," she said as if the distinction were important. "No, I shouldn't think it would. If those Kodiaks or Russians were fools enough to violate the temple, the common run of natives would go into such a frenzy that no one could stop the slaughter. Why? What are you thinking of?"

He didn't tell her what he'd been thinking because he was still undecided. He'd have to run faster than ever he'd run in his life. He said, "I was thinking, you don't seem much to care whether or not the Russians seize the port and island?"

"I don't much care?" she exclaimed like a flintlock banging off. "Pa's told me what would happen back in our world if these island ports were closed off! But Pa was afraid it'd be by the British. Scheffer humbugged him. Now Pa's a prisoner on Atooie, maybe killed because he cared so much. You think I don't care? Great stars above. I hoped to sail to Owhyee and warn the king. I'd have gone in an outrigger. Anything! I'd have tried to swim, even."

"Before I go I'll talk to Sam a minute if he's awake. You'd better come listen," Jeffery said.

A pale lavender light had gradually infused the cave's darkness. Sam opened his eyes and said so low Jeffery hardly could hear the words, "I thought you'd gone." He swallowed. He wiped at a thread of blood which had trickled from his mouth.

Jeffery opened Sam's wet jacket and saw a small caked spot near Sam's navel where the pistol ball had gone into his body. It wasn't much to look at.

"Sam—" Jeffery had a constriction in his throat. If a man continued very long to bleed internally he could drown in his own blood from having his lungs fill up.

"Why ain't you . . . down there fighting by now? Leave me with the girl."

"Sam, could you hold out for another couple of hours or so?"

"I'd rather die than git home . . . saying we were licked . . ."

Jeffery stood up. "I might have a chance," he told Susan, "to let those Kodiaks catch sight of me and lead them in a chase to the temple."

"You'd be killed!" said Susan.

"I told you I know how to run, didn't I?" He looked at Sam again. "I'd be delayed getting help for you, though."

Jeffery's throat hurt him. It burnt down in his chest and spread to his heart. He thought more of Sam than these islands or what the Russians did out here or of returning home in something like a blaze of glory.

Sam ordered harshly, "I ain't going to die. Do what I say . . . Git them Russians if y u can!"

"All right, Sam," said Jeffery. "I will."

He went out and Susan went with him. She said quietly, "You take my pistol and leave your musket. You can't run so fast with a musket."

"Take care of Sam, won't you? I'll get back or send help as quick as I can."

"I know you'll get back," she said. "Now, listen. You'll see three wooden oracle towers on top of the temple platform. If you get the Kodiaks or Russians to chase after you, once you put foot on the stone steps of the temple don't turn back or you won't have a chance. The biggest lane in the village goes by the temple. The natives'll see you and they'll jam into the lane. Run straight across the temple floor. Shoot anybody who tries to stop you. Head for the third and biggest oracle tower. If you get there, the priests won't want to kill you under it. They'll try to call you away from it, into the open. It'll give you a minute. When you get past the oracle tower, run for the edge of the stone platform. Mr. Davis's garden is directly behind the temple. Jump as hard as you can, even if you have to risk breaking a leg. If you can reach Mr. Davis's garden you'll have him to help you."

Suddenly she lifted up on her toes and kissed him. "Run! Run very fast, won't you?"

He started down the slope. When he was away from the cave he stopped and looked back. He saw nothing now but the thickets and morning-glory vines dark green against the red and black lava. Yet he could still feel her fresh warm lips where she had so unexpectedly kissed him.

6. He followed a northwesterly direction, keeping the bay to his left, two and a half to three miles distant he estimated, although he could see little of it through the sweeping mists of early morning. Up above him, to his right, towered the immense bare crags and ledges that rimmed the extinct volcano. As the night cleared, he noticed several thin columns of smoke

streaming from the crater bowl. The wind brought him the pungent smell of burning.

In the growing light, below and to the north, he saw a vast crooked finger of green extending between gigantic folds of mountains toward the bay. Down there was Nuuanu Valley. He paused, realizing it was not too late to change his mind. If he wished, he could continue north to the valley and there find the stream and go along the stream safely to the bay and have a good chance of slipping unseen into the village. A wave of disgust swept over him for hesitating.

He turned west, continuing toward Honoruru. The breeze from the bay beat through the mist, like an invisible animal nosing and huffing. Out of the mist again, he found himself on a rise of ground like a giant's pate. All the leeward side of the island was exposed to his gaze. A dozen miles away to his left was the castled rise of Diamond Hill. Directly before him, perhaps two miles distant and a thousand feet below, he sighted the promontory upon which the Partridge compound was marked by its pattern of red coral walls.

Once more he was overwhelmed by the threatening tranquillity of the land. He saw natives trudging along paths to their fields, but there was no sign of the Russians or Kodiaks. On to his right was the village, almost hidden within its grove. Like dots the ships rode the harbor, too far away for Jeffery to make them out clearly. But where in all this, he thought, were Scheffer's men?

He looked due west again, toward the promontory. Down there in the compound a flag was being raised. From where he was it appeared as though a small company of men were gathering themselves around the flagpole. Now up came a tiny square of cloth, the wind whipping at the Russian colors, the double eagles flying. Only a strong wind blew, not a shot was fired or a spear thrown. Natives continued to trudge unheeding to their fields. He went on then, directly toward the village.

He loped past three islanders repairing a mud dike; they turned their heads and watched him go. He entered a lane at the edge of the village expecting at every step to encounter Scheffer's sentinels. A quarter of a mile below him, high above the waving fronds, he could see the wooden towers which would belong to the temple. Where, he asked himself irritably, were Scheffer's men? He wanted very much to get it over with.

A sudden rustling off to his right from within a green hibiscus hedge at the end of a mullet pond became a loud whirring. Straight into the morning sky shot a yellow-winged bird. Jeffery walked perhaps five steps along the lane—and halted suddenly. Something about the bird's flight had not been right.

Then he remembered what it was. The hedge had continued to quiver and shake after the bird had climbed into the air. He turned, glancing over his shoulder. He felt something flutter within his chest as if the bird had given a last startled leap and then there was nothing but a sensation of gathering himself for effort. Somehow Jeffery had not been very surprised to see a brown, flat-faced, hairy little man rising from the green hibiscus.

Jeffery sucked in his breath and ran.

The Kodiak promptly lifted his musket and shot at him. Something like an enormous hornet hummed past, not far from Jeffery's right ear. He was astonished. The Kodiak had tried to kill him. Jeffery blinked. He heard a bird singing sweetly high in the air. The land was peaceful and lovely. He continued running toward the village.

Presently he stopped, for no one was running after him. Exasperatedly, he walked on, sighting around in an effort to find where the Russians or Kodiaks had hidden themselves. Everything was wrong; he had a notion he was about to make a great fool of himself.

The sun had lifted completely above the horizon by now. There was a refracted quality to the light which seemed to throw everything slightly out of proportion. It was as if the huts and noisy swarm of islanders and the tall palms were all floating away from him as he advanced. He followed a lane between apparently deserted huts. The village seemed very still. Ahead Jeffery saw the immense lava walls of the temple, gray and red with thick vines growing to the top. Past the temple walls was a large dun-colored structure, shaped exactly as Susan had described it to him, like an enormous barn.

He halted a dozen yards from the tremendous rise of worn steps that mounted the temple wall. Inside, he could see wooden and stone idols peering down at him and the three wooden towers which Susan had called oracle towers rising through black greasy columns of smoke from a fire burning on the great stone platform. He whistled softly through his teeth. He walked on past the steps. A few natives crawled from their huts and stared somberly at him.

When he looked over his shoulder he saw at least a dozen sturdy commoners collecting quietly behind him in the flowering lane. They were remarkably big fellows with skins ranging in color from light glistening brown to deep coral. Two were carelessly holding long sticklike weapons which glinted dully in the morning light from the shark teeth set along the edges.

Between Jeffery and the barnlike structure of the palace, a second lane came in at right angles. A Kodiak came pounding out of the second lane and stopped abruptly. At first glance Jeffery had the startled conviction it was the same Kodiak who had sprung from the hibiscus hedge back of the village. He advanced another step; the Kodiak showing yellow teeth in a mirthless face.

Jeffery looked back again. Five Kodiaks were elbowing through the growing group of islanders. He tightened his grip on his pistol and turned forward. The joints holding his knees seemed to loosen. Instead of the one Kodiak, a score of them had trooped into the lane.

Scheffer came running among them, lurching to a halt, peering at Jeffery. Scheffer's face was paler than when last Jeffery had seen it. His right arm was in a cradle of dirty silk suspended around his oxlike neck. He spoke across the space of twenty feet between them, "Tolamy! My men reported your approach to the village. The one who shot at you will be flogged, I promise you. I gave orders no harm was to come to any of you if you came peacefully. Where's Crowell? Where's Partridge's daughter?"

He advanced slowly toward Jeffery. "We should be able to accommodate each other. Early this morning some of your seamen were ill advised enough to row to your ship and throw my Kodiaks overboard. I want that cargo, sir. I'll pay for it in specie." Jeffery suddenly knew that this was what he had been waiting for. He had a vision of Scheffer enlarging before him, and behind Scheffer the bearded faces of Russian seamen, massing. He pointed his pistol and pulled the trigger. Scheffer dodged back. The pistol hung fire. Jeffery had already wheeled about, getting a knife thrust along his arm, when the pistol let go with a thud, its bullet smashing harmlessly into soft red dirt.

He saw the temple walls and deliberately ran for them. He smashed recklessly into a Kodiak. An instant followed when the islanders in the lane gave way, having expected the tawny-haired white man to go running toward the beach and wharf. Jeffery was followed by the Kodiaks in full cry, with Scheffer and the Russians behind them. He swerved violently and got himself to the top of the stone steps, paused to look behind him, and saw three Kodiaks darting up.

He went charging across the stone pavilion, between yellowish huts, wickerwork and wooden idols. A few white-robed men to the left leaped up and froze as though momentarily paralyzed. As he ran, two wooden towers seemed to flash crazily past him, one on each side. Beyond, he saw a third with white rags fluttering from the framework. The stench was foul, and a greasy smoke hung low over the center area of the pavilion. Jeffery's eyes smarted and momentarily he lost sight of the tower, but he kept on running. He heard shots. He burst through the thickest of the smoke, his head down, his legs flashing; and he ran as he had never run before across the two hundred yards from one side of the cluttered stone pavilion to the other.

His purpose was so single-minded that he forgot to leap when he came to the far end of the morai. He smashed headlong into a tangle of wet vines at the foot of the wall. Before he could extricate himself he heard a crackling from overhead, a thump, and down through greasy yellow smoke tumbled a hairy body close enough to graze Jeffery's right arm.

The Kodiak jerked and dangled, one leg caught in a vine, a spear sticking from his belly like a tremendous thorn. For several seconds before he died the Kodiak screamed steadily.

---

7.   A lane bright with hibiscus was below him. Across it, through gusts of yellow smoke, he made out a wall of reeds or sticks and a habitation which appeared to have something more to it than the clusters of grass huts under the palms. He re-

membered Susan telling him to try to leap into Mr. Davis's garden,
which he had not done. He struggled in the vines, while from the
pavilion above him the uproar increased. By now the noise was
deafening. A roaring mob of natives went running below him,
streaming out beyond the temple walls. Instantly Jeffery ceased
struggling.

When he judged it safe again, he tore at the vines with both
hands and, at the same instant, kicked. The vines gave. He plum-
meted to the lane with a thud that knocked the wind out of him.
He shook himself and got up, holding steady until his vision
cleared.

He skirted warily along the walls. The whole village was in an
uproar. He had a memory of Sam bleeding in the cave and of Susan
left to watch him. Doggedly Jeffery continued forward, trying to
orient himself. He had to get help.

In the brassy light of morning the wind had increased, carrying
rain in from the bay. He stopped, hearing a distant thud of cannon
fire. From the south came a rattle of musketry. He stiffened. Two
tall natives, running toward the bay, saw him, stopped, and went
on, all in a second.

Not far behind them came a black man. Two pistols protruded
from his belt, and he had a long-barreled musket in the crook of
his arm. Jeffery recognized him as the man he'd seen on the
Clymestre and called, "Mr. Allan!" He ran forward unsteadily.

The black man stopped. "You the one them Russians are after?"

"Yes. Where's Mr. Young?"

"Hard to say." The black man contemplated Jeffery for a long
second. "What you want Young for?"

Jeffery told him, shouting passionately at that dark face staring
at him in the rain.

"Young and the rest of us yesterday figured you were with Scheffer and the Russians. We figured something was stirring, but we
didn't know what. Young was waiting to hear from the king. Now
the entire village's gone crazy. You ought to see 'em swarming
down around the compound, thousands of 'em. The priests, the
kahunas, can't hold 'em back."

"Susan Partridge is at the cave with Sam, Mr. Allan—"

"Lemme think a minute. You can't git to Young. Likely he's

with the chiefs and kahunas somewhere to the south side of the compound where the natives have got at the Russians . . . I'll go with you." He peered down at Jeffery. "You ain't hurt?"

Jeffery shook his head. "We'll need a litter for Sam."

"I'll git you one from my kuleana. I live behind the village. Keep close along with me, Mr. Tolamy. This ain't too safe right now for white-skinned fellows."

The black man set a stiff pace, taking long strides while Jeffery strained to keep up with him. They got out through the village, taking a path Jeffery vaguely remembered having come down earlier that morning.

It would be no use trying to see Governor Young now, Allan said. The governor would be palavering with the chiefs. Everything had gone out of hand after the natives had fallen into such a frenzy, breaking the kapu protecting strangers. Maybe it was a good thing it had happened, maybe not.

"Tolamy! Oh, Tolamy!" From the smoky haze below Jeffery heard his name faintly called. The black man swung around, musket ready.

In another minute a thin, hatless man appeared, running upwards from between rows of deserted huts, running awkwardly as if one leg were hurt. Surprised, Jeffery recognized Captain Quorn, whom he'd met yesterday, the man who had brought in a cargo of sandalwood from one of the nearby islands.

"Tolamy!" he said furiously, his face drained of color under its tan. "By Christ! has the world here gone insane? Allan? You too? Have Scheffer and those Russians stolen your ship as well?"

"My sloop's safe at Pearl Island, Mr. Quorn. They got yours?"

"Half an hour ago." Quorn rocked on his feet. "I trusted Scheffer. He promised yesterday to buy my cargo . . ." He turned to Jeffery again. "They're after your ship, you know. Your men seem to be putting up a fight. Where's Crowell? I saw you and ran to warn you. My ship's lost. Gone, by God! If Crowell's with a woman—"

"He's been shot," Jeffery said.

"Shot? Oh, Christ!"

Allan said quickly, "Have they got Crowell's ship yet?"

"Not as I could see. What a savage mess this day's turning into."

Allan took hold of Jeffery's arm. "You look after your ship, boy. Cap'n Quorn—"

"I'll stand by him if we can steal a canoe from the wharf to make off in it. A few of my men are still on shore." The man looked at Jeffery, a bleak violence on his face. "I'll do what I can against those bloody Russians! Are you armed, sir?"

Allan thrust his musket at Jeffery. "You go for your ship if you'll trust me to do what's possible for Cap'n Crowell and Miss Susan."

Jeffery hesitated, torn between Sam and the ship. The wind crashed and moaned. Quorn and even the black man seemed small against the great rise of land.

Quorn's face contorted. "I blame Young for this. I blame the king! Why weren't we traders warned in time? Christ! Are you coming or not, Tolamy?"

"We was all caught," the black man said heavily. He gave Jeffery a push. "Git out there to your ship where you belong . . ."

Jeffery went stumbling back down the lane with Captain Quorn. In a crazy quilt of tawny browns and greens, the point upon which the compound was constructed came in sight, and it was as if Jeffery were sighting through rain at a drawing in perspective, across which streamed lines of smoke. The enormous bay was all to the west, and the entire area around the compound was thick with screaming heathen, attacking the walls.

Captain Quorn showed his teeth as he flung his arm in the direction of the compound. "Christ afflict 'em all, sir! Whether you know it or not, when you lost your head and led those damnable Russians after you to the temple you did a terrible morning's work against 'em . . ."

"Where's the Clymestre? I don't see her, captain."

"On ahead. Your crew has moved her further from the Russian ships. We'll sight her when we get free of this cursed smoke . . ."

In another ten minutes they had passed through the village on their way to the wharf and Jeffery saw a ship which looked like the Clymestre through the rain. The ship had lifted anchor. She was making headway slowly toward the south, the wind striking her storm sails. The waves rolled in heavily on the beach—and a long-boat near the wharf was being launched by a dozen men shoulder deep in the surf.

"We're in luck," cried Captain Quorn. "There's some of my men now and they seem to've located a boat for us."

Jeffery halted on the beach, surf washing his legs. He peered through the rain before turning with quick suspicion to Captain Quorn. "Look here, sir. Those men are Kodiaks—"

Something struck him down from behind.

It seemed to Jeffery that he came to in isolated pieces of perception with none of them fitting together. For how many hours or days it was he didn't know, but he had an awareness of being in Sam's berth, not his own, on the Clymestre. He thought perhaps men had entered to give him water to drink because he remembered choking and nausea, but all of that might have been a dream. Later, when he tried to get off the bunk, he discovered irons were clamped around his legs.

From the motion he knew the Clymestre was under sail—that was another piece of the pattern which began to form. In his mind he could go back as far as being upon the beach. He recalled going to the beach with Captain Quorn and at first he assumed Captain Quorn must have been killed by the Kodiaks but gradually he began to doubt it. He wondered how many other white men in addition to Quorn might have been secretly purchased by Scheffer.

Probably Governor John Young had had suspicions, he thought, which was why the old man had acted so strangely aboard ship the morning the Clymestre got into the harbor. It didn't explain, though, why Governor Young hadn't tried to beat Scheffer and the Russians to the mark. That was a mystery still, as upside down as ever. It was difficult to think rationally. The ship seemed to be laboring. They must be running into the storm which Sam had expected. Sam! The thought of Sam filled him with unutterable anguish.

When he came to again he struggled to remain conscious. It was like trying to climb up from a black well, slipping, falling again, once more being engulfed, and after an interval once again laboriously and painfully attempting the slow climb.

His body felt stiff and awkward. It was morning now and his throat was parched but his head was clearer. The irons were still clamped around his ankles. He wondered if they had forgotten him. Well, let them. The longer he had to get his wits collected the better. He was in the hands of the enemy—it came to him like that, flat and incisive, along with a dulled conviction of never having quite realized it actually could happen. It was like telling yourself the sky might fall on your head and then having it actually fall in pieces upon you.

He thought of protesting violently as soon as someone finally entered. He was a brevet captain in the United States Army, an officer of a nation at peace with Russia, but it seemed to him that his chances of extricating himself were far greater if the Russians and their agents assumed he were supercargo, someone arrived here without any particular design or knowledge. He resolved to hold his tongue and above all to admit to nothing of what Mr. Monroe had dispatched him here to do.

The sun must have lifted above the sea, for the light had become brighter inside the berth when the door opened and, without warning, in stepped Captain Quorn.

"Well, sir," he asked, looking down upon Jeffery, "how do you feel this morning?"

"Surprised," said Jeffery.

Captain Quorn showed his teeth in a grimace. "There's nothing like a rap over the head to give a man a feeling of surprise, is there? I've had it myself, Mr. Tolamy. You never can accustom yourself to it, either; I'll vouch for it." He laughed.

It came to Jeffery with a sense of wonder that such an evident ruffian as Quorn, despite the man's attempt at fine manners, must consider a rap on the head as nothing. He would be a fool to show resentment to such a man.

"Where"—asked Jeffery after a pause—"are we bound for, captain?"

"Atooie, Mr. Tolamy. Some call it the leeward isle."

Gazing up at that raffish face with its amused grin Jeffery felt sickened. He closed his eyes. Atooie? It was the first island he had learned about. Back in the Philadelphia City Hospital, that huge forlorn native, George Hoomehoome, had said Atooie was the name of his own island. Then Jeffery forgot George Hoomehoome and all he had learned from George during those ten months in the hospital and felt a constriction of his throat.

"What of Sam?" he asked.

"Captain Crowell? I can't answer for him."

"Have you killed him?"

" 'Twas you I was sent after, not Captain Crowell," said Captain Quorn negligently. "Ask Scheffer all the questions of that sort when you see him. I'll even give you a small word, if you're inclined to accept it? Scheffer's not a hard man to deal with if you don't cross him. He's acting for the Russian government to take possession of the Sandwich Islands and I'm under his orders. Now, sir, as supercargo you have the authority to dispose of the ship and her cargo when the ship's master isn't—available. Mind you," he added hastily, "if Crowell's dead, it wasn't by my doing."

Sam dead? No, Sam couldn't be dead. Susan had promised at the cave to take care of Sam. The black man had gone up there for Sam. Quorn was pretending and hinting at a knowledge he did not have.

"He's not dead," Jeffery said.

"I give you my word, I couldn't tell you. At least, he's not aboard and as supercargo you have the authority. Take my advice. Sign the ship and cargo over to Scheffer."

"That's what Scheffer wants of me?"

"I expect, Mr. Tolamy," said Quorn, faintly derisive, "Scheffer'll have what he wants out of you one way or the other."

For a moment Jeffery did not speak. At last, rather slowly, he asked, "You've killed our crew, have you?"

"We have only three of them to deal with. They're down now in the hold, thinking of whether or not they'll join with us. Now, enough questions, Mr. Tolamy. I would feed you this morning but the *Ilmen* has beat back, having signaled us to put you aboard . . ."

A quarter of an hour later men of the Kodiak crew carried Jeffery on deck. His legs were still bound; he was helpless.

Captain Quorn came to him, the warm wind blowing his cloak around his legs. He observed Jeffery for a moment and then said, "We're lowering you into the longboat. No attempt at communication, if you please, sir, with your ship's officer or the two men of the crew. It will go hard with them if you do."

"As you say, sir," and Jeffery, trying to smile. His voice was a croak, for he was parched, but he would not give this Yankee traitor the satisfaction of being begged for a drink of water.

He was let down and did as he was ordered to do. He saw the second officer of the *Clymestre*, a stocky man named Kegg Finn, in the bow, bound as Jeffery was; he looked hard at Kegg, who returned his gaze, but neither spoke. He got a wetting while being rowed the two cable lengths to the *Ilmen*.

They dropped lines and Jeffery was hoisted aboard. The leg irons were loosened. Hands and arms still bound, he was shoved up the companionway where three Russian ship's officers, swarthy and bearded, and Scheffer were waiting.

Scheffer puffed away at his pipe. Presently, in his toneless voice, he said, "I'm sorry to see you in this condition, Mr. Tolamy, but perhaps it can be remedied. As supercargo, you can release your ship and its stores to me if a payment I make satisfies you. I can take you below to our main cabin, where by signing a paper I have ready all can be arranged."

Jeffery said, "Let Captain Crowell attend to it, sir."

"I should like to have him do that, Mr. Tolamy, but your failure and his to accommodate yourselves to my proposals have cost him his life."

Jeffery looked back at Scheffer. "He's not dead."

He could look across the rail and see the *Clymestre* wallowing sluggishly. If Sam had been aboard he would never have allowed his ship to wallow as she was now, slowly getting underway again with those thick-fingered creatures swarming clumsily along her yards.

"Not dead?" said Dr. Scheffer, most gently. He looked down and Jeffery could have sworn the man's face was strangely kind. "I think I regret it as much as you do, Mr. Tolamy. Captain Crowell was a man who had attracted my admiration. I had hoped he might listen to reason and be persuaded it would be no loss to his honor were he to engage his talents under the Russian flag. I had even tried to warn both you and him about my Kodiaks. They are like dogs and like dogs sometimes lose their heads when attacked. They came upon Crowell and Susan Partridge sometime before we sighted you, and Crowell unwisely shot and killed one of their number. It was very brave of him, sir, because he was trying to give the Partridge girl the chance to escape but it was so very unnecessary. I had given the Kodiaks strict orders to harm none of you." He paused.

Jeffery said dully, "They killed him?"

"I'm sorry," said Dr. Scheffer and there seemed to be no make-believe about it. He was sorry. "Susan got away. At least Captain Crowell provided enough of a diversion for my Kodiaks—" Dr. Scheffer stopped.

It seemed to Jeffery that he could see Sam up there on the slope, crawling laboriously and painfully from the cave, trying to raise himself up to aim the musket while hoarsely ordering Susan to clear away while she could.

The deck of the Russian ship seemed to be tilting. Somehow the Clymestre looked very beautiful with her sails spread so whitely against the morning sky. Sam had always cherished her. She was making headway now, becoming smaller on the sea, leaving the Russian ship in her wake.

Much more briskly than before, Dr. Scheffer was saying, although still with much kindness, "With poor Crowell lost to us, I'm afraid I must now look to you to deliver your ship and her cargo to us, Mr. Tolamy. As soon as I can allow your release to return to your nation, you shall be paid in specie for both the cargo and the ship's temporary use. I think we can also allow a proper indemnity for Captain Crowell's death even though, in strict fact, I hardly believe any court of inquiry could say I was at fault. I must speak with some bluntness. As you are a neutral, I shall be required to detain you for a time on Atooie because you have acquired a certain knowledge of our plans. To release you before we have won these islands might possibly jeopardize our operations. There, now —can you ask for a franker explanation from any man? Sign the paper I have in my main cabin and I'll give you the best accommodations available on the island."

Jeffery made no reply. The Russians had both the Clymestre and her cargo, anyway. If by refusing to sign Jeffery someday could convict Scheffer of an act of piracy as well as for an action resulting in Sam's death he would ask for nothing better.

"Will you accommodate me?" asked Scheffer.

"No, I won't sign."

With his good hand Scheffer stroked his chin before saying equably, "I have at least tried with you, young man, haven't I? Your signature is of no great value to me, for a court of claims will uphold my rights in these waters to search and take over any ship inimical to my purpose. I wonder if you know how you have helped me to lose the port of Honoruru?"

Jeffery stared back more steadily than he felt at the eyes now probing at him. "How so?" he asked.

"To be blunt, you were a young fool, sir," said Scheffer, his eyes veiling. "By heedlessly rushing upon the temple, with my dogs of Kodiaks in full chase after you, you precipitated a disturbance which will cost me six months' delay before I can return with sufficient force to pacify the inhabitants. On my oath, if I believed you had done it by deliberate intent I would order you hanged. Be thankful I give you the benefit of the doubt. I shall put you on Atooie and keep you there until you can be released. And, sir, as a caution for you not again to interfere, knowingly or not, in an affair of no consequence to you, I shall order that you be given no privileges at least for the time while you are detained."

He turned on his heel, dismissing Jeffery, speaking in Russian to the officers. Then Jeffery was seized and forced below, into one of the ship's berths off the main cabin. Terribly weary, he felt himself slide slowly into blackness.

The next morning guards hustled him on deck. It was a time still before sunrise, the light having that greenish cast he remembered when Susan and he had been at the cave's entrance. One of his guards pointed past the bow, and said, "Wy-may-ah," and Jeffery knew the ship was coming into the port of Whymea on the island of Atooie, one of the two northernmost islands of the archipelago.

It was another hour at least before the ship cast her anchors, and preparations were made to go ashore. As he waited on the deck Jeffery gazed with great curiosity through a fine rain toward a jagged green land, even more rugged and precipitous than Woahoo had seemed. This was the island which Captain Cook first had seen. Captain Cook had made his first landing in January of 1778. Yes, and he remembered when George Hoomehoome Kaumuualii —George's whole name stuck in his mind like some faint thought of hope—had claimed his father was king of the leeward isle. His father was a vassal king who paid tribute to the old king of all the other islands.

Jeffery wondered if George's father were still alive or if it had been some other pagan chieftain with whom Ben Partridge had schemed a rebellion in advance of the presumed occupation by the British. Jerusalem, possibly it had been Russian agents who had spread talk and fear of the British plans to capture the archipelago in order more perfectly to screen their own advance.

In his torment it seemed to Jeffery that he had only two cards dealt to him for this game into which he had been thrust with so little experience behind him. As brevet captain on an urgent mission for Mr. Monroe at least he had been briefed in advance and had consequently a much greater knowledge of the total situation in the Pacific than Scheffer might think.

His only other card was his knowledge of the island language. He laughed a little at the thought. If he had not met George Hoomehoome in the first place, and, to while away the long weeks in the hospital, learned a little of the islanders' vernacular, he would never have been sent here to get into such trouble. But perhaps his having known George might still be put to use, providing he ever escaped from the Russians. If he escaped them he would have to find a refuge in a hurry if George's father were still the vassal king of Atooie—Jeffery's thoughts went streaming away with hope.

A new sharpness came over his mind. He stared calculatingly toward the land, determined to fix every detail of it in his memory. A bay of sorts was there, with a broad river emptying into it from between towering cliffs which receded into the distance. The river widened into a lagoon or lake before a sand bar against which the surf thundered. There appeared to be groupings of huts along one side of the lagoon and a promontory on the other, backed up under violet-colored mountains whose peaks were lost in mist.

He watched Scheffer going from the ship. A Russian officer came up the companionway, spoke a word to the two guards; and Jeffery was led down and thrown into a boat suspended from the davits aft. Men clambered in. He felt a sickening lurch; spray lifted high with a wrenching crash; and for another instant he was convinced the boat was finished and he with it.

His legs were freed before the longboat passed through the surf. He was able now to sit up. Half a league from shore, to the east of the river Jeffery saw more clearly that huge dark bulk which on shipboard he'd assumed to be a high promontory of land. It was an enclosure and at first he took it to be walls around a vast native village until he noticed a brassy glint of cannon at the embrasures of the walls. A fort! *That*—all that was a fort, he thought with fresh despair.

The seamen rowed closer in to shore where they expertly waited for a larger roller and then rode it up the sandy beach. They had landed on the west side of the river, across from the fort, and Jeffery was conducted at least a quarter of a mile over a kind of meadow country in the lee of the cliffs on this side of the river.

The morning sun had risen high enough to slant into the river canyon, melting the mist, and Jeffery could see more of the eastern bank of the river when he was rowed across in a longboat. To the north there were groves of coconut trees, with dense green shade trees growing up the sides of the canyon walls. The fort itself overwhelmed him. When he saw the dimensions of its walls, its monster size, its strength, the work already done on it by the Russians, Jeffery's whole being seemed to shrink. What hope could the old king on the lower island of Owhyee ever have of regaining his kingdom when the Russians had this massive bastion? Once engaged in their scheme of conquest, the Russians must have acted with incredible swiftness.

Entering through a huge wooden gate, Jeffery could see that the fort was not yet completed. Along the north wall were at least two thousand natives laboring amid a deafening hullabaloo.

Inside the gate, where barefoot soldiers stood on guard, three paths branched out like ribs of a fan. The shortest path ran to a large wooden building to the left of the gate; the second and third to the rear of the enclosure toward two large buildings of wood and stone.

Jeffery was taken to the largest of these two buildings, both reminding him of the soldiers' barracks outside Philadelphia. Inside, he was led through a small room lighted by candles and a torch, past a Russian in a ragged uniform.

A door was opened in one of the walls and he smelt an indescribable stench from below. Instinctively he recoiled. Hands grasped him and he was prodded down steps carved from live rock into a dungeon which had been dug and blasted from the soft lava and coral beneath the barracks.

He had a glimpse of something like a row of stalls, rather than cells, each having a heavy wooden door or front. He heard a muffled shouting from behind the doors and a beating of fists upon the wood. Then he was thrown into such a stall, himself. Irons were struck off his arms and his wrists unbound.

He was handed a pannikin of water, a calabash of something evidently food, and then the thick wooden door was shut. Through a narrow hole cut into the door Jeffery saw the Russian sergeant, the seamen, and the Kodiaks going up the steps, candlelight and torchlight vanishing.

8. He was able to reckon the weeks as they passed because the dungeons were cleaned every seven days. Early in the morning he would hear Atooie natives carrying down great loads of straw which were dumped in the narrow passage between the two rows of cells. One by one the doors would be unlocked, and when it came Jeffery's turn, he would be ordered to stand well back by a shouting Russian sergeant. By signs and gestures the sergeant had instructed Jeffery upon what he was to do until now it had become routine. With his hands Jeffery shoved old straw into the passageway and took up armfuls of fresh straw.

Unceasingly, he thought of escape. He had explored every inch of surface in his stall, reckoning it to be five feet wide, a little over perhaps, and twelve feet long. On each side of him were walls of lava, too thick for him to hear the sounds of his neighbors although he had tried tapping out signals. Below him was a floor of heavy planking. The barracks above had been built upon a foundation of stones lifting two feet from the level of the ground. At the rear, small openings a handbreadth wide and half that much deep had been left in the foundation to provide air and a very thin light for the stalls underneath. By leaping, Jeffery found he could grasp at the air holes to his stall and pull himself up. The foundation wall, he estimated, was at least two feet thick.

At first it had been all he could do to leap, to cling a few seconds by his hands, his chin at the opening, before weakening and dropping, but the determination never left him to keep in physical condition. When at last he could reach the opening in one jump, pull himself to it, and let himself up and down a hundred times before falling, by his accounting of time he had been over two months in the dungeons at Atooie.

Long before then he had explored all the possibilities of escaping from his cell, at first refusing to give up hope. He had torn away his fingernails by futilely trying to pry up the planks. He wove cords from the pili straw, making Indian loops to catch and kill the hungry rats scampering over him when he tried to sleep. He wove a larger and stronger cord and hid it away but a time never came when the Russian sergeant was careless enough for Jeffery to haul him in with the straw cord and snatch at a musket or pistol.

He had expected to have had a glimpse of Ben Partridge, Susan's father, and even a chance to speak to him but he knew no more of what had happened to Partridge than he had all the months ago when first Sam and he had sailed into Honoruru. It still hurt to think of Sam Crowell being killed. Jeffery dreamt of home, of his aunt, his uncle, of all the streets and lanes of Philadelphia—and he dreamt of Rebecca. It was a delight to recall her face, her tall slender figure; gradually it became Rebecca whose image was his companion.

Some nights the need he had for her was overpowering. He would imagine a door secretly opening in one of the lava walls as a door had secretly opened in an episode of that long heroic romance she had given him to beguile his days during the sea voyage. It was as though Rebecca would be in the stall with Jeffery, her skin as white as gardenias, her hair a sooty fragrant blackness, all of her translucent and melting, vanishing instantly when he lifted up his hands to take her.

He had a fear of going mad. He asked himself violently what in God's name was becoming of him. Damn Rebecca! He must think of something to put his mind to if he were to maintain his sanity and live and eventually get free to get at Scheffer.

To increase his torment, when he thrust Rebecca's image from his mind, it was Susan Partridge who appeared, at first vaguely and then with increasing vividness. He would see her thick chestnut-colored hair so entrancingly streaked by the sun, her bold forehead, her smiling eyes, her thin clever face, and the generous lips which, he recalled, had been so fresh and compelling—nothing at all like Rebecca's deliberate giving of herself.

In desperation he cast around for a means of filling his mind. Finally, he hit upon a project which even a few months ago he might have dismissed as completely fantastic. He determined very seriously to recall all he had learned of the islanders' language from George Hoomehoome. For nights on end, almost as if he had become the maniac he was determined not to be, he would talk aloud to himself, carefully pronouncing all the words he could recall. With the two thousand or so eventually dredged from his memory, he began to fashion phrases and sentences. "Na'u ka ĭa," he would say. "Mine, the fish." And, "Na'u ka rore," which was "Mine, the cloth." "Na'u ka wahine," "Mine, the woman . . ."

On the forty-seventh day of Jeffery's incarceration the door was opened early in the morning and he was taken out by two Russian officers. He was led through rain to a one-story stone house at the far end of the fort and brought into Scheffer's room.

The German didn't beat about the bush. He said the sergeant in charge of the dungeons was convinced a devil visited Mr. Tolamy each night. Scheffer could understand, he said, picking up his porcelain pipe, a man talking to himself. That wasn't unusual. Most prisoners in confinement sooner or later fell into that habit. However, the sergeant claimed the devil was speaking to Mr. Tolamy and receiving answers in the language spoken by the islanders. As a consequence the sergeant was demoralized.

"Now, sir, I want the truth. What are you up to?"

Jeffery stood there and presently he began to laugh.

9. Scheffer filled his pipe and waited until Jeffery had finished laughing; and again, very calmly, he asked, "Come now, sir, will you not share your jest?"

"I know a little of the language," Jeffery blurted out.

"Now, sir, I find that indeed hard to believe. Where have you had the opportunity to learn these islanders' way of speech when

you were but two days at Honoruru and have had the rest of your
time in my keeping?"

A small core in Jeffery's brain became like ice. Too late he
realized the danger to which he had exposed himself. It seemed to
him he could do no better than to tell part of the truth and trust
the ring of it would cause Scheffer to overlook the gaps.

"When I was in the Philadelphia hospital I learned a little of
the language from a native in the cot next to mine. He'd fought
with us in the war against the British."

Scheffer smoked his pipe. He asked thoughtfully, "You were
reviewing the language to yourself when my sergeant heard you?"

"That's right, sir."

Scheffer's eyes twinkled. It came to Jeffery that this man could
be uncommon agreeable. "My sergeant was a fool, but what can
you expect, sir, from such men? Thank you for relieving my
curiosity. Are there many islanders in your country now?"

Jeffery drew breath more easily. "They've been coming in the
past score of years—a dozen or more, I don't know the exact
count," he said politely.

Scheffer wagged his head. "Yes, these kanakas make good sailors.
I trust our Russians ships will employ them as well as your Yankee
masters must have learned to do." He gave another stare at Jeffery's
red-bearded face. "You believe I have dealt harshly with you, sir?"

There was nothing for Jeffery to answer to that.

"The truth is," said Scheffer, more and more agreeable, "another
man in my position would have had you hung or shot for the
trouble you have caused. If I agreed to improve your accommodations, I don't suppose you'd be willing to sign that transfer for
your ship's use and her cargo which I proposed some months
back?"

Jeffery had promised himself he would treat with Scheffer or the
devil if need be could any advantage be derived from it. God knew
there was no chance of escaping from Jeffery's present quarters.
Still, it stuck in his craw to sign a statement which later might
absolve Scheffer from having committed an act of piracy.

He said, "The truth is I've a five thousand dollar interest in that
cargo. My uncle and Sam Crowell shared the rest, with Sam own-
ing the ship. You've taken cargo and ship."

"For the Russians—"

"Exactly, sir. If you've taken ship and cargo for the Russians, I expect someday my uncle can get more from them by pressing his claims than I could now were I to sign, even if it was—" Jeffery paused. He shifted on his feet. "Duress, sir."

Scheffer surprised him by opening his mouth and laughing. "Handsomely said, Mr. Tolamy! Well, I shan't contrary you there, either. If the truth were told, I expect you were sent on the voyage by Mr. Monroe when that gentleman believed the islands might be occupied by the British. But you're overly young to be much of a ranking officer, I judge. Still, it might have been a happy chance for Mr. Monroe to have discovered a likely young gentleman such as you with a scraping acquaintance of the islanders' language?"

He had caught Jeffery entirely by surprise. He felt like a boy caught with jam on his mouth. He had been convinced he could hide the fact that he was an officer in the United States Army, and here was Scheffer, with that genial easy air, stripping him bare. At least Scheffer had realized the United States government would not much like having one of its captains strung up by a Russian agent; perhaps, after all, being brevetted a captain had saved Jeffery's neck, but nevertheless he had now no card or scrap of resource remaining to him except the fact that he had been a friend of the son of the king of Atooie.

"Now, this language of which evidently you have acquired at least the rudiments," Scheffer was saying, as if an idea had begun to take form, "it got you out here, to no avail either to yourself or to your nation. However, I have in mind a service this knowledge of yours might do me. Yes," he said, standing very big in the sweet glow of sunshine through the waxed kapa-cloth window. "I might be able to use you. Would you accept?"

"It depends," said Jeffery.

He heard Scheffer drumming his big knuckles on the rough field desk. He heard the steady dull thunder of surf foaming below on the beach.

"A very fair answer, too," Scheffer said at last. "Let me explain myself a little. I have been looking ahead to the time when we have all these islands under the Russian flag. The great disadvantage we have had in this affair is a lack of the language. Decastro, whom Governor Baranov sent before me to the islands, had first to waste valuable time by learning how to speak and understand. Myself, when first I arrived—"

"Decastro?" said Jeffery, surprised. "How many men have the Russians had in the archipelago?"

"Did you think we had gone into this blind, making an adventure of it as the English do? Governor Baranov is a man of foresight. I hope you may meet him someday when we have wound up this affair. But my point is this. Had Decastro, or myself or any others sent here in advance, possessed a dictionary of the language we could have spared ourselves valuable time. When we begin colonizing these islands, what will be more important? In short, a compilation of the language becomes a virtual necessity and I should like your assistance."

Even more surprised, Jeffery said, "I know no Russian."

"I am not so easy myself in Russian as I am in German and English. I have gone at such a compilation as a start in English, thinking that one of the learned societies of England might someday care to publish it. I have always had a fancy of retiring and living in England when I have finished serving Russia and—" he pushed his thumb down upon the burning tobacco in his pipe—"being well paid by them. But my time here is not my own. I've made little progress on a compilation either for my own use or to be translated into Russian for Governor Baranov. I could put you to it as a secretary, Mr. Tolamy."

"You'd free me of the dungeon?"

"Not quite that, I fear. No, but I should improve the accommodations. You will accept?"

"I believe not, sir," Jeffery said, "as long as you're determined to keep me in the dungeon."

"My oath on it, Mr. Tolamy, I can do no else with you! If I let you up I'd need guards assigned to you. I lack the men and haven't the time to be anticipating a trick from you. No, sir. You're here. And here you'll stay until it suits me to release you. I cannot allow your return to your country before the conquest of these islands is accomplished and Governor Baranov has announced the accomplishment to the world. You must know, sir, at present you are on Russian soil. This island has been rightfully ceded to Alexander, Czar of Russia. I have legal powers to detain neutrals of any other nation during this military emergency.

"If you doubt me," said he, his voice like new honey, "I can give you full proof. You're dealing with no filibusterers, Mr. Tolamy. Let me show you how we stand. Then, perhaps, you'll consider my offer more easily in your own mind . . ."

He promptly stepped to the door and gave an order in Russian to one of the four guards stationed there. He returned to his desk, dropped into the chair, hooked spectacles on his nose, and for five minutes became engrossed in papers there, apparently quite forgetting Jeffery's existence.

At the end of five minutes a young aide entered, clicked his heels, and handed Scheffer a parchment document.

Scheffer grunted and passed the document to Jeffery. It was, he explained, when the aide had departed, one which he had translated into English from the original signed by the king of Atooie and himself.

In the English translation handed to him Jeffery read, first surprised, next amazed, that the hereditary king of Atooie, Kaumuualii by name, stated his desire to have his island freed from the usurper and conqueror of all the islands to the south, Tamehameha by name.

The king of Atooie, Kaumuualii by name. . . . It was George Hoomehoome's father, Jeffery realized. The lines of the pages he was holding had seemed to blur before his eyes and become steady again. He continued reading.

As of June 2, 1816, the king of Atooie renounced his enforced vassalship under the usurper, Tamehameha, called King Tamehameha; and he formally placed his royal person, his subjects, and his entire dominion of the island of Atooie, including all villages and harbors therein, under the Russian czar. As an indication of loyalty henceforth the Russian flag was to be flown over the island.

With increasing dismay Jeffery studied the four conditions of the agreement signed between the king and Georg Anton Scheffer:

1. *The Russian-American Fur Company, under Governor Baranov, was granted a perpetual and exclusive monopoly of all sandalwood in Atooie, as well as the right to establish factories and plantations.*

2. *Half of the island of Woahoo was given outright to the Russian-American Fur Company to exploit . . .*

Jeffery raised his head. "Half of Waohoo!"

"At least," calmly answered Scheffer. "Read on."

3. Inasmuch as Woahoo at present was under the rule of Tame-hameha, the Russians agreed to furnish the King of Atooie with troops and armed warships for invading the island of Woahoo.

4. After the invasion the Russians were to receive complete control of all four harbors on Woahoo, including Honoruru, and as other islands in the archipelago were invaded and conquered, all ports there were to be placed under Russian authority.

Jeffery finished the document in silence and handed it back to Scheffer. It was difficult to believe George's father could have turned traitor. But here it was, convincing as the thrust of a knife.

He heard Scheffer remark that a document similar to the one Mr. Tolamy had read some months ago had been forwarded to the aging emperor on Owhyee. Jeffery didn't know whether it was a piece of effrontery to send a translated copy of this agreement to Tame-hameha or a strategical act to harass an enemy. He asked bluntly, "What happens to American ships stopping here if you gain the archipelago?"

"Let American vessels trade with Europe, sir," said Scheffer. "The American nation is on the east coast of the continent; its future is in the Atlantic, not the Pacific. All vessels not Russian will be warned off from these islands by next year." He spread out his fingers upon the edge of the desk. "Understand this," he said very seriously, "Russia has received the island of Atooie, not by revolution or even by conquest. The king of this island is its hereditary monarch. Tamehameha was the upstart, a revolutionary pagan chiefling thirty years ago. His gains were by conquest, aided by British subjects and British weapons. Tamehameha has never set foot upon this island, sir. His claim cannot be accommodated under any international law. I tell you this in case, after you are released and sail home, you are ever questioned by the heads of your own government. Of his own free will, as the original of this document now sent to Russia attests, the king of Atooie transferred his island to Russia. It is Russian territory now. It will stand under all law as Russian territory. It is as much a dependency to Russia as is Siberia or New Archangel."

Scheffer slammed a hand on his desk. "This much has been accomplished, Mr. Tolamy. God grant the other islands come swiftly. I have not forgotten that through your hindrance you delayed my getting upon Woahoo and Honoruru. That is past now. If I have had a grudge of you for what was done, I am not a man to harbor it long. Come, will you aid me? A dictionary of the Sandwich Island language will be an important achievement. The first men to complete such a work will be long remembered."

Hearing such talk from this man who had gone this far on the islands' conquest for the Russians struck Jeffery as the most absurd paradox he'd encountered. Here was Scheffer, by his own admission a man who made his living by selling his talents, who would be remembered as the man who'd taken the archipelago for the Czar, and he was talking of wanting to be remembered as a philologist and scholar. Well, Jeffery recalled, so had Napoleon and other men greater than Scheffer.

"It still sticks in my craw to have to work in that dungeon," he said, pressing as hard as he dared.

"Now, look you," said Scheffer, "I am trying to be patient with you, sir. This is not repaying me for my kindness. Mr. Partridge has tried to give me a hand. At first, I grant, he offered objections as you have seen fit to do, sir. But he came around. I even had arranged for native priests to visit with him to increase his vocabulary, but the work seems to languish. The truth is, he's an old man. The dungeon has not improved his health. Were you to join with us in this task, I have a mind to transfer Partridge to your cell. It would give you a friend of sorts—" The eyes became very sharp and shrewd. "I don't want the old man to die. Furthermore, I have need of Partridge's cell because two of our native chiefs have decided to be difficult. I shall give them a taste of our discipline. Your cell is second largest, sir. You can keep it and have Partridge move in with you; or, refuse to help me, and I except you will decide I am being harsh with you once again."

Amazed, Jeffery could have asked for nothing better than to have Ben Partridge placed with him. He counted it as a sudden and great change in his fortunes. He was wary, though, about showing his delight. So he stuck his hands into the tattered remains of his pockets and said, "I'm not certain it would please me very much to have Mr. Partridge alongside me day and night, Dr. Scheffer. If I agreed to take on—"

"Agreed!" exclaimed Scheffer.

"If I took on the job for you," Jeffery said in a rush, "and had

Partridge with me, I could work with more will if I was receiving better rations."

"Rations?" Dr. Scheffer's eyes twinkled a little as he regarded Jeffery. "Upon my oath, I swear it," he said in half a growl, "I've never seen a man in such a ragged state as you are and with such a stench. Yes, I'll give increased rations and water too, each day for bathing as well as drinking."

"Then I shall get at your work for you," Jeffery said soberly.

Abruptly Scheffer stepped to the door and bawled an order in Russian. He told Jeffery, "They'll take care of you and have Partridge brought in with you tonight."

He sat at his desk and picked up a sheaf of documents, reaching one hand for a quill pen. Jeffery and all else of little consequence had been dismissed.

Ben Partridge was transferred in with Jeffery that evening. He was a tall, ragged old man with a straggly white beard. There was nothing to remind Jeffery of that small quick daughter of his except the bold forehead, wrinkled though it was over his thorny white eyebrows.

He did not offer to shake hands with Jeffery but sat himself upon the matted straw, waiting for the door to close. Candles had not yet been supplied. The darkness was warm and intense, like thick velvet. Out of it Jeffery heard Partridge's whispery old voice, with its pronounced Connecticut twang, asking about his daughter.

Jeffery told him all Scheffer had told him . . .

"At least she's alive," said the voice. "The Lord be praised! My daughter's alive and I give thinks to the Lord. I've been able to think of little but what has become of her. I've a brother, Timothy, in Australy, who'd take her. I've wanted to get word to her to go by the first vessel to Australy, but Scheffer's told me all communications with the islands to the south have been broken. It's a terrible thing for a lone girl to be on these islands, Mr. Tolamy. But at least I know she's alive . . ."

The voice ceased, and then said suddenly, "But sit down. We'll get acquainted. Let me try to make up my own mind whether or not you've sold yourself out to Scheffer."

It hit Jeffery unexpectedly. "I've sold out?"

"Just keep your temper," said Partridge's voice flatly. "A thief and liar and even a traitor can shout as loud as an honest man. But you've done me bad harm, Mr. Tolamy."

Jeffery wondered if the old man had lost his reason because of his misfortune. "I've not done it knowingly, if I have," he said more evenly.

"It remains to be seen. Till I figger what was meant by having me come here with you, either you sit and talk and answer what I ask or I consider you an enemy."

After a pause Jeffery said, "Whatever you say, sir."

---

10. Until nearly daybreak, Partridge went at him in his old voice, having him, it seemed to Jeffery, repeat not once but a dozen times all that had happened to him. Slowly Jeffery began to relax. Clasping his hands around a knee, he made a point of answering completely and with as much good will as he could muster.

The thin whispery voice from the fetid blackness went on and on until presently there was a very faint light showing through the window slit.

"Mr. Tolamy, you have answered me like a gentleman except now and then when I could hear you swearing to yourself," Partridge said at last. "I'm obliged to you for what you have told me about Susan. I blame myself for not shipping her to her kin in Australy sooner, but it were hard for me to part with her. Now the Lord is punishing me for not thinking of her good. . . . I thought maybe Scheffer had put you to spying on me but I see I were wrong." Jeffery heard the old man sigh wearily. "I guess it were nothing but the Lord's will to have me removed from my cell just when I had meditated so hard and so long and at least were nearly ready to take myself up and walk away like a free man. Good night, Mr. Tolamy."

Jeffery pitied the old man. Talking of taking himself up and walking away like a free man! Jeffery cast himself down in the wretched mass of straw and fell asleep and dreamed that Susan

Partridge was smiling down from a great green slope, the air sweet and bursting with sunlight.

To aid Partridge and Jeffery, in an undertaking which at the beginning Jeffery had believed was preposterous and inconsequential and which very soon he found to be a most interesting distraction, Scheffer sent to them a kahuna. He was smallish, as island priests went, less than six feet tall.

The priest's hair was scraped from his head except for two braids hanging down each temple. Braided cords of whiskers dangled from his chin. Jeffery was fascinated by him. For dress this priest wore a loincloth of white kapa, a white kapa sheet wrapped around his shoulders to his knees, and around his scrawny neck was hung an amulet by a cord of braided human hair.

The amulet consisted of a sharkskin sack and when Jeffery, who had a passion to know the where and how of all things, asked what was in it, the priest stepped back in alarm, clutching at his sack. Probably it contained, Jeffery decided, bones and teeth and bits of feathers, and later by being patient he learned that indeed it did.

The three of them set to work for three to five hours each day, having a bitter shred of daylight and candles provided by the sergeant. Partridge seemed to be doing very well. Although he still seemed to stray off in his mind with long silences, by and large he spoke rationally and worked with good will. The priest's full name was Akahuakaninanaho'oleli'muimaiia. Jeffery solemnly wrote it down, memorized it to prove to himself he could, and called the priest "Aka" for short.

From having believed a kahuna was merely a priest who had some training in treating wounds, Jeffery now discovered the kahunas were wisemen, much more than priests. Aka explained, very slowly at first, as Jeffery began getting into the language, that there were kahunas who acted as engineers for building roads and fishponds; there were kahunas who were marriage brokers, surgeons, ship designers, bonesetters, astrologists, herbalists, obstetricians, soothsayers, judges, poets—and even those whom you could hire to pray an enemy to death.

At night Partridge either talked of the ways of the Lord which passeth a man's understanding, or about his daughter, Susan. More often than not he talked of Susan because it pleased Jeffery to hear about her. She was nineteen, her father told him. As he listened to her father it came to him that it would have been fun to have had as a young sister someone like Susan Partridge.

On the seventh or eighth night, Jeffery afterwards never quite remembered, the old man had been telling of how Susan a year ago had swum clean across the bay.

"That far?"

"You call that far, Jeff? You ought to see that youngster swim. For months I didn't think of nothing else but getting free to sail back to her, Jeff. It were terrible hard for me, too, because Scheffer had shoved those priests in on me for that dictionary he's in such a passion to have done. I couldn't very well refuse, either, because I wanted that big cell I was in. I had to let Scheffer think my mind was weakening. I hoped that would do it and give me more time at digging in the tunnel—"

"Tunnel?" said Jeffery.

"Yes," said Partridge in his whisper. "I guess maybe I was an old fool, being scared to speak sooner to you, but I've been humbugged so bad by Scheffer I wanted to be certain before I said anything. But I been praying to the Lord each night for guidance on you, and I've decided the Lord wanted me to come in with you for a good purpose—"

"You dug a tunnel in your cell?"

"Why, yes," said Partridge patiently, "haven't I been trying to tell you? Probably I wouldn't have finished it before the season comes for the big rains. It were the Lord trying to save me from a folly, is what I tell myself. If the Lord says I'm to stay here, I'll stay; but I admit, sometimes it goes hard against the spirit to do the Lord's bidding, don't it?"

Jeffery asked very softly, "Ben—if you've got a tunnel started in that cell you were in, wouldn't the tunnel be found by now?"

"By who?"

"Scheffer's had natives locked there the past week. They'll see where you've dug."

"I don't figure they will, Jeff. No, sir." The voice stopped. Presently it asked in a small whisper, "Just how loony might you think I am?"

It gave Jeffery a creepy feeling to hear that whispered question. Instinctively he edged away in the blackness. A hand reached and touched his arm and the skin on the palm of the hand was thickened like coarse coral. The whisperer ordered, "Feel that hand if you think I'm so loony. Every time I got up into the sunlight it worried me for fear one of those guards would notice the calluses on my hands. I got 'em by digging, mostly by digging with my hands like a mole."

He said his cell hadn't been covered with a floor of planking as this one was. Rock was underneath the straw in Partridge's cell. At one corner he'd discovered a kind of porous lava mixed with coral and, using a metal pannikin, he had scraped at the soft rock, inch by inch, month by month. Two feet below a base of over-lying lava he found he was digging into old mud and damp sand mixed with lava rock.

He realized he had located what he believed was an ancient lava tube going from north to south toward the sea. During the centuries the tube had become filled with hardened sand and mud, deposited by water seeping through, either from a spring some-where to the north or possibly from the river. By tremendous labor he had got six feet down to the tube and had managed to follow another ten feet or so south under the dungeon's floor; the packed sand and conglomerate becoming softer and easier to dig with each night's added work.

Jeffery listened and his excitement became intense. Partridge said his fear had been that the rains might come too soon. The seepage of underground water could increase to such an extent that within a few hours it would fill in the hole he'd dug, drowning him if he wasn't prepared to stop his efforts and recommence in the spring. At noontime last week, the guard fortunately had informed him in advance to prepare to be transferred into a new cell. Partridge had had three good hours to tamp down the opening and to hide his digging. It was dark as pitch in his cell, without candles, no opening to daylight, either, as here in Jeff's. He doubted if the native prisoners would find the opening.

"It warn't the Lord's will for me to escape," he said. "He works in mighty strange ways, Jeff. It passeth my understanding. Sometimes it passeth my understanding so much I'm plagued nearly to tarnation with it, but it never did a man good yet to cry over milk that's spilt. Now, if you will excuse me, Jeff, I shall say my prayers."

As usual the kahuna arrived early next morning to continue work on the word list but this morning Jeffery had lost his eagerness. His mind was not on the task. He could think of nothing but the lava tunnel.

Finally, the priest asked disgustedly of Jeffery, "He aha kau noho wale nei?" Why was Jeffery remaining idle?

Jeffery said he didn't know. "Aore o'u ike."

"Owau ke kumu," said the priest severely. He was the teacher. "I mia iu'u. Aohe ou rohe?" Speak to him. Didn't Jeffery hear? Jeffery promised to get to work. Jerusalem! He wished the day were gone and night were here to go at Partridge again.

As soon as it was night, Jeffery questioned him. What exactly were lava tubes? Partridge explained that when a volcano exploded hot lava gushed forth and often it bored through the earth, melting rock and coral, to form a long opening leading miles and miles to the sea. Owhyee had many such tubes. Woahoo might have a few but most of them were filled by now. Atooie had nearly as many open tubes as Owhyee had.

Well, what about the lava tube Partridge had located in his cell? It was ancient, Partridge believed. The centuries had packed it nearly full with sand and hardened mud. That wasn't quite the point, Jeffery said. That tube came down from the north, didn't it? If hot lava followed a fairly straight course wouldn't the tube pass somewhere under this end of the dungeon? Lord save them both, Partridge said, straw rustling as he sat up; yes, it ought to.

"Shouldn't we find out?" asked Jeffery.

"I'm not sure it's the Lord's will."

Jeffery wished Partridge would stop referring to the Lord's will. He waited, saying nothing.

"We can't do much tonight," said the old man's whisper. "Yes, 'twon't hurt maybe to give the Lord a reminder for a clear sign from Him. We'll have a look tomorrow night."

The next day Scheffer sent for Jeffery to see how the famous word list was progressing. While walking to and from Scheffer's stone house between the guards, Jeffery seized the opportunity to pace off the distance between the barracks and the southwest walls. He reckoned the distance as about one hundred and twenty-six feet.

That night Partridge warned Jeffery they had only two months to go before the big rains could be expected. Unless they wanted to risk being caught deep below the earth and drowned they'd be compelled to hold off for months, until next spring, after the rains. By then Scheffer's campaign against the islands ought to be done with, the prisoners here released.

Jeffery said passionately, "There's two of us now. We've at least two full months to get on with it."

"All right, Jeff. We'll have a try . . ."

That night they begun. They lit a candle and set fire to a small mound of straw in one corner of the stall, planning to burn through the end of several planks in order to get down to the rock. But the smoke set them to coughing. Furthermore, it lifted upwards—and they were greatly alarmed, afraid soldiers asleep above them in the barracks would smell the smoke. Hastily they blanketed the tiny smoldering blaze with their hands.

Jeffery said, "That kahuna smokes tobacco, why can't we beg a supply from him tomorrow and puff out enough tobacco smoke tomorrow night to hide the burning smell?" The next night Jeffery puffed furiously on a stone pipe while Partridge charred a plank, slowly and carefully. When morning came they hid what they'd done with straw.

It was slow going, Jeffery discovered. On the fourth night they finally got one plank free and used that to pry up a second plank—and had to waste the remaining hours before dawn by learning how to fit the planks back in place.

By now Partridge was as eager to get on with it as Jeffery was. On the fifth night they made such a discovery that for a few minutes they acted like crazy men, hitting each other on the back and dancing around, all in a wild desperate silence. The surface under the planks consisted of hard-packed sand and fillings thrown in after the dungeon had been excavated!

By the eighth night, digging with both metal pannikins, they were nearly two feet deep in a hole whose diameter was a little larger than a man's body. Jeffery was in the hole, stooping, tearing at the surface between his feet with the iron pannikin, when of a sudden the bottom shifted, dropped, held for an instant—and next, plunk down he went into a dark shaft, sand and small rocks pouring on him.

He was terrified. He thought he was going to be smothered to death in coral sand. He moved. He got his head free. He sat up, feeling a sharp hard incline at his back. He could hear Partridge whisper anxiously to him, "Jeff, are you all right? For God's sake, Jeff!" Partridge lay flat and reached down his long arm. "Grab hold if you can."

Jeffery shoved upward and caught hold of the big calloused hand and felt himself yanked hard. Then he sat there in the cell and shivered and felt as weak as a cat, while Partridge promptly went about covering the hole. Partridge managed to jam three lava rocks together in an arch over the hole, covering them with the two loose planks. Jeffery began to feel better, realizing they actually had succeeded in digging into the ancient lava tube.

Partridge whispered, "You might have busted your neck with that fall."

"I didn't, though—"

"That were a sign of warning from the Lord," said Partridge solemnly, "that were the Lord's sign for us to cease. It isn't meant for us to dig ourselves to freedom."

"You're not going to quit now?"

"It is exactly what I am going to do. Jeff, I've had my doubts all along. The season's too advanced. We're bound to have rain before we get a tunnel to the sea. If we were in that tunnel when it rained, we'd be drowned like rats. No, sir. We're done with digging. I made up my mind. I'm going to get on my knees and give thanks to the Lord for saving us in time."

---

11. For two nights they argued while the planks remained over the hole. Ben Partridge would not budge from his decision. He was not going to allow either of them to risk his life in that ancient crack of lava. If Jeffery persisted and attempted to do it alone, Partridge promised he would go to Scheffer.

Jeffery sat in the darkness, inwardly raging, trying to hang on to his temper and persuade Partridge to change his mind. Finally he said, "Ben, you'd make a fine early Christian martyr. How do you do it?"

"Suppose you never come up against that heathen in the Philadelphy hospital who learned you his language? Suppose you never knew a word of it? Neither of us would be here together, would we? A man needs a friend to jaw at, Jeff. I tell you, it's the Lord's design."

"I wish He'd designed something else then. If I'd never encountered George Hoomehoome in Philadelphia I wouldn't be in this dungeon. Have you considered that?"

"Sure, true enough. But maybe the Lord wanted you humbled down. Plague take these fleas." Partridge scratched at his skin vigorously enough for Jeffery to hear him. "Was that the heathen's name—George Hoomehoome? You never told me."

"I tried to tell you but you never listened. George came from—"

"I guess I been by myself so many months I got out of the habit of listening. Jeff, I declare. There, now! I'm sorry. Where did you say this heathen was from?"

"This island."

"Was he, now? That reminds me. Susan lived near a year here, too. She taught King Kaumuualii's wives and daughters how to talk proper English."

"The king's George's father."

"Susan was treated fine by— The king's what?"

"George's father is the king here."

"No, that can't be. Your heathen couldn't be the son of the king of this island. There's only one king of Atooie. That's Kaumuualii. I don't know why Kaumuualii hasn't helped me, either," Partridge said. "You'd think he would, too, when I was his friend. I haven't heard a word from him all this time I been in Scheffer's dungeons."

"Ben, do you think I could get a word in?"

"Why, sure. There! I declare, I get to rattling on, don't I."

"I wanted to say George's father *is* King Kaumuualii. George's whole name was George Hoomehoome Kaumuualii."

"He was lying to you, Jeff."

"I'm positive—"

"I tell you, Jeff, he was lying. Why, King Kaumuualii's only son, heir to all this island, years ago was taken—"

"Ben, I know all about that. George told me when he was in the hospital. Years ago as a boy George was taken to America by a Yankee and sold into slavery."

"Sold into slavery! That boy was killed."

"Ben, last November George was as alive as I am."

"Now, wait a minute," said Partridge, breathing very hard. "You swear you never picked up that story from the traders in Honoruru?"

"I wasn't in Honoruru long enough to hear any story. In Philadelphia, George Hoomehoome told me his father was king of Atooie. As a boy George was shipped off to America."

"I—just—can't believe it."

"Well, it's not important."

"Not important! Jeff, listen here. How do you know this George of yours is the king's son? Did he ever mention his pa?"

"No, not much. Usually—"

"Not much? Jeff, didn't he say anything?"

"Well, he told me about a rock somewhere near his village. He remembered being taken up there by his father and shown an arrow cut in it and his father telling him Captain Cook years ago had—"

"Jeff, that won't do. Any heathen father could've taken his son up to Cook's rock! All the natives know about the arrow Cook had cut in that rock when he landed here on the island."

"Well, George said something about an amulet."

"An amulet? Lord help you, Jeff. Every native wears an amulet."

"Well, George learned what was in his father's. He ran off with it once, and opened it. George told me his father gave him a beating and afterwards said the lock of hair in the amulet had been given to him by Captain Vancouver and it was great magic—"

"Jeff, don't you have any notion of the thundering thing you're saying?" cried the old man. "I've seen King Kaumuualii's amulet. I never knew it held a lock of Vancouver's hair but the king admitted to me it contained magic he'd received when Vancouver landed on Atooie in 'ninety-two!"

"Well, there you are. Why are we arguing?"

"Arguing? Arguing? I had to know for sure." The old man seized Jeffery's arm in a grasp of iron. "It's the Lord's own workings. Don't you know what news you have got? Let me tell you. For years everybody on these islands has heard how King Kaumuualii of Atooie gave his only son to a Yankee ship's captain back in eighteen hundred and six or seven. He sent off that son to receive an American education—and never heard from him again! Ever since, the king has believed the Yankee captain killed the young prince. Why, don't you see? Can't you get it into your head? Here you been carrying this around and never knew! *Don't* you understand? After the king dies, everything he owns—island—his wives—his daughter—his people—all go to King Tamehameha—and why? I'll tell you. It's because the king of Atooie hasn't got a son. All he's got left are daughters. Is it any wonder the king of Atooie hates Tamehameha? Why in the nation do you think the king ceded Atooie to the Russians?"

"Because he's a traitor and Scheffer talked him—"

"Traitor! No, sir! And no white man could ever have talked King Kaumuualii into doing such a thing, either. He ceded his island to the Russians because he didn't have a heir of his own to leave it to and he wanted to cheat Tamehameha from getting Atooie. *That's* how Scheffer got here so easy. More than that—King Kaumuualii wanted to prevent Tamehameha's fat useless son from eventually getting this island. Why, Jeff, if King Kaumuualii can be convinced there's a good chance of his son being alive in America it might turn all the tables on Scheffer's schemes. Yes, sir! Jeff, it just might!"

Jeffery drew his breath in sharply. It was beginning to come to him. He could begin to see it now. He heard Partridge moving in the darkness. "What are you after, Ben? I can get it for you."

"What am I after? I'm after lifting those planks from the hole. We got to get ourselves out of here to bring the news to John Young and Tamehameha. With the Lord's help, someway, somehow, we have got to get off this island with the facts. I'd stake my life that the king of Atooie'd revolt against the Russians were he convinced he's got a son to inherit. I was wrong to think it were the Lord's wish for us not to keep digging. I was proud and high in my mind; and I spoke harsh words to you. Now, give me a hand here," Partridge said. "Rain or no rain, we'll put our faith in the Lord and dig!"

By the middle of September, Jeffery estimated, they had gone nearly forty feet along the tube toward the south walls. Using a shark-tooth knife, which Jeffery had borrowed from the priest, they had managed to saw off the end of one of the planks, and shape a rough spadelike digging tool.

Jeffery had never seen a man so clever with his hands as Partridge was. By heating one of the iron pannikins over a candle, bending it, and having infinite patience, Partridge had fitted the rough wooden digging tool with an iron cutting edge.

They had need for haste now. Any time after another thirty days, Partridge warned, they could begin to expect the rain, with water flooding into their hole and forcing them to stop.

Once Ben warned Jeffery solemnly to trust their secret to no one except Governor Young if they finally managed to reach Honoruru. "Young'll know what to do. But after I got took in by Scheffer, I wouldn't know who else to trust, the Lord forgive me for saying it. Look at Quorn. He took you in. Who else has Scheffer bribed at Honoruru? I wouldn't know, Jeff."

Jeffery recalled Scheffer had mentioned the name of a man evidently sent to the islands as an agent before Scheffer had arrived. He asked Ben if he had ever heard or met a man named Decastro.

"Decastro? Elliot Decastro?" Ben's face hardened. "Yes. He used to live on Owhyee three or four years ago. Come to think of it, he also got into the good graces of Tamehameha by acting as his physician. Yes, Decastro visited at Honoruru a couple of times and stayed the first time at my compound. Spoke English, too. I think he said his mother was an Englishwoman. He was a black-haired, slippery sort of fellow. I wouldn't have him in the compound on his second visit. Susan—" He hesitated. He said harshly, "Decastro tried to have her run off with him but even if Susan was young she had too much sense. She laughed at him and told me about it when he was gone. I'd have shot him. I heard he sailed off to New Archangel. That was six months or maybe a year before Scheffer showed up." He stopped. "You don't mean Decastro was also—"

"Evidently," Jeffery said, and told Ben what Scheffer had said.

"That shows how the Russians have been planning, don't it? I never did care much for that fellow Decastro. That explains him sailing to New Archangel and Scheffer arriving after he had gone and seeming to pick up so much about the islands in such a short time. Decastro was the fox to be sent first. Scheffer's the wolf."

"And Governor Baranov at the north?" said Jeffery. "The lion waiting to take all after fox and wolf have done their tasks?"

"The lion? The bear," said Ben Partridge.

Partridge was invaluable in preparing plans for escaping from Atooie in anticipation of the time of emerging from the tunnel. If Jeffery and he happened to be separated, he told Jeffery to try to work his way across the Whymea River. West along the beach Jeffery was certain to find native dugouts drawn up under the grass canoe shacks to protect the boats from the weather. The dugouts always contained calabashes for water, but Jeffery or Partridge would have to remember to fill them with fresh water from the river before embarking.

The island of Woahoo was separated from Atooie by the Kaieie-wahoo channel, a two hundred and fifty mile stretch of rough water, the prevailing winds from the east to southeast. At this time of year, Partridge counted upon intercepting whaling ships sailing to their winter anchorages in Honoruru Harbor and hoped to be saved from the arduous passage by native canoe. If necessary, he could navigate by the stars. He knew the channel. The problem would be to keep themselves alive without food. It might take a week or more in bad weather to get a canoe across to the other island. In the cell they cleaned as best they could one of the two wooden slop pots and set it aside, gradually filling it with poi, which would keep without turning rancid . . .

Jeffery obtained permission from Scheffer to go out several nights, under guard, with a kahuna-kilo, one of the priests versed in the stars. He had the Pleiades pointed out to him, the "Makali'i" the priest called them. The North Star was the "Hoku-paa," the steering star. The third night, Jeffery noticed a great showering of fire falling from the western cliffs, sparks flying high into the night.

He inquired about the fire and the priest explained the king and his warriors were there on the heights to celebrate the beginning of the tax-collecting season, a time of religious frenzy, when there was a peace-kapu throughout all the islands.

Five to six hours each night, Partridge and Jeffery took turns digging along the course of the tube. In a few more weeks they should be passing directly under the walls. Their constant fear at present was that the passage might fall in upon them. They were following an underground stream—a tiny trickle actually, which flowed along a channel of its own at the base of the V split in the lava. The stream helped carry off the mud and sand which they dug to enlarge a passage. No longer did they have to carry up dirt by handfuls to scatter carefully over the straw, later to be carried out and dumped in other masses of straw and excrement when the cells were cleaned.

---

12. The rains held off, and, by the night of October eighteenth, Jeffery estimated the passage underground had been cleared to a point fifteen or twenty feet southwest of the line of fort walls—but still there was no indication of an exit. It now required nearly fifteen minutes merely to crawl along the tortuous narrow way before beginning to dig.

Often, for two or three nights at a time, they would be aware of a faint current of air coming in to them. Then it was easier to work. Jeffery lay on his side or his belly, the water coursing around him in the pitch darkness, digging with the makeshift iron-tipped spade—or with his hands and fingers—passing the larger clots and rocks behind him for Partridge laboriously to break into pieces, tiny enough to be swept away by the stream. Some nights would be without a breath of freshness—the stale air musty and thick, seeming to clot on Jeffery's tongue and in his throat.

Partridge believed the opening was alternately filled and exposed by the tide, which accounted for the periods of fresh air and the periods of stagnation. During the last days of October they had the first storm of the season. It rained until it seemed that sky and earth melted together. The tunnel filled. For two days after the storm it was impossible to crawl ten yards in the tunnel without going under. Gradually, the water drained away. Partridge was more than ever convinced his conjecture about the opening was correct. During low tides evidently it came out somewhere along the coast above the sea.

It took them nearly to November to clear away the debris washed down into their tunnel. On the first night of November they came against a dead stop, which resisted their flimsy tools. Partridge crawled back, and returned with two candles, steel, and flint. They

had agreed it wasn't safe to exhaust their scanty air by using a light
—but this was an emergency. How Partridge managed to get the
candle lit in that narrow hole was beyond Jeffery; he did though,
the flame burning thin and blue.

Before the light flickered and went out from lack of air, they
saw what was blocking them. A section of ancient tree trunk,
shaped like an inverted Y, appeared dimly, the wood still partially
encased by hard sand and mud deposited ages past. At the very bottom, water had forced a little channel through the two inverted
branches of the Y. Jeffery attacked the packed sand with his
wooden shovel.

"Watch out!"

Partridge pulled him. Sand clumped down. A rock fell. As Jeffery
apprehensively wriggled backwards to escape, he felt more dirt and
sand fall upon his body. Earth, ground, and night were thirty to
forty feet above him. He lay there, the water lapping along his
ribs and his arms and flowing on. He expected to be engulfed. Very
steadily from out of the blackness Partridge said, "I'll guide your
legs, Jeff. Easy now. Try not to kick your feet against the sides until
we back out of this slide area."

Once again in their stall they covered the opening with the
planks, from habit, dried themselves with straw, pulled on the tat-
ters and rags remaining of their pants and jackets. Next, methodically they lit a candle to inspect themselves.

Partridge whispered, "Maybe after the rains the sand'll harden
enough for us to remove that buried stump."

"Have you ever seen such rotten, unaccountable, damnable
luck?"

"What the Lord wishes passeth all human understanding."

Jeffery looked bleakly at Partridge in the candle shine, both of
them gaunt and ragged, one red and the other white of beard, their
eyes like burnt holes. Jeffery sucked in his breath as if it scorched
his nostrils.

"If there's a Lord," said Jeffery, "He's forgotten us. Damn Him
if it's His will to block us with that tree stump."

The old man dropped instantly to his knees. Presently he stood
and quavered, "Me and you'll have hard words between us in another minute, for which I would never forgive myself. I'll pray for
the Lord to give you understanding. Good night, Jeffery . . ."

It rained the next day and Jeffery felt an almost uncontrollable rage. A few more days of rain and the tunnel would start filling with mud and sand. Jerusalem! Jerusalem! Jeffery couldn't say he hadn't been warned. It was agonizing, though, to have their chance at freedom so very near and find themselves blocked by a tree stump a thousand years old. Jeffery didn't eat when the food was brought that night.

Partridge waited until they were sure of no interruptions before morning. Then he said slowly, "I know what you're thinking. If you try to dislodge that buried stump, you'll bring forty feet of sand and mud upon us."

"If we wait, the tunnel will fill. We'll never get into the tunnel."

"Next spring we can try again if it's the Lord's will."

"Next spring?" said Jeffery in an ugly tone.

Partridge didn't say a word. In silence he watched Jeffery lift the two planks and make preparations to climb into the tunnel. When Jeffery started to pull off his jacket, to strip as usual to the skin, Partridge stopped him.

"All right," he said. "I'll go down with you. Don't take off your clothes this time. Neither of us will ever see this cell again. Either we'll get past the stump and find the opening tonight or we won't. We'll require something to protect our skins from the sun when we're at sea unless it's the Lord's wish for us to be buried and never again see daylight."

"Fair enough," said Jeffery, and took a last look at the stall before letting himself down. Partridge hadn't hesitated. Inch by inch he slid into the hole until only head and shoulders remained. He asked Jeffery to pass him the wooden spade and the remaining pannikin, worn thin now; he said not to forget the wooden calabash filled with their store of poi. More than anything that brought it home to Jeffery that one way or another this was the last night he would spend here. He lowered the candle he was holding, preparing to follow after Partridge—and once more paused.

"What are you doing?" Partridge whispered.

Jeffery picked up sheafs of paper from the table and kicked them down into the hole beside Partridge. He gave a short laugh. "There goes Scheffer's dictionary."

"All that work we done?"

"All that work. If Scheffer wants to be honored for compiling a Sandwich Island word list, I say, let him earn the honor."

He descended after Partridge, trampling the hundred-some sheets into the mud and water. Wedging themselves along the blackness, they reached the point where the ancient tree trunk was embedded at the bottom of the split between the lava rocks.

Jeffery tried to light the candle, failed, tried a second time, nearly dropping the flint into the water. At last he succeeded. It was like being crowded with another man inside a long barrel, water streaming along the bottom, and attempting to hold a light for the other man to work awkwardly at the obstruction at the barrel's far end.

Partridge was chipping at the lower section of tree trunk, hoping to widen the inverted Y enough for Jeffery and himself to crawl through. It was cruel work. Jeffery and he exchanged places.

Jeffery used one edge of the pannikin as he would an adze or knife, slicing away with short careful strokes. The air became thicker. When Partridge lit the third Chinese candle, the light flickered and died out. He relit the beeswax. After a few minutes, light spilled into blackness. Water slopped at Jeffery's face. He had to stop hacking at the embedded wood to feel with his hands and clear away the clogged channel. He heard another soft gurgling, the water once more sucking itself through. His arms ached. Partridge said quietly it was time to change places.

Soon he lost count of how many times the two of them had pushed and shoved back and forth over each other. He tried not to think of the enormous weight above him, and of the chances of the conglomerate suddenly shifting to drop only a few inches, enough to smother Partridge and himself. At intervals, he had an urge to rise insanely upwards as if he could miraculously claw his way to the surface. Again, he had to fight an instinct to twist himself around and scurry back and back until he was inside his stall with space to stretch his hands and legs and to stand erect.

"You'd better take over a spell, Jeff."

Partridge had given Jeffery a long rest this time. The wood was like iron, it seemed to Jeffery. His right shoulder pressed an outcropping of lava and he was half coiled in the blackness, a knee jammed against the other side to give him more leverage. Cold water soaked him to the bone, and it became more and more difficult to breathe. A piece of falling lava invisibly grazed his forehead, splashing dully near him.

"Easy, Jeff," Partridge's voice warned from behind.

"I think—I've got it opened."

"Watch for a slide."

"I'm going in, if I can, Ben."

"We haven't cut away enough wood, I tell you. Here—"

But Jeffery had pushed his head through, worming forward until his shoulders stuck fast. He scrabbled more violently, clawing out with his hands, pushing with knees and feet. He felt sharp pain where ancient wood or a point of rock was tearing at his ribs.

Muffled, Partridge's voice said, "Jeff, get back quick."

Jeffery dug his hands into water and mud, scraping forward a minute fraction of an inch. He thrust harder. He gathered himself for another effort, and gave all he had to it—and it was like a cork being blown from a bottle. He lay there a moment, water and mud pouring over him. He raised his head, lifting himself on his hands. He discovered that he now had more space above him.

Partridge? Jeffery twisted back as wet mud and sand still flowed against him. Somehow the passage had changed. "Ben!" he called. The trunk had shifted. Jeffery buried his face in water and sand, holding his breath, scooping sand away and drew back, getting his breath; melting blackness closing in around him. Now he could reach through. He felt Partridge's hand feeling for his.

Partridge's voice was miles distant. "I can't get through."

"Give me the pannikin."

"You'll bring down another slide if you start digging."

"Are you all right?"

There was a pause. Then Partridge said, "Yes. You?"

"I'm clear through. It's wider on this side."

"You'll have to go on alone."

"My God, I can't."

"Hear me. Search for a canoe on the west bank of the river or along the west beach. You'll have south winds. Sail by the stars."

"Shove back," said Jeffery, "and I'll crawl through to you."

"You'll bury us both," said Partridge's voice.

Jeffery had to go on alone. Partridge repeated the instructions. Jeffery could tell Susan about King Kaumuualii's son because she'd see how important it was, and would help Jeffery with Governor Young. But Jeffery was to be on his guard. Scheffer had agents in

Honoruru. Partridge spoke as if he had no doubt of Jeffery's eventually reaching one of the other islands. He spoke as if Jeffery were merely departing for a night's easy sail.

Lying there in darkness, his hand thrust through water and sand and mud to touch the other's hand, the hard block between them, it was as if Jeffery could almost see Susan's father on the opposite side. What would Scheffer do to Partridge when the escape of Jeffery was discovered? The old man urged Jeffery to go. Jeffery gripped hard at the hand.

"Ben, are you all right?"

"I'm fine and I know you'll get through safe to Honoruru. Listen. Tell Susan she's not to try to wait till I'm released. She's to get the first ship for Australy and stay with her uncle Timothy."

"Yes, I'll tell her."

"Tell her to be a good girl till I get to her and never to have any fear. Tell her . . . I cherish her . . . and we'll see each other when it's willed by the Lord . . ."

"Ben!" cried Jeffery. He could not desert him.

But the old man had pulled his hand loose from Jeffery's. "Go now quickly," said the muffled voice. "Godspeed, Jeffery."

Half an hour later, in the early hours before dawn, Jeffery discovered he'd been crawling for how many minutes he didn't know along the bottom of a muddy crevice, with stars showing above his head. He got down to the beach. Surf rolled him, tossing him upon a sand bar.

He recovered his breath and got across the bar, plunged down deep into one of the narrow courses cut through to the sea by the river, was washed a hundred feet toward the sea, picked up by surf, slammed back again, and staggered to higher ground. He rested there for a time. He started crawling again, until he came to a second channel.

This time he held his breath, keeping himself afloat. He felt ground rise under him and twisted and squirmed and crawled and got upon the sand, gasping. He looked up into the night sky and thought the sun was rising, red in the sky, realizing he was sighting toward the cliffs and seeing the smoldering embers high up there from one of the ceremonial fires.

He reached the meadows. He walked, fell, walked and staggered through pili grass, the land gradually rising. The sound of the surf to his left helped to guide him.

He stumbled on. The marshy ground became solid. He walked around the wide flat meadows at the river's mouth and headed across hard sand mixed with lava blocks toward the west, under the deep shadow flung by the cliffs.

Presently he was aware of a wetness under him. He had come to the flat banks of sand. He struck something hard. It took him time to realize it was a shack. He tried to remember snatches and phrases of the language, planning to promise untold rewards if the natives in the shack would hide him. He crawled forward, finding a large opening and a sort of shallow track into it. An outrigger was in here, nothing else.

It was twenty-five feet long, with a prow built up at both ends, thatched sail folded around a mast of kou wood and laid along the keel, the two outriggers hung up on the sides of the shack like giant scythes. Jeffery had a general notion of how the separate parts should fit together. He found rolls of tough braided cords neatly arranged in the boat. Each outrigger pole fitted into a grooved block.

The tide was high; the hull of the boat was slippery from hog's fat; there was a natural slope toward the sea. Jeffery stumbled upon a pile of wooden rollers. He had enough intelligence to know what they were here for. A pig had wandered in, grunting at him. He knocked the pig on the head to quiet it, afraid he'd be discovered.

The boat slid clumsily down the rollers and splashed into a flood of surf and lifted and whacked hard against the sand, tipping to one side, the outriggers lifting like spider legs to the other side. He remembered he should get fresh water for the voyage. He didn't have time. It was a mile, two miles, east to the river.

He flung the dead pig into the dugout; the surf flooding the beach again, lifting the hull. Jeffery leaped and water swirled. Surf roared and bellowed. It plunged at him and lifted him; by and by he pulled himself from the sea into the hull and lay there, hearing the wind.

He inched his way to the stern. The mast troubled him because it wouldn't fit into its socket. The wind caught the cords, flinging them away from Jeffery's hands. He didn't know how to rig the sail after he'd got the mast set, the cords tied—tied badly, most of them —along the crude cleats at the gunwales.

The sail wasn't of cloth; it was of woven pandanus strips. It was hard and tough—sailcloth would have ripped and stripped away ten times under the clumsy treatment Jeffery gave it.

He discovered the sail was set for a triangular rigging. The wind caught it; the outrigger swinging in more easily now, making head-way against the great current which flowed from east to west around the southern angle of Atooie.

A paddle was tied along the stern. Afraid he'd fall unconscious from fatigue, Jeffery went to great pains to tie the end of the paddle to his right wrist before he began to steer with it. The stars were fading.

At dawn there was only a greenish reflection of Atooie far to the north. He saw no ships that day. The sky was cloudy, rain sweeping in now and then. Rain made little puddles at the bottom of the canoe. When Jeffery tried to drink, the water was salty from the sea slopping in. He lowered the sail to catch rain water in it and man-aged to swallow several gulps. That night he sucked blood from the pig.

The next two days were blazing hot. Jeffery searched the horizon endlessly for sign of land. He was afraid he was drifting too far to the south. At night he had the stars and he attempted to tack back in a northerly direction, the canoe proving lubberly against a wind, having no keel to hold it. He never gave up hope.

On the morning of the sixth of November when the bark *Nelly Taylor* hove to and sent a longboat off to see if anyone was alive in the dugout, Jeffery was still conscious. He lifted up his head and croaked, "Boys, you almost took too long in coming," and passed out.

When he came to he was in a ship's bunk and a black-bearded, one-eyed fellow with a carbuncle on his nose was sighting down at him. Jeffery looked up at what was the most hideously genial face he'd ever seen, and asked faintly, "Don't I know you?"

It was Bully Jim Hollister, a ship's captain Jeffery had met exactly once when on leave during the war. They had encountered each other at the Red Lion, had got drunk together while Jeffery listened to Bully Jim's tales of capturing a dozen British ships of the line with a Portland sloop manned by himself and ten other roaring tigers. He had lent Bully Jim ten dollars and never expected to see him again or be repaid but he had never forgotten that terrifying and yet, somehow, wonderful countenance.

Jeffery tried to rouse himself up from the bunk. He had a state of mind so perilously close to extinction that it contemplated the incredible and found the absurdity of it. It came to him with abnormal clarity that meeting Bully Jim after an interval of three years was a coincidence the like of which was not to be found in that romance Rebecca had given him to read. Only in actual life could you meet a man on one side of the world for a brief time during one year, get drunk with him, lend him ten dollars, and three years later be picked up at sea by him on the other side from where you both had been.

Bully Jim Hollister said, "You got the best of me. Can you say your name?"

". . . ," Jeffery said. "Ten . . . dollars . . ."

"What's that?" Bully Jim leaned over the bunk. He shook his head at his first officer. "Poor creature's plumb out of his mind. Wants money."

"Philadelphia . . ."

"Philadelphy? We're in the Pacific Ocean, not . . ." Bully Jim bent again over the red-bearded thing on the bunk. "Why, by God! Why, by God A'mighty! You can't be. You ain't that feller? The one who lent me ten dollars back when the war was on to get to New Jersey and my sloop? Yes, I am the biggest jackass in creation. Jesus, God, and the Ghost! What was your name again? Don't speak! Jist don't try to talk. Tolmy? Tol-a-my! To think you're young Tol-a-my! Sure, I remember. I never did get back to Philadelphy or I'd have hunted you up. I'll stuff black powder down every pagan's gullet I meet for what they done to you. I'll set fire to 'em all. No, don't try to speak. Say nothing more, Mr. Tol-a-my. Your own ma wouldn't have recognized you."

"How quick . . . to Honoruru?" croaked Jeffery; and before Bully Jim Hollister could answer, Jeffery's eyes rolled up, his face shriveled, and he passed out a second time.

13.   When Jeffery recovered enough to understand what was being said, Bully Jim promised to sail him to Honoruru. The *Nelly Taylor* had been twenty-four hours outward bound from Honoruru toward Monterey on the California coast at the time the dugout was sighted, Bully Jim said, and he could stand losing another day's sailing to square accounts for the favor Jeffery Tolamy had done him. So, on November seventh, Thursday morning, the *Nelly Taylor* sailed through fine rain into the passage. She was towed by canoes into a harbor empty of foreign ships, and anchored not far from the wharf.

Jeffery was conscious of being lowered into a longboat and of Jim waiting at the stern. He felt arms helping him again. He had a confusing impression of a great crowd of natives, of a greenness beyond, of heat, of rain, and of the fresh moist smell of land.

Now a man with a bulldog face had arrived and stilled some of the noise. Jeffery heard Jim asking loudly if this was how a feller was to be treated after being kidnaped by the Russians and making his escape? The hard-faced man in charge was suspicious, wanting to ask questions. Jeffery wondered if they thought he was a spy sent here by Scheffer? Wasn't there anyone here who remembered him?

Now he seemed to see a black face thrusting from the circle, and as from a long time ago came a recollection of a tall Negro, one as straight as a hickory tree and having an Indian look to him despite his shiny blackness. "Mr. Allan! Don't you remember me?"

Jeffery must have been carried from the wharf then, although he had no memory of being taken anywhere. He couldn't have told when the knowledge first came to him that he was back in the stone sleeping chamber which once before he had briefly occupied.

It had been months ago, after Sam Crowell and he had rowed ashore from the *Clymestre* and had been taken into the Partridge compound. Off to his left from the bed he distinguished his books all in a neat row along one stone wall, resting on a plank of wood. They looked as if someone had frequently wiped them to protect them from mold and dampness. Not long afterward he was conscious of a soft rustling sound. He followed the sound to its origin and dimly saw a girl stationed at the other side of the bed.

Later, he saw her more clearly. She was slowly fanning flies from him with a long tufted pole. Her hair was a gleaming chestnut in the unsteady light, brushed back hard from a bold forehead. He felt his heart swell. "Susan? It's you?"

"I didn't mean to wake you, Jeff."

"You're really here?"

"They've turned our compound into a fort. But I wouldn't let Governor Young ship me away until I heard if Pa was alive."

"He's alive, Susan."

"Oh, Jeff! How is he?"

"Good enough health . . . Worried about you."

All in a rush, he was saying "Susan" and she was saying "Jeff" as if they had never been separated. He tried to tell her about the tunnel and how at the last minute he'd been blocked off from Ben. He wanted her to know her father was safe. He told her that while Scheffer would probably be hard on her father for having helped dig the tunnel, Scheffer wasn't needlessly cruel. Besides, Susan's father was too valuable as a possible hostage. He remembered Ben's message. He said her father didn't want her to remain here, waiting for him to be released. Susan was to take the first ship she could find to carry her to her aunt and uncle in Australia where her father would come to her as soon as he could.

"I got a letter last month from Uncle Tim, but I had to stay here until I could hear about Pa."

Jeffery remembered something more. "Ben told me . . . he cherished you . . . he'd see you when the Lord willed it . . ." Jeffery realized he was tiring.

He saw her gray eyes had become big, all wet and shining and smiling. She said swiftly, "No more now. Tell me everything later. Oh! I'm so glad Pa's alive and so glad you got back to tell me!"

It must have been next morning when he awakened and found the tall black man gazing cheerfully down at him. Accompanying Tony Allan was another man, a head shorter, with a bulldog face and watchful eyes; something in the formal way he held himself was of one officer waiting to be introduced to another of at least equal rank.

Allan asked, "Feel easier today?"

Jeffery did feel easier, surprisingly so. He heard Allan introducing Captain George Beckly, who'd been sent from Owhyee by King Tamehameha last June.

Captain Beckly explained that Governor Young was still on Owhyee with King Tamehameha. The governor was expected next Sunday, a week from today, for a big meeting of the Honoruru chiefs. Last Friday, however, Beckly had sent a fast-sailing canoe to Owhyee. The canoe would land at Owhyee today or tomorrow. By Wednesday or Thursday there ought to be a reply, if not the governor in person, to greet Captain Tolamy.

Captain Tolamy? How had they discovered he had been brevetted a captain?

Beckly was continuing. Although they were hoping to surprise the Russians, Captain Tolamy had earned the right to know the situation as it now stood. On the islands to the south the king was building a thousand war canoes and half a dozen small sloops. The king had decided to resist. Instead of waiting to be attacked, the king was planning to invade Atooie at the end of the Muckahitee season.

Then Beckly was mentioning a Russian warship. The king couldn't risk his fleet across the sea channels until something had been done about the Russian warship which was expected within the next four or five weeks. That was one reason Governor Young was in Owhyee now, to lay plans for fighting off the warship. They'd had sailor's luck, sir, learning about her. Last summer two Russian trading ships in want of water had come coasting as bold as you please into the bay of Kailua where the king was in residence. One ship's captain had actually rowed ashore, demanding water and provisions and permission for both ships' crews to have a night ashore. Beckly said he was a Yankee, no offense meant, sir, one of the dozen or so renegade Yankees who had sold themselves to the Russians. The man had been given a barrel of water and half an hour for his ships to sail. He had blustered, lost his temper, and in the end threatened that the town would be left in smoking ruins this winter after a big sixty-gun Russian warship arrived to support the Russian advance down from Atooie. Beckly paused . . .

Jeffery raised his shaggy head. He said thinly, "We thought we had news for you."

"We hope you have. When you've a day or so more of rest, we'll want all the information you can give us. Partridge's safe, I hear from Susan?"

"He helped me escape. Without him—"

"It's hard rocks for both Partridge and Susan, cursed hard rocks. Partridge has lost his compound. The king's had to take it over. Partridge also lost both his ships. Did Susan tell you?"

"No."

"Last month the Bordeaux came in from Australia, bringing Susan a letter from her uncle. One of Partridge's vessels was lost to the Malay pirates this summer and the other's been missing for months."

What dismal rotten luck for both Ben and his daughter! Jeffery thought.

"She's been here all this time?"

"Governor Young's been cursed perplexed what to do with her but he didn't have the heart to ship her out until we could get news about her father. There's been no communication between us and Atooie. Several of our chiefs have tried to get here, but we've not heard from 'em. Her uncle and aunt'll take her, all right. Welcome her, in fact. The Bordeaux ought to be on her return voyage now from the California coast and when she stops here we can put Susan aboard. At least, it gets her safely out. Well . . ." Beckly bobbed his round head. "We can't risk fatiguing you too early. Honored to have you here, sir . . ." He was opening the huge koa-wood door. "My wives or Susan ought to be in soon to see if we've tried you too severely. If there's anything you need, don't hesitate to ask, Captain Tolamy."

"I'll ask one thing now, Captain Beckly."

Beckly inclined his hard round head. "Happy, sir."

"You've called me 'captain'?"

"That?" Beckly showed white teeth in a silent laugh. "Sam Crowell told Governor Young and Tony and myself after he learned how things stood and decided he could trust us."

"What! Sam lived long enough for you to talk—"

"Lived long enough? Curse it, didn't Susan tell you? Sam's been on Owhyee since August. The king's made him the alii over five hundred makaainanas building the war fleet."

Sam, alive! Jeffery thought his heart would split. God damn Scheffer for the cruel lie . . .

He tried to sort out his thoughts, but before he made much progress Susan had entered to say good morning. She was covered in pewter-blue silk and had a ginger flower in her smoothly brushed hair. With her were two large, well-proportioned young native women whom she presented as Captain Beckly's wives. Both wives were well over six and a half feet high, sisters, and full chiefesses of the Shark clan, Susan said, her eyes crinkling as she watched Jeffery gape.

Jeffery told her at once how very glad he was to learn Sam Crowell was alive.

"I told you I wouldn't let Sam Crowell die, didn't I? I knew you'd get back, too, just as I know Pa'll get back."

"I can't quite believe I'm back."

"Sam never gave up hope, either. It's why he stayed."

"What happened to the rest of the Clymestre's crew?"

"Most of them shipped out, finally. But Sam said he wasn't leaving until you and Pa were rescued and he'd settled his score with Scheffer. It was what he wrote your uncle."

"Sam—wrote my uncle?"

"As soon as he was well enough. It was in—" When she shut her eyes to remember, he saw he had forgotten how long her lashes were. He had a brief passing wonder as to why a girl's eyelashes should be so much longer and silkier than a man's. She said, "It was about a week after I sent my letter on the Comet to Aunt Cora and Uncle Tim, telling them Pa'd been captured. That was early in June. Sam showed me his letter. He wrote your uncle you'd saved Honoruru but you'd been taken by the Russians exactly as they'd done to my pa. But he was certain both Pa and you were alive."

"Good for Sam. Captain Beckly says you'll be leaving for Australia as soon as the ship gets back from the American continent."

"Yes, I suppose so," she said unhappily. "There's no reason for me to stay any longer, I guess." She sighed. "I wish I could be a man and do something like you did."

"Like being made a fool of?" said Jeffery.

Her eyes opened. "Jeff, you don't know what a hero you are! Governor Young even enclosed a letter in Sam's dispatch for your uncle to give to Mr. Monroe."

"To Mr. Monroe? What for?"

"Governor Young wrote he was writing officially for King Tamehameha, who was commending you for valiant action. Aren't you pleased?"

He saw she was very pleased. He felt a flush of pleasure, too, though he was ashamed to be honored for failing. When he was stationed at Grey's Fort during the war, he recalled having envied several friends who'd seen action and had received official commendations for valor. He reminded himself that the island government was hard pressed. It was no doubt good diplomacy for Governor Young to write the Secretary of State in praise of a young captain whom that dignitary had dispatched.

"Well," he said dubiously. "Yes, I'm pleased."

"Is that all you think of it? Sam and I agreed it was a great honor. Oh, there's mail for you. Sam had to open some of the letters to know what was best to write your uncle, but I've saved them all. Shall I bring them in?"

"Yes, please." He wanted very much to see his mail.

There were three packets filled with letters. The first packet had been mailed the second of January, 1816, from Philadelphia. Someone, probably Susan, had noted on the enclosure it had arrived in Honoruru the fifth of June by the *Boston Princess*. This merely held a short Christmas letter from his uncle and a longer one from his aunt. The second packet had been mailed a month later, the third of February, it arriving the tenth of June by the whaler *Mary Fillmore*. His uncle wrote of the political situation. His aunt's letter expressed concern because Jeffery was so far away. Jeffery was acutely disappointed because Rebecca still had not written.

The third packet was much thicker, covered over with wax sealing wafers which were now broken and notations and scrawls by various hands indicating it had changed ships at Valparaiso. It held four letters in all, two from his uncle, one from his aunt, and a fourth which caused Jeffery's heart to beat more rapidly as he recognized the handwriting. He deliberately saved the fourth for last.

His uncle's third letter was dated the twelfth of March, the first two pages giving Jeffery political news. Congress had voted a million a year for eight years to build warships. The Second National Bank had been established for twenty years with a subscribed capital of thirty-five million. On the final page, as if still merely re-

counting the news, Congressman Perkins had written he'd heard
Rebecca Koch's father had invested a quarter of a million in the
new bank. Then in the next paragraph, he wrote that Jeffery's and
his "Friend," capitalizing "Friend," had received new intelligence
of developments in reference to the matter mentioned last November
in Mr. P's letter.

Hastily Jeffery opened his uncle's last letter, written the four-
teenth of March. Now his uncle had become plainer spoken, mentioning Mr. Monroe by name. Mr. Monroe, it seemed, had received
disconcerting news of plans for conquest in the Pacific by Russia,
not Great Britain. He was in urgent need of a full report from the
islands. Jeffery was ordered to return home at once by the first
available vessel. Jeffery read the last page twice:

     . . . If you are still at Honoruru to receive this letter, you are
to return immediately. Drop everything else. If Sam Crowell decides to stay on and assist the native government against attack,
go by any ship which can supply you passage. Enclosed are your
military orders, signed by General Hackly, instructing you to
make all haste in getting back. I've seen Mr. Monroe this morning. He wants no dallying. Several times he has enquired of me if it
might not have been a mistake to send so young a man to the
Sandwich Islands where he understands temptations are great for
a young man to dally.

     Jeffery, Get Home! Your enclosed army orders will assist you
in getting passage on any American vessel you encounter. Don't
hesitate to show your orders to any one of authority in the native
government if it will allow you to obtain aid in clearing more
quickly for home.

     I wrote last week to Rebecca and Mr. Koch, telling them of
the confidence Mr. Monroe placed in you. Along with your enclosed army orders I also enclose a letter Rebecca sent to me from
Philadelphia, asking to have it forwarded to you. Your aunt and I
wish you God speed, and hope before many months to have you
home . . .

Jeffery glanced swiftly at his orders. They were precise. He was
charged to terminate his mission and to make all effort to return at
once. Well, he thought fleetingly, he'd wanted the honor of being
brevetted a captain. Now they weren't allowing him to forget he
was under military orders and regulations. This last letter had been
opened as were all the others written by his uncle, Sam Crowell

having evidently rightly decided he should read them before writing to Jeffery's uncle.

But none addressed by Jeffery's aunt had been opened, nor had Sam broken the seals enclosing the fine French paper with Jeffery's name, "To Captain Jeffery Hooke Tolamy," written in a girl's fashionable slant script.

Jeffery did not torment himself any longer. He neglected his aunt's final letter. He opened Rebecca's.

Evidently Rebecca had written in great haste, not long after his uncle had informed her and her father of the real reason why Jeffery had sailed into the Pacific. She wrote that both her papa and herself were terribly excited. To think Jeffery had been brevetted a captain and asked to sail by the great Mr. Monroe! Twice she wrote, "Captain Jeffery Hooke Tolamy," with exclamation points as of great satisfaction.

"Dearest, dearest," she ended. "Hurry home. Hurry! I can't wait before we send our invitations: 'Captain and Mrs. Jeffery Tolamy beg the honor of your acceptance—'" She had broken off, Jeffery saw, starting a new line. "Everyone will be at our reception after the marriage, won't they? You must be in a splendid new uniform. I shall command a new dress from Paris for the occasion." She had signed her letter, "With all my heart, Rebecca."

Evidently when he returned to Washington and Philadelphia it would be considered he had made a name for himself. He could look forward to marrying Rebecca in a blaze of glory. He should be satisfied; he should want nothing more.

---

14. When he awakened Monday morning, November the eleventh, he was feeling much better and the sores were beginning to heal cleanly on his skin. George Beckly stopped in for a moment when the servants brought food. Two of the important traders, Mr. Winship and Mr. Davis, had asked if they could present their compliments later this morning to Captain Tolamy.

"You remember them, don't you? They said they met you last spring." In addition, Beckly added, they were bringing Señor Marin along. Señor Marin, or Manini, as the natives called him, was one of the most useful white men on Woahoo. He had a passion for horticulture and for a number of years had been settled on an island in Pearl River, an hour's sail east of Honoruru. He had laid out his river island into gardens and lemon and orange groves. Señor Marin, even if he was a Spaniard and a foreigner, was a splendid fellow, very much of a gentleman, Beckly said with no awareness of the incongruity of labeling someone not an Englishman a foreigner on these islands.

After Beckly had shut the door, Jeffery hoped Susan would come in. He had not forgotten her father had advised him to confide in her. He was impatient to tell her about Prince George Hoomehoome and hear what she had to say, but that morning he had no opportunity to see her.

When Jeffery was dressed, Beckly installed him on the lanai, where he greeted Mr. Winship and Mr. Davis when they arrived from the village. With them they brought a small neat-looking Spaniard whom they introduced as Señor Francisco de Paula Marin.

The Spaniard looked like a man who would be the opposite from taciturn but, Jeffery noticed, he seldom spoke. When he did, it was to the point. Even George Beckly seemed to loosen his dignity slightly to defer to him. After they had settled on the Canton-made chairs, Winship lighting a seegar of rank native tobacco, Jeffery recalled Ben's warning and made no mention of George Hoomehoome. He wished he could have. It might have cheered them. They looked very solemn when he described having seen the agreement which King George Kaumuualii of Atooie had signed the second of June with Scheffer.

"Yes," Beckly said in a hard tone. "Scheffer got a copy to us months ago, curse him. It was pegged to one of the trees near the wharf. No one knew how it got there. We're in want of everything, maps included. Can you give us an indication of how the fort looks, captain?"

"I can try," Jeffery said . . .

Inside an hour, he had drawn a map of Whymea harbor on Atooie, a second of the approaches to the gigantic fort at the river's mouth, and a third of the fort's interior. On the second map he had noted the high cliffs to the east of the fort, the village to the south along the river, and the trading house located between the river and the fort. Here, he said, a determined group of men might be able to make a landing from the river and use the trading house as a shelter from cannon fire.

No one said very much after Jeffery had finished. He decided they were thinking of King Tamehameha's plans to invade Atooie after the peace season in December and, as he was, wondering glumly how many of the ten thousand or so warriors might manage to swim ashore after the fort's cannon had smashed the armada. The only chance the invasion would have would be if the Atooie king and his warriors joined in against the Russians.

Señor Marin arose and said he must get back to his island and Winship and Davis got up with him. Then Marin stared down at Jeffery's maps for a moment. Softly he said, "Donde una puerta se cierra, otra se abre," as if to himself. He looked up and told Jeffery, "W'en one door is shut, another we mus' find to 'ave open, yes? The king will find the door. I know him. It is not so hopeless. Now I mus' go. But tomorrow I bring you nice oranges. Miss Susan, she will tell you I 'ave the bes' oranges, for they grow the bes' in all the worl' here. Someday I think it will be the fruit, the orange, the lemon, the grape, perhaps the piña for why the ships come to these islands, not for sandalwood or for the pretty wahinis."

"What's piña?" Jeffery asked.

"He means pineapple," said Winship. "He's even got wild South American pineapple growing on that river island of his. Wal, Captain Tolamy, I guess we all hev got to pitch in to help the king find thet door Marin was speaking of, don't we? I hope to see a lot of you in the future." He thrust forth a leathery hand. Jeffery had an unexpected impression of being very welcome here.

After they had departed, it made Jeffery redden with pleasure when Beckly warmly complimented him on the maps. Beckly said they were the most accurate and detailed he had seen of the fortifications and he was certain King Tamehameha would want them for the invasion.

As he saw more of the Englishman, Jeffery could not help but be impressed by the man's evident ability and determination. Even while the traders had been here, Jeffery had noticed that Beckly constantly was glancing over the compound, missing nothing that was going on.

At the south end where seven cannons were ranged in an embrasure, at least a hundred makaainana workmen were increasing the thickness of the wall by building another layer of lava blocks over the clay and coral. A whole community lived in the compound. Half a hundred small grass huts covered the grounds to the west. Cook fires were burning in stone ovens. But when Jeffery sighted across the compound it all seemed very small compared to his memory of that vast fort on Atooie and from the noise and confusion he had an impression that one white man, even as able as Beckly, was greatly handicapped in trying to make trained troops out of pagan recruits.

Beckly glanced at Jeffery, stuck his thick thumbs in his pistol belt, and said rather grimly, "I can guess at what you're thinking, sir. 'Struth, my men need a good year more of hard drill. We lack muskets. We lack cannon even. I wish we had more cannon but the king's spared us all he can from Owhyee. We can't foresee whether we'll be hit first at Honoruru or on Owhyee and we must divide what precious little we've got to defend ourselves, captain."

As if he were receiving a title which he hadn't earned, it still gave Jeffery an uneasy feeling to hear himself addressed as "captain" although he could remember a time not much more than a year ago when he could not have imagined anything more satisfying.

It put him in mind of when he was in rank at Grey's Fort during the war. Grey's Fort had also been in want of cannon. Jeffery's commanding officer had ordered two pine logs painted black and mounted on wagon wheels in an attempt to give the fort at least a look of being adequately defended. He told Beckly of this hasty stratagem, wondering if the same device could not be used here.

After a short silence, Beckly pointed out three cannons among the seven along the south wall. He said those three were no better than logs for they were all cursed old and corroded. It wouldn't greatly astonish him if they all burst at the first round of firing. Then there was something more of a silence than ever, Jeffery finding he had nothing to say.

He hoped very much that both Governor Young and Sam would get in the day after tomorrow. Until he could tell them of George Hoomehoome it was as if he were shackled to these islands and their desperate situation.

Beckly said they could have lunch on the lanai. Jeffery had expected Susan would eat with them but Beckly explained she was with the women in the women's yard. There was a kapu preventing women from eating with men. Since her situation had changed and she found herself living as a guest in the compound which her father had built, she had preferred to follow the kapu and eat with the women. She had been a problem, Beckly said. He was pleased it was finally settled and she would take the Bordeaux as soon as the ship arrived.

Jeffery asked, "When do you expect the Bordeaux?"

"The end of this month. She went to California to pick up guns and powder for us if the Spaniards will sell."

That meant that Susan would be on her way to her aunt and uncle in Australia within twenty-odd days. Suddenly time seemed to be going by very rapidly after all the months on Atooie. Jeffery realized he ought to ask about his own chances to get a ship home.

"The Traveller of Philadelphia ought to be in any day now."

"That sounds like a ship from my own city."

"I dare say she is." Beckly rose. "Captain, I think we've put too much on you for one morning. I'll give you a hand to your room. We can discuss your leaving after Young gets here."

The damp hotness of the stone room depressed Jeffery. Toward evening he went down to the beach not far from the fort and bathed in the shallows. Afterwards, the servants poured fresh water over him. He dressed lazily, told the servants to clear off, and flung himself on the warm sand under the shade of the palms. As he breathed in the sweet clean air he had a sudden qualm for Susan's father so far away, still breathing the fetid air of the dungeons.

He had not intended to fall asleep; but he did. When he awakened it was near sunset and he saw Susan sitting cross-legged not far from him, the Chinese silk skirt covering her knees and tucked neatly under her legs and sandaled feet. She said she had been waiting for him to wake.

The palm trees hid them from the fort. It was secluded here and he could speak to her without anyone else hearing. She was eying him, smiling a little.

Rather more solemnly than he meant to, he said, "Susan . . ." and for the next twenty minutes held her intent while he told her all there was to tell about George Hoomehoome. He watched her gray eyes open wider. He ended by saying her father was convinced King Tamehameha and George Young could raise a banner in the young prince's name.

"I tried to tell you sooner but I didn't have a chance. Your father warned me not to tell anyone except you and Governor Young."

"Jeff—" She clenched her hands tightly. "It's such tremendous news it scares me. Won't Governor Young be excited! You actually saw the young prince? He's really alive?"

"I saw him for months. Before leaving Washington, I gave his name to Mr. Monroe. It shouldn't be difficult to locate him."

"It'll take a whole year to send a ship for him and bring him back. Suppose the king of Atooie won't believe his son's alive? Jeff, it would be dreadful to have a chance to save the islands and have it lost because the king of Atooie decided it was a trick or lie to persuade him his son was alive."

"Governor Young and King Tamehameha have got to persuade him it isn't a lie."

"They must," Susan said. "Oh, they must, Jeff!"

She offered to run to the fort to have a litter sent for Jeffery, but he said he could manage by himself. He had never seen her so stirred. Her face glowed.

As she took his hand to help him up the stony path he felt her silk skirt flick out and rustle against his legs and he had such a sense of her nearness that it was all he could do to speak with any coherency. Near the fort's gate, he stopped and looked somberly at her. "It won't be many days before you're gone, will it?"

"No, I'm afraid not."

"I'd like—" He hesitated. "I'd like to know if you get there safely."

"I'll write you if you like?"

"I would, very much. All you'd have to do would be to remember my uncle's name, Congressman Jonathan Perkins. Any letter sent to Philadelphia—"

"Yes, Sam told me. I'll remember. Oh, Jeff," she exclaimed unexpectedly, "I wish you were staying. If King Kaumuualii can be convinced his son is alive, there *should* be a chance still for the islands, shouldn't there? At least, as you told me Pa told you, we could delay the conquest perhaps long enough to get help from the other nations."

"I can't stay."

"I know you can't, not with your orders. But I wish you could."

When he got back into the stone chamber, his legs aching from the walk to the fort, he thought of everything he hoped to have, all waiting for his arrival in Philadelphia. His future was there, not here. He had been deterred once from his future by listening to Mr. Monroe. Nothing, he knew quite clearly, ever could deter him again.

Next morning, Beckly thrust a hard round cleanly shaven face in long enough to announce that no ship or canoe had arrived from Owhyee. "Sometimes during this month and next you get queer weather," he said. "A ship might get becalmed two or three days. They'll get here as soon as they can, captain."

Jeffery had been stropping his razor. It still made him uncomfortable to be addressed as "captain." Before Beckly could shut the door, Jeffery said impulsively, "I don't know whether Sam ever told you. But I'm not much of a captain. Mr. Monroe decided he wanted me to be an officer. I got as high as a sergeant's rank during the war."

"I could use a good drill sergeant. They're hard to find."

"I doubt if I'd certify," Jeffery said. " 'Tolamy's' good enough for me. You could call me that or 'Jeff' but 'captain' strikes me as a little too—" He didn't say. He ceased, slightly embarrassed.

Beckly stuck out his hand. "George, sir. George Beckly. Very pleased, Jeff. Very pleased, indeed. There's too cursed few of us here to have any formalities between us . . ."

Somehow, too, after that, Jeffery was very pleased. It was as if between one word and another he had found a new friend. He finished shaving. It was still a luxury to shave and to feel his cheeks, hard and taut, without a beard covering them. He wondered what time it was. He heard the sounds of men at work in the compound and he suspected it was fairly late in the morning. He wondered what Susan was at. He checked himself. He did not give a damn what she was at.

However, when presently she rapped and he heard her voice he sprang at once to open the door for her. She said she had stopped by to see how he looked this morning. He looked back at her in the doorway and he thought she had never looked prettier.

She glanced over her shoulder to be sure no one was coming down the hall and whispered, "I was so excited after what you told me yesterday, I couldn't sleep last night."

"I wish Young and Sam would get here to tell them."

"It's awful to wait, isn't it?"

He knew what she meant. She had waited months to hear from her father. The unexpected compulsion to comfort her caught him by surprise. He stood awkwardly in front of her, not moving, having a glimpse of the reflection of his face in the Chinese looking glass hanging on the wall beyond her. It was the face of a stranger, the hair cut short and bleached a light tawny color by the sun, the features all gone to bone, the chin longer and heavier than he remembered, the eyes looking out with a cool distrust.

He heard her saying, now openly, no longer in a whisper, "Mr. Allan was here half an hour ago to see how you were. But Captain Beckly said you weren't to be disturbed."

"Is Tony Allan a trader, Susan?"

"No, he has a cordage yard behind Honoruru. Pa liked him."

"A cordage yard?"

"Yes. Didn't you know the best rope comes from Mowee and our island here? Our olono fiber's even better than Manila hemp. Mr. Allan learned the trade in New York State. About fifteen years ago he jumped ship here and went back to his old trade."

"Was he a slave?"

He saw something briefly flick in her eyes. "Does it make any difference what he was?" she asked. "King Tamehameha gave him a grant of land and a wife from the Lizard clan. This morning Mr. Allan said he hoped you'd visit him."

"I'd like to. Will you go with me?"

She hesitated. "I can't today."

Jeffery discovered he urgently wanted one afternoon with her before Sam and Governor Young arrived. When they came, this little lull which somehow had become very pleasant would be ended. Then time would move faster and faster.

She saw he was disappointed. "I'm sorry, but I'm too busy sewing uniforms."

"Has Beckly got you making uniforms?"

"No. It's King Tamehameha. He wants all his principal chiefs to be in military uniforms. Captain Alex Adams's wife is doing what she can on Owhyee to show the alii women there how to sew. It's my job here." She paused a moment at the door. "There's not much wind today. Perhaps we won't hear from Owhyee tomorrow."

"Jerusalem," Jeffery said. "Don't say that."

She eyed him. "I was going to suggest we could go tomorrow if nothing came in. However—"

"Please," he said almost humbly.

Jeffery looked down at his neat row of books and pulled back his foot to kick at them and thought better of it. What was he going to do with himself for the rest of the day? Why was the old king of the islands so determined to have military uniforms for his chiefs?

All that day Susan was occupied in the women's yard. He saw no more of her. He walked himself down to the beach, swam cautiously in the shallows, and walked himself back. He had lunch, eating ravenously. During the afternoon he watched Beckly drill at least five hundred warriors massed in ranks in the dusty compound. That night at dinner in the big room he asked Beckly if there was a chance of the *Traveller of Philadelphia* being delayed.

Beckly said, "There's always a chance, but she ought to be in soon. I know her master, Wilcox. He's a first-rate captain."

"The *Traveller* has military uniforms for us aboard from London, but her course lay around by India and Australia. The king ordered those uniforms two years ago. Now he's in a hurry, so he's set his alii women to making some of sailcloth."

It puzzled Jeffery because there appeared to be so much concern about military uniforms. He would have assumed if a cargo had been ordered from England it would have been a cargo of guns and ammunition, not uniforms. You did not fight with uniforms. However, when he asked, George Beckly's face became quite blank. He said the king wanted his principal chiefs in uniforms and that was all there was to it. Jeffery let it drop. He finished eating one of the oranges supplied from Señor Marin's Pearl River island gardens and asked, "I shouldn't have any trouble getting passage for home on the *Traveller*, should I?"

"She's an American and Sam Crowell told me your military orders gave you the right of passage on any ship of your nation, Jeff . . ." Beckly appeared to find something of interest to stare at in his empty wooden plate. "Your orders were definite?"

"Very. I'm six months late already."

"Curse it," said Beckly, "I wish you were staying," and Jeffery remembered those were the same words Susan had said Tuesday.

On Thursday morning the bay was like glass. Beckly said any ships trying to work their way up from Owhyee probably were becalmed. There was no need to worry. Why didn't Jeff go on and take Susan with him to Tony Allan's this afternoon and stop trying to worry up a wind? The only way to bring up a wind was to stick your hands in your pockets and whistle and not care.

Allan's cordage yard was two and a half miles north of the village and fort. Jeffery learned he had not gained back his strength as rapidly as he had assumed after going with Susan along the beach, wading with her through Nuuanu stream, crossing the flats, and climbing higher and higher on the green slope until the air was like fresh Pennsylvania cider.

He had little breath for talking with Susan; but he did say he thought she should look forward to finding herself in Australia.

"Why?" she asked.

That took him aback.

"Well, your father wanted you to go," he said.

"I'm going," she said, "but I don't have to look forward to it, do I?"

"Ben didn't like to think of you growing up with savages."

"They're not savages."

"They're—heathens."

"That doesn't make them savages, does it?" she asked. "If you want to know what I think, I think they're a lot more civilized than what Pa used to tell me about the way women had to live in Connecticut. Do you think I want to go to Australia and right away have Aunt Cora think she has to teach me how to cook? Why shouldn't the men do the cooking?"

Jeffery was relieved when he saw Tony Allan ahead of them in the path, waiting to show them their way to the cordage yard. He had not known it would be quite so difficult to make Susan understand the advantages to be derived from living again where people were civilized.

When they returned late that afternoon, it was easier walking down to the village than it had been up the steep mountain grade.

As they came down through the rushes bordering Nuuanu stream, by the warm glowing afternoon light the town on the other side, spread under the palm trees, had a primitive and secluded look. The air was scented from the yellow piles of sandalwood along a white beach. The sound of surf was gentle.

Susan and he had followed the curve of the beach toward a point, until a quarter of a mile distant from them they saw the fort, its walls red in the red twilight. They were passing near a grove of banana trees which, Susan said, were about three-quarters through their twelve months' span of existence. He hadn't known bananas grew this size within only twelve months.

It was cool and shadowy within the grove and he had a sense of being removed with Susan from everything else. She was looking up at one of the flowering buds. He saw only her. He surprised himself by kissing her. He must have surprised her, too, for she tried to draw back, laughing a little, pressing her hands to his shoulders.

"Susan—" he asked.

She let him kiss her a second time and this time she did not draw away too quickly; and then she did, firmly and quickly. They walked in silence to the fort.

That night in the humid darkness of his chamber he seriously took stock of himself. He could not have Susan as well as everything else and his determination to have everything else had not changed. Without Rebecca and her dowry he would have nothing, or next to nothing. He could not go very far, he reminded himself, on love alone.

He was not even certain he knew what it meant to be in love. He decided it probably meant you were prepared to sacrifice everything for the one you loved. He was not prepared to go that far.

Friday morning a sailing canoe came in from Owhyee. It had letters from both Governor Young and Sam, which had been written last Sunday. But the letters were not the letters Jeffery had anticipated.

Mr. Young wrote that he was detained by the king. He planned to leave Wednesday to arrive in Honoruru Saturday, if the wind had freshened, or by Sunday. He asked Captain Beckly to present his compliments to Captain Tolamy; to say he looked forward to

meeting with Captain Tolamy as soon as possible; and that H.M.
King Tamehameha had also expressed the greatest of interest in
hearing Captain Tolamy had escaped, sending his warmest con-
gratulations.

Sam's letter was short. Jeffery did not know what to make of it.
It left him with a stunned feeling. Sam wrote he was too occupied
with getting ships built to come to Woahoo. It was cheering news
to hear Jeffery had escaped. Now, both of them would have a
chance to get their whack back at Scheffer and those goddam
Russian dogs. He wanted Jeffery to sail to Owhyee next week, as
soon as Governor Young had got to Honoruru and had talked to
him. Sam had a house of his own. He was living like a royal nob,
he wrote. Jeff could come to Owhyee and he and Sam would share
the house together and Sam promised to fix it with King Tamehameha to have Jeff put on the same sloop Sam was sailing in on
the invasion . . .

Friday night, Beckly said you could climb the slope of Punch
Bowl and, when the weather was clear, sight past Diamond Hill to
the sea far enough to see if any ships were standing out beyond the
reefs.

Jeffery awoke before daylight, Saturday, and set out for Punch
Bowl slope. By the time the sun had lifted he was halfway up the
slope, his legs wobbling but still carrying him. The grass was as
high as his hips. He reached a crest, vaguely remembering from that
time long ago that the cave was not far above him. He saw no ships
or canoes at all beyond the reefs and was greatly disappointed,
having hoped Governor Young would arrive this morning. He could
not understand Sam's letter. He had wanted to ask Governor Young
why Sam was staying on and why Sam had assumed he—Jeffery—
would stay despite the strongest orders to the contrary. It hurt him
more than he cared to admit because Sam had merely written and
not sailed promptly to welcome him.

He trudged a little ways downward, stopped to drink from a
rivulet of running water, and took himself under the shade of a
lehue tree and wished bitterly a ship for home would arrive. What
had come over Sam? He was exhausted from the climb. When he
awakened Susan was there, waiting for him.

"Hello," she said. "Why didn't you tell me you were climbing
Punch Bowl? I'd have come with you."

"I thought you'd be too busy with those uniforms."

She merely smiled and said, "Are you hungry?"

"Have you brought food?" asked Jeffery, realizing he was smiling back, despite himself. Of a sudden he was not feeling as morose as he had believed he had felt.

"Captain Beckly started worrying when you didn't get back. I told him you'd probably fallen asleep. I knew you'd be hungry."

She opened an old leather sack, which he thought most likely had belonged to her father, and took out baked chicken, wrapped in aromatic ti leaves. They ate and said little. Afterwards she wiped her fingers and face with soft new pili grass, native fashion, and he did the same.

He remembered he had decided he was going to see as little of her as possible and never alone and now she had come of her own volition to him. He was very glad she had. He looked at her and she looked back, candidly, neither speaking. The slope shimmered with heat. The ridge towered behind them in a golden haze. He looked away; but while sighting toward the bay it was as though he still had her before his eyes, seeing the thick chestnut web of hair, the small freckled face, the forthright curve of brow, the coral lips, and the young body so lightly clothed in yellow silk.

He heard her ask, "Do you remember the cave we hid in that morning? I've never been back. Shall we see if it's changed? It's not far."

He looked at her bleakly as she stood. He had honestly tried, he told himself. But he hadn't thought of it being inevitable whether he resisted or not. He made a final attempt. His voice sounded rough in his ears.

"No, thanks. Let's go back."

"Jeff, what's wrong? Is it because of Sam's letter?"

"Damn Sam . . ." he said.

And before he knew what he was saying, he said he was falling in love with her. That was what was wrong.

As directly as a high-ranking alii girl might ask, she asked, "Is there anything wrong in that? I started falling a little in love with you ever since that terrible morning I watched you go running toward Honoruru from the cave. I thought you were the bravest man alive."

He knew better than she, he thought bitterly, what he was. But it was all happening too quickly for him to establish any of his thoughts. She had let herself be drawn closer. When he kissed her, she kissed him back, half frightened this time, and half smiling. Without a word between them, they went toward the cave. The cave was cool and dry and nothing had changed. When again she came into his arms he had a disturbing sense that she was very young with him, expecting him only to kiss her. When he touched her he knew he had taken her by complete surprise. He had no longer any exact knowledge of what was happening to either of them except that it was now something which must have been inevitable from the time they had first seen each other. He felt her strain belatedly, trying to resist.

Next, he heard her astonished whisper, "What are you doing to me, Jeffery?" but it was too late.

---

15. He went on ahead, making a way for her through the dense sharp grass. Once he felt her bare arm brush his, and both drew self-consciously away, one from the other. He had not meant to glance at her but he did. Her eyes looked blurred.

They reached the path leading to the village, a line of hau trees to their left. From behind the trees came the noisy babble of water where, hidden by trees and thick clumps of wild hibiscus, a stream flowed down to the bay.

"Jeffery," she asked, "will you wait for me, please?"

As he stopped, she quietly slipped through the green hibiscus, going down to the stream. He waited, it seemed an age, although it could not have been more than ten or fifteen minutes, before she returned as unobtrusively to the path as she had left it.

She said, "I'd better fix my hair before anyone sees us."

Spent, he leaned on the trunk of a breadfruit tree on the other side of the path. He did not like to think of how she might feel. He heard his voice ask, "Are you all right, Susan?" and resented his clumsiness in asking.

She nodded silently. He had an impulse to put his arms around her and hold her tightly but forced himself to remain where he was. It was ended. She finished braiding her hair. In silence, they continued along the path toward the village.

When next he let himself glance at her he saw the sun was rapidly drying the wet silk holoku. She looked less spent than before, he thought. He felt her hand touch his and she asked, "What are we going to do? How can we be married here?"

Married! *Married!* Jeffery rocked and halted. "We can't," he said flatly.

"I know," she said. "It's dreadful, Jeffery. If I could sail with you, we could be married at sea. But I can't go to Philadelphia with you. How would Pa know where to find me? Suppose he was released and you and I had started back to the islands with Prince Hoomehoome?"

Jeffery had not realized that Susan had assumed he would return to the islands with Prince Hoomehoome. He felt very awkward and ungainly, standing before her, not speaking, deliberately not speaking, deliberately allowing her to hold such an assumption.

After a long pause, she said, "I'll have to go to Australia. I'll have to. I'll have to go there and wait for both Pa and you. It won't take you more than a year to return with Prince Hoomehoome and come for me to Australia, will it?"

He heard himself lie. "I'll come for you as soon as I can."

"Oh, Jeffery!" She clasped her arms around him, pressing her face against his shoulder.

It was ending, he thought. He would write her six months from now in Philadelphia. A year or so from now, in Sydney Cove, Australia, she would learn how he had betrayed her.

On the way to the fort he silently asked himself, what possible other choice was there? By losing the *Clymestre* he had lost his small inheritance. If he persuaded Susan to sail with him and had a Christian marriage at sea and brought her to Philadelphia as his wife, what would there be for her or himself? At best, it would be a miserable existence. He had argued it out with himself, logically and reasonably. But he knew exactly what he was being. He was being a blackguard.

Back at the fort they learned from Beckly's excited wives that, less than half an hour ago, a runner had crossed from the east side of the island to report that King Tamehameha's bark, the *Taamana*, had been sighted in the channel. The bark appeared to be drifting, becalmed, and Captain Beckly had immediately departed in a swift canoe, manned by twelve paddlers. He was certain Governor Young was aboard and wanted to get the governor off and brought to the fort tonight instead of waiting for morning's wind and tide.

Beckly's canoe did not return until long after the stars had come out. It must have landed at the wharf, because Susan and Jeffery first heard the clamor of shouts from the village. Then flares were lit in the compound and a great crowd went down to the gates as Beckly arrived with Governor Young.

In the red flaring of light, Jeffery decided the governor appeared older than he had six months ago. The old man was dressed in his sea cloak, a kapa-cloth apron wrapped around his middle, native fashion, a pistol strapped around the wrapping of kapa, his scrawny legs bare. He kissed Susan on the forehead. In that surprisingly deep voice of his, he greeted Jeffery. He explained he had only come to the fort for a few minutes to pay his respects to Susan and to congratulate Captain Tolamy upon his escape.

"Look here," protested Beckly. "You've got to eat, you know."

"A bite, if ye insist."

"We'll have food in ten minutes."

"Susan—" The old man looked at Susan. "Ye'll join us? I 'ave seen too little of ye and I think ye could break the kapu for once."

When they entered the big room, Jeffery noticed Governor Young was not too old nor too weary to think of Susan. The old man had her sit in a chair at his right, and with that same old-fashioned grave English courtesy asked Jeffery to sit at his left. Then Governor Young seemed to relax, his head falling forward, all of him of a sudden very shriveled.

The servants entered noiselessly, like shadows, with goat stew, fruit, poi, raw fish, and a whole baked chicken. The governor raised his head. "Susan? Ye'll 'ave some with me?"

She shook her head, smiling.

"Captain Tolamy?"

"No, thank you, sir."

"Beckly, 'elp yerself. No ceremony."

"You'll want the maps I told you Tolamy made for us."

"Fill yerself first. We can talk later."

The governor ate a little of the stew, helped himself to one of Marin's Pearl Island oranges, sat back, silently filled his pipe, lit it, and when Beckly had finished, said, "Now, if ye'll get the maps, George?"

Beckly grinned. "You're in a hurry tonight."

"Somew'at," said the governor. He puffed on his pipe while Beckly left the room. He regarded Jeffery. " 'Tis a godsend to 'ave ye escape. I tell ye plain, we 'ave desperate need for all the intelligence ye can give us. Beckly says ye've learned of the Russian ship's coming?"

"Yes."

"Will she 'it us 'ere at Honoruru, or at Kailua on Owhyee where King Tamehameha 'as 'is residence? We can't say. Ye see, we 'ave to plan both for the ship and for the invasion—"

"Here you are." Beckly returned with Jeffery's maps. The makaainanas swiftly cleared the table.

The governor told Jeffery, "Afore I forget: Sam Crowell sends ye 'is greetings. So does the king. But we can go into the amenities tomorrow. I'm 'oping ye can show where may'ap we can land in some safety . . ." He had unrolled Jeffery's maps. Now he bent over one illuminated by the candlenut torch held so silently by a makaainana.

Jeffery did not want to be nervous but he was. He gripped tightly the carved arms of the teakwood chair. "Before we go into details, sir, I think there's something more important. Ben Partridge told me I was to mention it to no one but you, although he did give me leave to discuss it with Susan."

"What's this you haven't told me, Jeff?" asked Beckly, hitching himself forward.

Susan said very clearly from the shadows, "Jeffery was nearly ten months with Prince George Hoomehoome in the Philadelphia hospital. The prince wasn't killed as a child, Mr. Young! He can be brought back!"

Governor Young had jerked around his head. "W'at's that ye say? *Kaumuualii's* son's alive?"

"Who," George Beckly asked loudly and plaintively, "is Prince George Hoomehoome?" No one seemed to be listening. "Curse it, you don't mean— Curse it, everyone knows—" Then Beckly's eyes seemed to bulge. "The boy wasn't killed by that Yankee captain years ago?"

"No," said Jeffery, "he wasn't . . ."

And while they listened, he told of first encountering a native in the bed next to his, of being taught a little of the language, and of discovering that George Hoomehoome had been transported years ago as a child from Atooie.

After Jeffery had finished, there was another silence. Jeffery had not realized he had been speaking for so long. His mouth felt dry. Governor Young slowly got up, still not saying a word.

George Beckly exclaimed, "After giving his island to the cursed Russians, won't Kaumuualii eat dust when he knows his son's alive!"

"Ay," said the governor. The deep voice was like a single drumbeat. He sighted again toward Jeffery. "Ay, captain, I believe ye 'ave given us a new sword 'gainst the Russians. Ye must not be thinking I'm slow to thank ye. My mind is too filled with the need of deciding 'ow to use this sword. If we can get the word quick to King Kaumuualii and 'e believes us, it will spare thousands of lives w'en we go to invade Atooie. But afore we invade, we 'ave to plan to deal with the Russian warship."

"Can you?" asked Jeffery.

"If she strikes Honoruru, we 'ave the fort. If she strikes at Owhyee, we 'ave our fleet and fire canoes. Either at Honoruru or Owhyee we 'ave near to a thousand men who can swim like sharks, sir, to come up under 'er 'ull, if all else fails. They'll wrench at 'er copper sheets, to pull and bore and dig 'oles through the wood. They'll swarm up 'er sides at night to set 'er afire if the fire canoes 'ave not done it afore, to chop, to kill, to fight like men ye 'ave never seen fight before."

"Then you invade?"

"Not till the first of the year. We still 'ave the Muckahitee season to finish. Ye know of the Muckahitee? 'Tis the season of peace and we are in it now. 'Tis all over the islands. The natives'll fight if their 'omes or persons are attacked. But 'tis 'gainst their superstitious 'eathen beliefs to go into a battle. 'Tis the same on Atooie. Scheffer cannot count upon using 'is auxiliaries till after the season ends, any more than can we. 'Tis a stalemate, ye see."

"How long does this last?"

" 'Tis a 'eathenish thing, but it comes at our Christmas season for an ending, close to the first of our new year. We will mount ten thousand men and send them to Atooie afore the ending of the first week in January, 'oping to beat the Russians to the attack. 'Tis at the invasion yer great news of King Kaumuualii's son being alive can, I'm 'oping, win the Atooians to us . . ."

He stood from the table, old and gaunt and small, the leathery shoulders gleaming nakedly in the red light. He picked up his cloak. He said, "Beckly tells me 'e means to put ye on the *Traveller* when she gets in from Australia. Ye'll make yer report to Mr. Monroe and locate Hoomehoome for us and we can count on ye getting 'im 'ere in the least possible time?"

Jeffery said, "Yes," and did not look toward Susan. He had the first workings of a dull resentment at having to continue on and on as a blackguard with no letup to it. Why should everyone, even the governor, assume he was planning to return with George Hoomehoome? He had done his share by now. He had had enough.

"Good," the governor answered, the voice like a cannon's far-away booming. " 'Twill be a year 'ence. But even so, we can give the king of Atooie assurance that the ambassador sent from America 'as promised to get 'is son back—"

"Ambassador?" Jeffery swallowed. He found he was being badly embarrassed. "I'm no more than Mr. Monroe's agent, sent—"

"Ye'd be surprised, captain," said the old deep voice, " 'ow so far away from everything, a great title can 'ave weight. Don't let it worry ye, w'at we might say ye are to Kaumuualii to 'elp convince 'im 'tis the truth ye bring. But that's looking to the future . . . Now, Beckly, I think 'tis best if the aliis of the island as well as Prince Krimoko 'ear from Tolamy's own lips w'at 'e's told us tonight."

"I'm with you on that," said Beckly immediately.

"Captain, I want ye to speak to our chiefs tomorrow morning at the palace. Beckly can take ye. Ye say ye know the language?"

"I can try," Jeffery said. "Who's Prince Krimoko, though?"

"King Tamehameha, me, and Prince Krimoko—'tis the order of 'ow we stand in the government. The traders 'ave started calling Prince Krimoko 'Billy Pitt' atter William Pitt of England. W'ile such a great name might make ye laugh, it won't atter ye've seen 'im tomorrow. I'll want ye at the palace an hour atter sunup. Beckly, ye'll see 'e's there?"

"I'll have him there, sir."

"Atter Captain Tolamy 'as finished with the chiefs, I want 'im dispatched to Owhyee."

"To—Owhyee?" said Jeffery, sitting very straight.

"King Tamehameha'll want to see ye and to talk with ye. Ye must get to Owhyee with not a day of delay."

Jeffery hesitated. He would see Sam there. He felt a stirring of excitement when he thought of at last approaching the old king of the islands who, for so many months, had been as something dim and huge and shadowy waiting below the horizon.

"If the *Traveller* comes in while I'm in Owhyee, I'd hate to miss my ship."

"I'll manage that for you, Jeff," promised Beckly. "I told you I know Wilcox, master of the *Traveller*. Wilcox is with us, hand in glove. I'll ask him to sail the *Traveller* to Kailua to pick you up there for the homeward voyage."

" 'Twill give you more time at Kailua," said the governor. He stuck out his hand to Jeffery. "Ye'll forgive me if I'm somew'at in a 'urry, but I 'ave Krimoko waiting for me. I'll give ye a note in the morning to Oliver 'Olmes, who was vice-governor of Woahoo afore 'e went to Kailua to be counsel to the king. 'Olmes'll take ye to the king and stay with ye till I get there. Now, captain. Tomorrow morning. Good night to ye . . ." He turned, throwing his cloak over his shoulder, pausing before Susan. "Ye're sailing on the *Bordeaux?*"

"Yes, Jeffery said Pa wanted me to go to Australia."

" 'Tis best for ye. We two'll 'ave a talk together w'en I clear some time for us. Ye look tired. 'As George Beckly been working ye too 'ard?"

"No," she said. "I wish there was more work for me to do."

The old man gave her a long look. He kissed her forehead. Then he nodded, and without another word went out into the compound where, Jeffery saw, guards had been waiting patiently, their lurid flares smoking in the hot fragrant night.

Beckly had conducted the governor to the gate; and in that short interval Susan came around the table to Jeffery. "Tomorrow? So soon? Jeffery, you'll be gone."

"I can't believe I'll be going," Jeffery said, and he looked at her and he could only begin to realize by this time tomorrow he would have gone from her forever.

"Why couldn't we tell Governor Young we are in love with each other and I want to sail with you to Kailua?"

"Where would you stay?"

"With you," she said. "We could ask King Tamehameha to marry us?"

"Susan," said Jeffery, "you know what a native marriage is. It won't do. We can't. No."

Because he knew by now what a native marriage was, for an instant he had been greatly tempted. It was merely a barbaric ritual which publicly celebrated the decision of a woman and a man to have a joint sharing in their daily labors. It could be terminated by either the one or the other by mere announcement.

She was smiling at him. "Why can't we? We wouldn't have the public feasting afterwards, and I shan't cut off my hair for you like the pagan girls do. Later we could be married again in church when you came for me in Australia."

"Don't even talk about it."

"Jeffery—"

She never finished. Beckly had opened the door. They stepped self-consciously away from each other.

Beckly's hard pink face floated forward, his teeth very white. He laid a hand on Jeffery's shoulder. "I ought to hold it against you, Jeff, for not taking me into your confidence. But, curse it! It's such great news, I'm much too cheered to quarrel with you."

Susan said meekly, "Jeffery did what Pa asked him to do. Pa's had so much bad luck trusting people, you can't much blame him, either."

"You won't quarrel with me, either of you. We'll have this island stirring like a beehive with the news tomorrow. Jeff, you'd better pack tonight. We'll have you off before noon. With those sailing canoes there's no need to wait on tides or wind, you know. They're not like one of our ships. They go by paddle as much as by wind. Susan, did you think Jeff was leaving us as soon as this?"

"No . . ." Jeffery damned Beckly's heartiness. He saw Susan's eyes fill. "Good night, Jeffery."

"Good night, Susan." At least, he thought, it was better this way.

He assured Beckly he could pack for himself. After he had shut the door to his sleeping chamber, he realized there was very little for him to pack in his sea chest, which some days ago had been dragged here from one of the storerooms. The clothes he had brought with him from Philadelphia had rotted and were not worth saving. He dumped them in one corner. He had his books. He did not want to leave them. He filled the chest with the blue volumes of *Polexandre*, noticing now that all of Susan's care had not prevented the dampness and heat and mold from attacking some of the pages.

He would have a chance to see Sam, he thought, taking up several volumes of Cook's *Voyages*. Sam's letter had constantly bothered him. He hoped to persuade Sam to sail home with him. He could not understand why Sam had consented to stay. Sam and he, Jeffery thought bleakly, had both pushed their luck to the limit. It was time they both got home.

He had taken the sixth volume to drop among the others crowded into his chest. Now he paused. He sat upon the bed, absently staring at it by the light of the stone lamp. In a few days he would be seeing King Tamehameha. It was in this sixth volume, he remembered, that he first had read of the king of the islands. It had been when aboard the *Clymestre*, still bound toward the islands.

The sixth volume had been written by a Lieutenant King who had continued Cook's own narrative after the explorer's ships had been anchored at Kearakekua, Owhyee's great harbor, in January, 1779. Jeffery opened to the pages where Lieutenant King had described the interviews with the island chiefs during the days before Captain Cook had been murdered by the aroused natives. Among these chiefs was one whom Lieutenant King evidently had noticed more than all the others, for he had written:

His hair was now plaisted over with a brown dirty sort of paste or powder & which added to as savage a looking face as ever I saw, it however by no means seemed an emblem of his disposition which was good natur'd & humorous although his manner showed somewhat of an overbearing spirit & he seemed to be the principal director of this interview . . .

When nearly a year ago Jeffery had first read that paragraph he had immediately reread it because this heathen who had so impressed Lieutenant King was Tamehameha, not even then a principal chief but merely a young attendant to the principal chiefs meeting Captain Cook. But it had been the young attendant who had been neither too awed nor too abashed by the strangers arriving in ships of such huge size who had stepped forward and become the principal director of the interview.

He put aside the sixth volume of Cook's Voyages. He got up from the bed to select the third volume of Vancouver. From his readings last year he had learned Captain Vancouver, after sailing with Captain Cook, had returned to the islands fourteen years later in command this time of ships of his own. Upon first reading Vancouver's account of his own expedition to the Pacific, Jeffery had seen Tamehameha's name mentioned again and again—but no longer as merely an attendant to chiefs. Tamehameha had been a man of middle age and the first man on the archipelago when he had welcomed Captain Vancouver's second arrival.

And as Jeffery had understood it, from Vancouver's writing, in all the millennium of time in which these remote islands had been populated, split up, divided among countless chieftains, King Tamehameha was the first to unite the archipelago and to hold it united by the power and will of his intelligence. It was very strange. In effect, after having read Vancouver's narrative, it had appeared to Jeffery that King Tamehameha had done in regard to the eight islands of the archipelago all that Napoleon had tried and had failed to do with the eight principal nations of Europe. Granted the desperately primitive resources of the one, compared to what the other possessed, you might be led to think, Jeffery had decided, that the presumably heathen monarch had revealed much more address and skill in his military campaigns than had Napoleon. It was an untenable proposition, Jeffery knew, but it had stuck in his head. He was reminded of it when reading tonight.

He turned to the paragraph where Captain Vancouver had written of again meeting with Tamehameha:

I was agreeably surprised in finding Tamehameha's riper years had soften'd that stern ferocity which his younger days had exhibited and had changed his general deportment to an address characteristic of an open, cheerful, and sensible mind; combined with great generosity and goodness of disposition . . .

On another page, Captain Vancouver named him as "One of the most princely nature . . ." and in other pages he praised him repeatedly for his wisdom, his ability, and his diplomatic talents. Moreover, Captain Vancouver had also met with John Young in those days. John Young was then a man also of middle years, a former boatswain, Captain Vancouver had written, who had been captured in 1789 by the natives and had been rescued by Tamehameha. The great English navigator wrote and the civilized world had read that this humble British sailor was a man of integrity and had been of immense value as a counselor to Tamehameha.

Jeffery closed the book. It was suddenly as if he were touching history and very great events. Only a little time ago he had been talking to John Young, the same man, the identical man who a long time ago had talked with Captain Vancouver and whose name was here in this book along with King Tamehameha's.

He knew Mr. Monroe would want him to have an interview with the old king of the islands if it could be managed without losing passage home. In a few days he would be in Owhyee, standing before this same pagan who had welcomed Captain Cook and perhaps, for all Jeffery knew, had assisted in Captain Cook's murder and who had been a friend of Captain Vancouver. Jeffery would be able to return to Washington with nothing left undone. He had been a prisoner on Atooie. He would have had his interview with King Tamehameha. He thought of himself eventually standing before the second highest man of the nation in Washington, D.C., making his report. He caught himself thinking of what a stir it would cause; and he became aware of already being on the way toward trying to forget Susan.

---

16. Before dawn, Beckly sent servants to awaken Jeffery . . .

Someday, Jeffery thought, he would look back to this time. It would all be like a dream. In a week or so, he would be on the *Traveller*, homeward bound. It would be in the past then, something sweet and sad and bitter and hopeless, all far behind him. He had not even kissed Susan. He had not even briefly held her a last time in his arms.

When Beckly finally had to come for him, Jeffery was sitting on the edge of the bed, blindly staring at the stone wall before him. "Here now," Beckly said, "are you worrying about those fellows at the palace?"

"What fellows?"

"Curse it! The chiefs. Krimoko. Come along, you want some food in you. That's what you need."

"I ought to be hanged," said Jeffery. "That's what I need."

"What's come over you?" Beckly clapped him on the shoulder. "Come along now. Get some food in you . . ."

Beckly had told him the palace was a stone's throw from the wharf and a quarter of an hour's walk from the fort. Jeffery's legs had grown stronger in the time he had recovered at Honoruru and it was no great effort for him to keep up with Beckly on the winding path above the beach.

As they rounded the point, Jeffery had a view of the canoe sheds along the beach near the wharf. The sheds were like huge loaves of freshly baked bread. He saw a large double-canoe resting on its rollers before one of the sheds. It had twin hulls almost as long as the bark *Taamana*, now anchored in the bay; and the hulls seemed to be bridged across by a platform or deck consisting of many poles lashed together, with a mat house lashed on top of the platform and a mast forward. Was that, he wondered, the thing on which he was to sail? It was bigger than he had expected.

Beckly said abruptly, "Take my word. If Billy Pitt believes you, the king of Atooie'll be easier to win over. The king of Atooie'll trust someone like Billy Pitt where he won't King Tamehameha. He hates Tamehameha. You know, Tamehameha tried to have him assassinated when that first invasion was stopped back in eighteen-three."

"What invasion? Assassinated?" What was Beckly talking about?

"After Tamehameha conquered all the islands except Atooie, he got together a fleet and nearly ten thousand men to sail across the north channel. But King Kaumuualii of Atooie lost his nerve and wouldn't risk a fight with Tamehameha. He offered to pay tribute and Tamehameha took him up on it. But afterwards, Tamehameha got him down here to Honoruru and curse me if he didn't try to poison him. Young got wind of it, somehow, and put a stop to it."

"By God," said Jeffery, "you begin liking them and suddenly you get brought up with a jerk to realizing what savages they are."

They were going up the lane now which Jeffery remembered from the time long ago. They had passed the great stone morai, Jeffery seeing the palace ahead of him. Beckly told him the palace had been built about ten years ago. That was when the king of the islands had held court on Woahoo, before he had gone to the island of Owhyee to stay out the rest of his years.

Governor Young was waiting for Beckly and Jeffery at the palace entrance. He was attired in a magnificent robe, woven of thousands of yellow and red bird feathers. "Gentlemen," he boomed, very formally, "we can go in . . ."

"Hold on," protested Beckly. "I want Jeff to see our flag."

It was the flag of the Sandwich Islands, a British Union Jack in the upper quarter next to the mast, and a field of alternate blue, red, and white stripes. Beckly said it was being flown for the first time today in honor of Prince Krimoko and the governor's arrival.

"You like it, sir?" asked Beckly. "It's time we had our own flag, y'know. I designed it. Designed it myself, and had Susan sew it for me two days ago."

Jeffery stared up at the flag, floating in the soft wind. "Yes," he said. "A flag gives you something to fight for, doesn't it?"

Although he knew as a rule he was not very good at expressing how he felt, this time he had the impression of having said what was exactly right. His comment had pleased George Beckly. He even saw Governor Young's old head turn to him for a moment, the light shimmering in rainbow colors over all the thousands of brilliant feathers.

After a slight pause, Governor Young said, "We 'ave got two 'undred and more aliis waiting on us, gentlemen."

The inside of the palace was one enormous room receding off into shadowy distance. Shafts of dulled sunlight speared down from a few narrow windows of oiled silk into the great hall. Walking between Beckly and Governor Young, Jeffery had the sense of going much farther than he knew he actually was.

The timbers, side posts, and the row of strong pillars supporting the massive ridgepole had been cut by stone adzes and polished until they gleamed. Three large cut-glass chandeliers, imported from England, hung empty and useless from the ridgepole. Along the walls were crimson sofas, French tier tables, and pier glasses.

As Jeffery approached the far end, he saw a fine ebony table around which was a full score of portly nobles, men and women. Gathered in circles of ten or more, lesser chiefs sat upon mats.

They had come to the end of the hall. Upon a raised platform was a large chair and in the half-light Jeffery became aware of a man sitting there, idly fondling a fat grayish dog with pricked ears. Jeffery looked harder, because the light seemed wrong, increasing beyond reason the dimensions of the man up there. Governor Young said, "Captain Tolamy; Prince Krimoko, Prime Minister—"

"Bill-ee Pit-te," said a very pleasant voice, making four syllables of three.

The man in the chair who was called Billy Pitt, having no awareness of the name's incongruity, started rising. Although it could not have taken more than a second for him to stand erect, it seemed to Jeffery to take a very long interval. When at last Billy Pitt was standing upon the platform, Jeffery gazed and gazed again and thought he must be dreaming.

As a boy he had been taught in Sunday school that once, ages ago, giants had walked the earth. He had not been taught to believe giants still existed.

All the babble and talk and rustle of noise inside the palace had ceased. The intelligent face regarding Jeffery was dark amber in color, no wider than an ordinary face. The soft voice started speaking to Jeffery in its own language, slowly and deliberately in order for Jeffery to understand.

Billy Pitt welcomed Jeffery in the native tongue; and, afterwards, in English which was not an English ever spoken in Philadelphia. He sat. He waited for Jeffery to begin. Because by now Jeffery had so often repeated his story of having met Prince George Hoomehoome, he found he was much more fluent than he had anticipated. For the first time in his life he had the experience of holding a great many people as by a spell while they listened to his words.

After Jeffery had concluded, Billy Pitt once more stood and

spoke. "Nui roa mai-tai," he said. Jeffery had done well in telling of the great news. It was good. It was tremendously good.

Now Jeffery with something of a transfixed feeling watched Billy Pitt's head slowly bend down through moist warm space. A nose like a coarse block of lava stone grated against Jeffery's nose.

Billy Pitt, still bending down, was smiling. He said, "Good. Now I talk more to aliis. We bring Prince George here quick. Very quick." He smiled again, said, "Alora," to Jeffery, "Alora oe." Then he was going, not huge, but very tall, high above the other chiefs.

Jeffery followed Governor Young through a throng to the entrance and saw the sun was much too high; it was midday. He was incredulous. It had seemed less than an hour.

Governor Young said, "I'll go down with ye to the wharf. Ye're packed?"

"This morning."

" 'Ere's the note I 'ave written for ye to give Mr. 'Olmes." He stopped, giving a dispatch to Jeffery, not precisely a note at all. " 'Olmes can read it to the king. King Tamehameha speaks our language but 'e don't read it. The crew'll land ye at Kailua. That's the village and the bay. Ye'll 'ave chiefs or someone asking what yer business is and yer kahuna of the ship'll send off to 'ave 'Olmes fetched for ye. 'Twill be a crowd and uproar for ye at the landing because 'tis the Muckahitee season and 'tis like a big fair at Kailua this time of year. But the ship kahuna'll watch out for ye till 'Olmes arrives. Squat where ye are on the beach. Don't budge."

"All right," Jeffery said.

"I wish I could be sailing with ye but Krimoko and me 'ave still a few more days 'ere. But I'll see ye at the end of the week unless the Traveller surprises us all and anchors 'ere before then."

"You'll send the Traveller to Kailua?"

"Don't ye be concerned. Beckly's a bulldog w'en 'e 'as made a promise."

Beckly said, "We'll get you off on the Traveller, never fear, Jeff."

"Now, w'en ye see Tamehameha, don't act feared of 'im. Speak up bold. 'E likes boldness in a man. And—" Governor Young halted in the lane, rubbing at his nose. He eyed Jeffery a moment. When the governor had halted, behind him had halted the guards and fan carriers and a cavalcade of nearly half a hundred aliis.

"Don't," said the governor at last, "seem to remark too much on 'is size, though. Tamehameha don't like to be thought uncommon big, ye see."

"How big is he?"

"Ye'll see 'ow big 'e is. That's w'at I'm saying."

"Well, look here, sir. He can't be any bigger than Billy Pitt?"

"Billy Pitt? Billy Pitt's no giant. Billy Pitt's just grown bigger 'ere and there, Captain Tolamy. Tamehameha's a giant, the last giant w'at probably lives on the planet."

Jeffery had a strong sensation of staring. Was Governor Young attempting to tell him something about Tamehameha that he was failing to understand? A giant? If Billy Pitt wasn't a giant, what, then, was a giant?

Then for the time being he forgot about giants and of thinking about Governor Young's attempt to warn him because George Beckly had exclaimed, "There's Susan. She's come to see you off."

Jeffery turned instantly. He saw Susan advancing toward them on the lane. At her right lifted the colossal structure of the morai, and behind her was the massed green background through which he could dimly see the huts of the village.

"Susan," he said, "you did come, after all."

"Jeffery, I've thought all morning. I want to go with you. A year's too long for us to be away from each other if we can't have a few days at Kailua—"

"W'at's *that* ye want, young lady?" asked Governor Young.

"We love each other," Susan told him. "Jeffery's coming for me next year, when we'll be married in a proper church in Australia. But why can't I go with him to Kailua? Why can't I wait there until he sails on the *Traveller*? The Bordeaux puts in first at Kailua, doesn't it? I could go aboard the *Bordeaux* at Kailua. After Jeffery goes, I could stay with Mrs. Adams. It wouldn't be for very long. King Tamehameha can marry us. Even if it isn't a Christian marriage, an island marriage will do for Jeffery and me until we can have better. King Tamehameha is the king. Our country recognizes him. England recognizes him. Please, Governor Young. Please!"

Jeffery had never suspected how merely the sight of a girl with her brown hair curling crisply in the sun and her eyes looking excited and eager could cause scruples to vanish.

Later he was to remember that it was Sunday, November the seventeenth, not many days before the Russian warship arrived in

these waters, when the sight of her had struck down all his great
resolutions.

———————

17. The first landfall was made shortly before sunrise,
Wednesday morning, the twentieth of November.
Since Sunday noon, the stone-hewn peleloo—as Jeffery had learned
these seafaring vessels were called—with its double hulls, deck of
lashed poles, and its great triangular sail of matting hoisted to the
wind, had moved majestically down the long course from Honoruru.

The lookout gave the first cry from the carved prow of the port
hull, the crew taking it up. Jeffery heard Susan calling to him.

She had crawled from the deckhouse, which was actually no more
than a lean-to of poles and pandanus mattings. Kala, Beckly's
younger wife, had crawled out massively behind her. Governor
Young had refused to allow Susan to make the voyage as the only
woman aboard, and Beckly had said Kala could accompany her.

"Look, Jeffery!" Susan was pointing. "There's Mauna Huararai.
It's the next largest volcano on Owhyee. In another hour we ought
to catch a glimpse of Mauna Roa."

All during this Wednesday morning the peleloo steered upon a
south by southeast course, the prows gradually turning more and
more eastward until the smaller volcano peak had shifted toward
the port side and the greater peak of Mauna Roa was now well to
the starboard. For nearly three hours Susan and Jeffery watched a
rugged coast line approach and go sweeping past them. Waterfalls
tumbled down distant heights. Cliffs arose and went marching like
stone giants to the rear.

The peleloo bore around a rocky point of land which extended
three or four miles into a heavy sea. Through the blaze of spray in
the sunlight, Jeffery saw the sail being struck. Susan called to him
to lie flat and to hang on. The men in the hulls were paddling
furiously to catch the roller. The point of land seemed to turn and
veer away and now Jeffery felt the peleloo hurled forward by a huge

wave. It was over very quickly. The foaming roller gradually lost its impetus, flattening into a long wet green flow over the smooth amber-green water in the shallows. The men took their paddles. Jeffery sat up drenched and felt Susan's hand on his arm as she steadied herself. Her legs glistened. The hot light beat down upon him.

Near the water's edge was a large morai, near enough for Jeffery to see clearly the idols and wooden towers. Having visited Kailua twice with her father, Susan could identify nearly everything he saw. The temple? That was the king's temple. No, all those straw houses among the palms weren't the town of Kailua. They quartered the king's servants and the aliis and aliis' families who were attached to the king's court.

The village of Kailua came slowly into view. Jeffery saw hundreds of thatched roofs, with what appeared to be lanes and even streets passing through the town. Some of the larger houses looked to have walled courts or gardens. It wasn't a village at all, he thought. It was a large town, almost a city.

When the twin hulls grated over a sandy bottom, he felt the deck shudder. The crewmen leaped into water up to their armpits, pushing and straining; others splashing forward to haul the level keels higher on the black sand. Jeffery jumped to the hard wet blackness of fine lava sand, Susan following before he could reach for her. Kala came down like fluid copper in the bright sunlight. The kahuna was already on his way toward the king's court in search of the haole alii, Ho-mee, as Mr. Holmes was called in the vernacular.

Jeffery looked around in a long, sweeping glance. He was not high enough on the sloping beach to see very much of Kailua except the rooftops but he could make out a winding road coming down from the mountains to the north. The entire semicircle of bay was thickly dotted with a swarming people who had established hundreds of camps for themselves. They were probably down from the hills for the Muckahitee.

Warriors were leaning on their spears, watching the crowd on the beach. They wore crested helmets of feathers which might have been blazing copper, their shields of wood or leather or wickerwork hanging down their backs. Jeffery stared at them angrily. What would happen here to all these thousands of people, to this bay, to the town of Kailua, to these warriors, when in a few weeks the Russian warship stood out a mile or so and unloosed her cannons? Anyone was a fool to hope the old king of the islands could do better than all the other brave pagans out of the past who had lifted shields of straw or wood or hide against steel and powder and shot. Jerusalem, Jeffery thought, he'd be out of it in a few days. So would Susan be, bound for Australia.

"You've a dreadfully black look, Jeffery," Susan said beside him. He turned with half a start. "Have I?" he said.

"You've had a black look ever since you sailed Sunday." Her eyes were very direct.

Instead of replying, he looked around to see what was causing such a commotion among the crowding of makaainanas on the beach. Then he saw three runners come down from the road, crying, "Noho! Noho!" for the crowd to fall back. They were followed by the kahuna who had gone off for Mr. Holmes. Now, all along the beach, hundreds were squatting, hastily removing leaves and gourds covering their heads. Servants appeared bearing a litter upon which sat, cross-legged, a neat portly little man with a hat of palm leaves shading a pink cherubic face.

Susan ran forward. "Mr. Holmes!"

As soon as the litter was lowered, Mr. Holmes hopped to the ground and had his hat knocked off his head by Susan rushing to him and hugging him.

"My dear, it's you." Even as he spoke, Jeffery saw him extend a hand apparently into thin air, not once glancing at the makaainana who had instantly bent to snatch up the palm-leaf hat. Mr. Holmes's hand received the hat from the makaainana, while the face was still beaming at Susan.

As Susan and Mr. Holmes moved toward Jeffery, a whole little cavalcade followed. Jeffery stared. The first servant carried a black umbrella, a second carried what was no less than a rocking chair, a third carried a small box, a fourth carried a tall feather-tufted fly-pole, and the fifth carried a Chinese fan.

Susan said, "Jeffery—Mr. Oliver Holmes. Captain Jeffery Tolamy —Mr. Holmes."

"Pray forgive my little procession, captain," said Mr. Holmes, "but these people here are very much like the people of Boston.

They all enjoy a parade. As king's counselor I must do my best. Will you excuse me if I sit, Susan? Very few of these people have ever seen a man in a rocking chair. It will delight them immensely to have me sit on it."

Susan grinned. "Do, please."

Mr. Holmes reached behind him with his hands to spread the tails of his ancient black clawhammer coat. He sat in the rocking chair, pulling at the knees of his neatly mended blue trousers. He opened his coat, removing a square of Chinese silk from a tail pocket. Delicately he mopped his face, his neck, his chest, and finished with a quick circular motion over his plump stomach. Jeffery watched, entranced. He was not certain Mr. Monroe would believe him when he attempted to describe Mr. Holmes.

Susan said, "Sam Crowell's no doubt told you about Jeffery?"

"Yes, we know all about Captain Tolamy down here. I might say the king thinks very highly of him. Captain Jeffery Hooke Tolamy, isn't it?"

"Well, yes," said Jeffery, taken by surprise.

"Now, Susan. What have you come down here for?"

"You can't ever guess."

"My dear, Young told me he meant to put you aboard the *Bordeaux* by force, if necessary. Seeing you here, I should surmise you've decided to go aboard her of your own free will when she comes in from California. Recalling your stubbornness, I also surmise Captain Tolamy must have brought word from your father that you were to stop your nonsense and take yourself to your aunt and uncle in Australia without any further delay."

"I'm going to Australia. But that's not all. Jeffery and I want King Tamehameha to marry us before I sail," Susan said all in a breath. "Governor Young gave us permission. Pa would, too, if he was here. Pa and Jeffery became friends on Atooie."

Jeffery hated himself and Susan and Mr. Holmes. He listened to Susan explaining that he had to get back home to Mr. Monroe. He'd take the *Traveller of Philadelphia*, which was expected any day in Honoruru and would be sent south to Kailua. That was why they wanted King Tamehameha to marry them before both of them were off to the opposite ends of the world. But Jeffery would get back to the islands as quickly as possible; and go on from the islands to rejoin her at Sydney Cove in Australia. She paused.

Jeffery said, "Here's a dispatch Governor Young gave me to give you, sir, as soon as we found you."

Mr. Holmes unwrapped the oiled kapa cloth from around the dispatch Jeffery had given him. He humped forward, spreading the papers on his knees. There was a silence. Jeffery felt the silence. He thought nearly five hundred people had gathered around them. He had an impression of all the faces turning to stone, only the eyes alive, watching the king's haole kahuna receiving an unutterable message from a few pieces of paper having magic scratchings on them.

Mr. Holmes read what Governor Young had written, thrust the dispatch in a pocket of his clawhammer, for a moment silently rocked back and forth, and then stood from his chair.

"It does not astonish me in the least, Captain Tolamy, to learn young Hoomehoome's alive. I've never quite believed that story of him being murdered by one of our Boston sea captains. A Boston man would be too smart after a profit to kill off what could be sold." He regarded Susan for a moment. "My dear, we must decide what to do with you before I try to break in on Tamehameha at the temple with this urgent information."

"I can wait here with Jeffery and Kala."

"My dear, I think that's not indicated. I shall do what I can, but there may be more of a wait than you expect. I think Mrs. Adams is indicated. At present, Captain Adams is on Mowee. But I think Mrs. Adams can find a place for you until Tamehameha can attend to a marriage ceremony. I think Mrs. Adams is indicated, Susan."

Yes, that would be the very thing. Captain Tolamy and he would conduct Susan to the Adams place in the valley, fifteen minutes' walk from here. He would send a runner to have Sam Crowell meet them at the Adams kuleana.

He spoke to the servants. The precious rocking chair was lifted from the black sand. Mr. Holmes sent a runner streaking through the crowds on the beach to Sam Crowell, who was at Kohononi Point. Now he was telling Susan she must travel by litter because he wished to talk to Captain Tolamy on the way up into the valley.

Jeffery watched Mr. Holmes hand her into the litter. It came to him that Mr. Holmes thought very highly of Ben Partridge's daughter, that a number of the king's advisers at both Honoruru and Kailua must have watched Susan growing from a young girl into a young woman and shared her father's pride in her.

They went forward, then, all of them, Susan borne ahead in the litter, Kala marching at her side, Mr. Holmes and Jeffery, the whole cavalcade behind. They followed a pebbled lane perhaps half a mile to the south of the city or town of Kailua. The lane ascended steadily, running past pleasant straw houses. Jeffery could see watermelons, green and striped, in the fields of sweet potato and sugar cane. He had not known watermelons were so common on the archipelago. Mr. Holmes explained that watermelon seeds had been brought twenty or thirty years ago, by the first trading vessels.

Mr. Holmes wanted to know about Susan's father. How did Ben look? How was he treated? How had it happened that Ben hadn't also escaped? Jeffery answered but he was not very certain he had answered with any great credit to himself. He felt the old distress which he had felt at Honoruru.

He was short of breath from answering questions and from the steep climb when at last the small cavalcade entered a clearing of several acres, hau and mountain-apple trees all around, a green rise of cliffs not far beyond. In the center of the clearing was a new house of wood and thatched grass, half European in style, half native. In the rear were eight or ten smaller huts.

Susan called Jeffery to introduce him to Mrs. Adams, who had skin the color of smooth porcelain, hair as black as jet, and slanting, amused eyes. She wore a single cool garment closed from her throat down to her tiny feet, something on the order of one of Susan's holokus. It shimmered like gold and had a dragon in red glittering down the back, and Jeffery realized that Susan had forgotten to tell him that her friend at Kailua, Mrs. Adams, was Chinese.

He was drawn along with the others into a large, airy room of the great new house. There were cries, exclamations, Susan explaining, laughing, becoming confused, glancing at Jeffery, laughing again at her own confusion. Jeffery listened to Mrs. Adams's sweet, tinkling voice. She spoke a round, precise English, with no Chinese in it that Jeffery could distinguish.

Then Mr. Holmes was bowing. Yes, he must depart. Captain Tolamy had given him an urgent letter from Governor Young which had to be brought to the king's attention. Captain Tolamy could expect the king to send for him. He suggested that Captain Tolamy remain here, though. It might be several hours. It might be even very late at night. He bowed again.

Susan followed him to the door, where she asked impulsively, "But our marriage—"

"I shall do what I can." He patted her hand. "I'm afraid the king's business does come first, though, doesn't it?"

Mrs. Adams put an arm around her. Susan must have a bath of fresh water in the tub Captain Adams had built. Then Mrs. Adams would call in the makaainana women to anoint her with sandalwood oil and brush her hair and she would give her fine fresh new clothes to appear even more beautiful for Captain Tolamy. Then she would cease having such a doleful face because Mr. Holmes must think first of the king's business.

Jeffery opened his hands and closed them into tight hard fists. He was sitting on the stone steps leading to the great house, watching two naked children scrabble in the dust, when Susan put her head through the door, closing one of Mrs. Adams's shimmering golden robes about her throat.

"I'll wait taking a bath if you think Sam'll be here fairly soon?"

"I'll have another look."

He was halfway to the lane when he heard Susan give a pleased cry from behind him. He stopped, seeing a figure outlined against the sky as it lifted over the lee of the hill. Then Sam Crowell came striding down toward the little valley. In that afternoon light, he looked very thin, Jeffery thought. His face was all bone as he approached, his hair much grayer than Jeffery had remembered.

Jeffery met him halfway. "Sam!"

"So you got away from those damned Russians, after all!"

For an instant, Sam's big arm plunked around Jeffery's shoulder in the old familiar style. But he stepped back, frowning, seeing Susan.

"Susan! You ain't down here, too? I got it out of that runner that Jeff must have been one of the two haoles to land but I never believed Young would let you—"

"Great stars, Sam! Why shouldn't I come?" She looked up at him. "Don't they feed you at Kailua? You've got thin as a rail."

Sam went straight to Susan as if Jeffery had never been there. He awkwardly kissed her on the cheek. "I missed you. I guess maybe I'm glad you did come."

"Sam, you don't look well," said Susan, frowning.

"Me? I never felt better."

"Sam," said Jeffery, "that bullet wound of yours is all cleared up by now, isn't it?"

Sam looked at Jeffery as if he had nearly forgotten Jeffery was here. Instead of answering, he asked, "What ship did you and Susan git down here on? I didn't see anything in the bay."

"We came on one of Beckly's peleloos."

"You didn't bring her on a reg'lar ship?"

"Sam," said Susan's voice, "Jeffery and I are going to be married. Why shouldn't we take anything we could get to get down here?"

Jeffery walked in silence with Sam up a slant of ground. That was after all the explanations. Mrs. Adams had said she would have her makaainanas attend to Captain Tolamy's sea chest. Meanwhile, would the two men go off someplace by themselves until Susan had a chance to wash off the salt scum from the sea voyage and get her breath back?

Sam asked how Jeffery had managed to escape from Atooie. By the time they had climbed above the cliffs, with a great view of Kailua Bay before them, Jeffery had finished his story. Sam sat himself on a stump of koa tree. He pulled out a seaman's knife and began whittling off a piece of vine as if something was on his mind. He said gruffly, "I want you to know I wish all the best for Susan and you. But you better take her to Philadelphia, 'stead of letting her sail alone to Australia. Why can't her old man meet her in America?" When Jeffery was silent Sam looked all around. "You wasn't thinking of gitting to Philadelphia first to have time to ease off with Rebecca? But, no. You ain't that sort. You'd have told Susan straight away."

"Well," said Jeffery, "I haven't."

"You haven't told Susan you were engaged to marry Rebecca?"

"No, I haven't."

Sam looked down at his feet. Presently he muttered, "It ain't none of my business, Jeff. But I'd think with a girl like Susan—

you'd maybe want to tell her you'd broken off with Rebecca 'stead of waiting till you married her and took her to Philadelphia."

"I'm not going to break it off with Rebecca."

Sam opened his mouth and then breathed through it instead of speaking. He seemed slowly to straighten and grow very tall. Jeffery had expected it would be easy to explain to Sam, who should be the one man who could understand. He looked up at Sam and felt a wind blowing coolly down the slope against his hot face.

"I've got myself into a—problem, Sam. I'd like advice."

"You ain't going to marry Susan?"

"No."

"You told Susan you were going to marry her?"

"I'm trying to tell you. Last Sunday I thought I could go through a temporary marriage. But I started thinking about it on the way here. Sam, I can't do it. I can't do that much dirt to her. Sam . . ."

Jeffery did not quite understand what next had happened because he found himself flat on the ground, his ears ringing, and his mouth filled with the taste of his own blood. He felt himself being hauled by the scruff of his neck to his feet. He heard Sam shouting in a terrible voice, "You goddam little bastard! You white-livered, sneaking, puking Mister Palmer!" Then Sam hit him a second time.

---

18.   Jeffery got up, shook his head, and charged at Sam. He hit Sam once and instantly was blindly aware that it had been too easy. He stepped back, wiping at his mouth with his arm; and he saw Sam had dropped his arms. Sam wasn't even trying to protect himself. Jeffery spit blood and felt himself shaking as if the ground was trembling under his feet. He tried to remember how it had started. All he could remember was telling Sam he wouldn't marry Susan.

Sam muttered, "To think of you and me fighting over the same girl."

Jeffery had started to turn away. He stopped. He said stupidly, "Susan?"

"I ain't too old yet to git married."

Sam? Susan? It had never crossed Jeffery's mind. He felt a shock greater than the shock of having Sam knock him down.

"She never said a word to me."

"I never told her. I wanted first to help git her old man off Atooie. When I did say something, she'd know at least whatever she wanted all she had to do was point and I'd try my best to git it for her."

It was unthinkable. Sam and Susan! Jeffery had never thought of a third person being caught in the net which his folly had cast for Susan and himself. He felt as if all three of them were poised on the edge of a precipice. He said slowly, "Sam, I'd better explain."

"I don't want to hear anything more," Sam said heavily. "I guess you ain't the first feller to go off from your girl and start looking at another. I see it now. There you were, fresh from Atooie. You were somebody exciting to Susan. It'd be nat'ral for a girl even as sensible as she is to think both she and you were being serious, but why didn't you tell her the truth when you saw she was taking you serious?"

Almost angrily, Jeffery said, "If you want to know, I lacked the courage. I never thought Young would agree to an island marriage. But he's been here too long. So has Holmes."

"Probably they never figgered you meant to take advantage of the island law to break your marriage with Susan when you sailed."

Jeffery winced. "Probably not. Everything you said before you knocked me down was right." He had a sensation of everything crumbling inside. He turned and started almost blindly down the path.

Sam ran after him, grabbing him by the arm. "What are you going to do?"

"I'll tell her now."

Sam pulled his arm. "We got to do this right. Don't you see you can't go down to her and relieve your conscience as easy as all of that? Think of her. Not jist of making it as easy on yourself as you can."

"I'm not going to make it as easy on myself as I can."

"Because you and Susan've had a few days of sparking, you got yourself in a whirl about having made a damn fool of yourself.

The king won't have time for a wedding ceremony till he's fixed about what can be made of this Prince Hoomehoome. You finish first with Tamehameha today or soon's he's ready to see you. Then go to Susan when your mind's clear. Start by putting doubts into her head about a native ceremony. Say you been thinking her old man might not approve, after all. If that don't work, git to hinting of there being a girl waiting for you in Philadelphia. Let Susan be the one to break it off. You know how proud she is. All she needs is an inkling you ain't so sure. Ain't that right?"

Jeffery turned it over in his mind. Sam was right. "Yes," he said, "I'll talk to Susan as soon as I've seen Tamehameha."

The runner found them ten minutes away from the Adams kuleana, where the path went south past a field of old sugar cane and pitched down toward the little green valley notched between the rise of cliffs. The runner said Holmes was at the kuleana waiting for them. Tamehameha had gone from the temple to his court and would see young Kukay at once. Jeffery understood the runner's message and felt a flicker of excitement touch him like a small flame at the thought of now at last going to see the old king of the islands. But he did not understand being called "Kukay."

Sam explained, "The king got your middle name twisted last week when Young read Beckly's report to him about your escape. Beckly likes to be formal and he had it written 'Jeffery Hooke Tolamy' but the king got it as 'Jeffery Cook Tolamy.' Next thing he was calling you 'Kukay.' "

"Kukay?"

"Sure. That's what the natives called Captain Cook. They still remember him from forty years ago. They called him 'Kapena Kukay.' Both Holmes and Young told the king you wasn't any kin to Captain Cook. But all the king did was give 'em a funny look and say you was young 'Kukay' and ask Young to git on with the letter."

It was slightly disconcerting. "I thought Cook's only son died some years ago," Jeffery said. "Am I supposed to be Cook's bastard or merely a distant connection?"

Then it struck him and he began to laugh. Sam and he were still laughing when they came down to the entrance of the kuleana, where Susan, Mrs. Adams, and Mr. Holmes were waiting for them.

Mr. Holmes had already told him about the two houses of stone which Tamehameha had built for himself and his three wives after retiring to Kailua. The stone houses even had glass windows in them which had been brought all the way around the Horn from Boston. Now Mr. Holmes led Sam and Jeffery through the clamor and smells and turmoil of the courtyard toward the larger house, its white-limed lava stones gleaming in the early dusk among the banana and ohia trees.

A score of aliis were squatting upon the broad lanai of the king's residence, beginning their evening meal with fish, steamed sugar-cane pith, boiled dog legs, and a large communal bowl of grayish poi. Every few minutes female makaainanas stooped with polished wooden bowls of sweet water in which the aliis languidly cleansed fingers big around as rake handles. Other makaainanas were engaged in clearing the air of flies with long-handled poles to which tufts of brilliantly dyed feathers were tied.

At the far end of the lanai was a large table of carved teakwood. When Jeffery managed to shove through the crowd of nobles, catching up with Sam and Mr. Holmes, he halted, seeing two chiefs facing him at the table. These two were both baking profusely in what appeared to be frock coats worn over gaudy checkered waistcoats. A third man in a red-colored waistcoat, his shirt sleeves showing, had his back to Jeffery and was eating his food in silence. This third man had a very broad back—and when Jeffery, startled, again looked at it, somehow the back seemed even broader than before.

The two chiefs in the extraordinary civilized garments as well as the third one were all engaged in eating with iron knives, forks, and spoons, instead of with their fingers. Every now and then, as if upon a hidden signal, all three would raise small China cups and gulp down the contents. In the midst of that racket upon the lanai, extending outward to the yard, there was something almost unreal in seeing these three men, silently sitting at the table, trying to eat European fashion.

The two nobles facing Jeffery were hideously tattooed. One had black whiskers knotted and tufted like a tassel below his chin. The other's black hair was shorn and cut and stiffened with pig's fat until in shape it resembled a Spanish conquistador's helmet.

At first Jeffery had conceived of them as being rather small. It was not until he gradually perceived all of the third man in the red waistcoat that Jeffery knew he was looking at two large men and at a third who was something more than merely large. He did not have the same shocked feeling he had had last Sunday. Billy Pitt had been out of proportion to himself as well as everyone else. The red-waistcoated man at the table was in proportion to all his parts. His shoulders, his hands, his feet, were not too large or too broad for the rest of him. Nothing about him was too big. It was simply that everyone else near him had suddenly shrunk in size.

All his life, Jeffery thought, he would remember this frozen moment. He knew now. He knew who it was. It was not necessary for Mr. Holmes to touch him lightly and explain, "Those two chiefs facing you are John Adams and a Kohala alii whose name I've forgotten."

"John Adams?" Jeffery had assumed Captain Adams was a white man and was in Mowee.

"Not Cap Adams," hastily whispered Mr. Holmes. "We've got two Adamses in Kailua. Cap Adams is in Mowee. He's the one married to the Mrs. Adams Susan's staying with. That 'John Adams' at the table is the name the chief's taken for himself. Now don't move for a minute, Mr. Tolamy. The Kohala alii appears to be having difficulty with his lesson in eating. Tamehameha's determined to have all his principal aliis learn how to eat white man fashion."

Jeffery watched intently. He did not even think it ludicrous any more to hear a tattooed chief had given himself the name of the second President of the United States. He started back—the Kohala alii had leaped away from the table, upsetting a chair, yelling furiously. The alii had spilled poi from his iron spoon down his jaw, down his yellow waistcoat, and now he flung the spoon to the floor and stamped on it, bellowing passionately. The man in the red waistcoat, scarcely looking up, gave the alii a casual whack, and continued drinking coffee from the cup held by the other hand as if there hadn't been an interruption.

Jeffery decided that whack must have echoed on the other side of the bay. He watched the tattooed chief falling. He heard others laughing. He watched the chief get to his knees, shake his hideous head, and get on up to his feet, breathing heavily. Jeffery expected a fight; but the man in the red waistcoat finished drinking the coffee as if nothing had happened and nodded casually toward the spoon on the floor. Like a child obeying its parent, the big tattooed noble stooped meekly, recovering the spoon. He sat quietly in his chair, once more desperately trying to spoon poi from a wooden bowl to the unsteady opening below a nose having sharks tattooed on both sides. It was hard going, but he made it. The third man wiped his mouth. Jeffery heard him give a grunt of approval.

Now the third man had shoved back his chair and was standing. He was still all in proportion. He still did not seem unusually big. He started coming toward Jeffery, who had the peculiar notion the man wasn't moving at all, but that the lanai and everyone upon the lanai had started sliding gently toward him. Later Jeffery realized that you no more thought of him moving than you thought of a cliff moving. If you approached a cliff, part of it passed entirely from view, but all that remained within the range of vision was so normal and solid you had no idea of marveling at what you saw. It was something like that when Tamehameha advanced and halted and regarded Jeffery.

The face was no longer so very savage, Jeffery saw, feeling rooted there by the eyes sighting upon him. The hair which once had been described as covered with a brownish sort of paste or powder was now a grizzled white, cropped as short as iron shears could do it. The nose was much flatter than most noses on these islands. The lips were thick, the upper one turned up so that the face in repose looked sulky, almost petulant, with nothing in it for Jeffery to find of that good humor and openness which had once been described. Three of the lower front teeth were gone. Tamehameha was dressed in a colored shirt stained by his sweat, a red waistcoat gaping at the chest, a black handkerchief tied around the stout swarthy neck, worn velveteen breeches big enough for three men of Jeffery's size, worsted stockings on his legs despite the heat, and large military shoes. His grizzled head was crowded up under the roof of the lanai.

He looked down at Jeffery with no perceptible change in the face, the peculiar configuration of his upper lip with its half-petulant sneer still giving him the expression of sulkiness. "Him, Kapena Kukay son?"

"Your majesty," said Mr. Holmes, "Captain Tolamy is not Captain Cook's son."

"Him, Kapena Kukay brutta son?"

"No, not even a nephew."

"Nay-foo?"

"Brother's son. But he is not any connection. Captain Jeffery Hooke Tolamy. *Hooke*."

"Him Kukay," said Tamehameha. "No more talk."

Jeffery wished he had only seen Tamehameha and had never heard Tamehameha speak. He did not know how he could convince Mr. Monroe that a pagan who could not tell one name from another would be able to hold his kingdom against the Russians even for a few weeks, let alone ten to eleven months until help could arrive.

Tamehameha had left off scowling down at Jeffery. He nodded to Sam. "Alora oe, Ammay. You come," he ordered, an explosive whistle of breath escaping through the gap between his teeth. "All come. Kukay come . . ."

Tamehameha's English was spoken as evidently he had learned it, during the past quarter of a century, from British and Yankee sailors. It was monosyllabic, soft, very soft. At first the voice had startled Jeffery, a breaking of the nervous tension giving him an urge toward laughter, for the voice issuing from the enormous cavern of chest was not thunder, nor as the roar of the surf, but a high reedy sound.

Tamehameha went on through his chiefs and was gone, Mr. Holmes following in his wake. Jeffery had not realized he was still standing there until Sam gripped his arm. "We're supposed to follow him."

Jeffery said disgustedly, " 'Kukay.' I thought he knew more than that."

---

19.   The residence had rooms and halls in the fashion of civilized houses. Jeffery followed Sam into one of the largest rooms, he looked around, trying to see everything at once. Large pier glasses were placed at the four corners of the room,

which Jeffery decided was the throne or gathering room. At one end was a high teakwood commode. Upon the floor was spread a fine Chinese yellow rug. Along one edge Jeffery noticed a hole which evidently had been eaten by rats, one of the greatest plagues of the islands.

He was struck by the casualness of the household, the noise, the general confusion. The king had seated himself in an outsize chair, and all the time the king was there a young makaaiana with small rosy breasts and hair like heavy spun coral waved a tufted pole of royal yellow above his head to clear away the flies. Before asking Jeffery about either Atooie or Hoomehoome, Tamehameha had Jeffery tell him of that morning last May in Honoruru.

The feeling Jeffery had of being made the butt of an obscure joke had now passed. He decided the old king merely had made a mistake and was stubborn enough not to wish to admit having made one by believing Jeffery was a descendant of the great Captain Cook. There was a silence. Jeffery felt a change come over the assembly. Next, Tamehameha asked what was this, now, of the inheritor of Atooie, the son of Kaumuualii being alive?

Jeffery had decided previously to speak in the island language. His experience before the assembled chiefs and Billy Pitt at Honoruru had been as a rehearsal and it helped him address the king more easily and in an even more convincing manner. He had no need to search for words.

He spoke for half an hour, perhaps forty-five minutes. The candles were lit while he was speaking. When he sat down he was surprised to discover the room was packed with chiefs, numbers standing in the hallway, the rumor having spread all through the yard that a momentous thing was taking place. Then Jeffery saw that on the king's face the petulance had vanished. A gargoyle's grin was beginning to form.

Jeffery heard the excited murmuring of the aliis. Mr. Holmes stepped forward to explain the problem facing Captain Tolamy, who planned to leave for America on the Traveller of Philadelphia, which was expected any day in Honoruru. Five or six months from now, when arriving in his country, Captain Tolamy would be summoned before his own chief, Mr. James Monroe, and asked if the islands would hold until ships bearing muskets and cannons arrived from faraway America. What message had Tamehameha to give Captain Tolamy to carry back to his chief?

Tamehameha now rose and said very simply that he had only this to say. At the end of the Muckahitee, Tamehameha would sail for Atooie with ten thousand men. King Kaumuualii would regret having betrayed Atooie to the Russians after it became known on Atooie that Hoomehoome was soon returning. Olohana—Jeffery had to remind himself that "Olohana" was Governor Young—had already dispatched emissaries to Atooie. If the first emissaries were killed before they could get to the king, others would be sent until the king finally heard and believed and instead of going with the Russians against the forces from the south, at least he and his men would retire to leave the forces from the south free to reach a decision with the Russians. All that, Kukay could say to his chief in the far land.

The king sat. There was a silence. Kukay again! Jeffery thought. He saw the intelligent old eyes gazing at him. For an unbelieving instant, Jeffery imagined seeing a reassuring twinkle. He recalled that Ben Partridge had believed there were two factions at the court of the Czar, one faction strongly in favor of risking a war with Great Britain and the United States of America to obtain the Pacific, the other faction still holding out.

He now mentioned what Partridge had said.

Tamehameha nodded his vast head. Makoa. Very good. Tamehameha agreed. It was well reasoned.

"But the Russian ship?" Jeffery demanded. "What am I to tell Mr. Monroe?"

When the ship was sighted, Tamehameha would place a kapu on it to prevent his subjects from attacking. The ship would be allowed to approach in peace. When the Russian captain landed, Tamehameha would protest strongly against Scheffer's actions. He would make it clear that these islands were a civilized country, having an established government. Had Kukay seen those chiefs on the lanai attempting to learn how to eat in the haole fashion? Perhaps he had been tempted to laugh? It was a solemn thing. Tamehameha had already selected a score of his greatest chiefs to be with him when he undertook to negotiate with the Russians. These island nobles were to be dressed in civilized uniforms and have an understanding of haole manners of eating. If possible, the women aliis also would wear haole wahine clothes.

Now, at last, Jeffery had the answer to what had mystified him in Honoruru when first he had learned of Tamehameha's obsession with military uniforms.

"Is that all?" he asked.

No, it was not entirely all. Tamehameha explained his plan of attack exactly as Governor Young had previously explained it to Jeffery at Honoruru.

Jeffery said slowly, "If you had sufficient cannons here and at Honoruru I'd be willing to recommend to Mr. Monroe that at least you had a fighting chance to drive off the Russian ship. Those cliffs inland are natural fortifications. When I sailed in this morning, I even hoped they were bulwarks Tamehameha had raised—"

He stopped. He looked at Sam. He said, "Sam, you remember me telling you what we did at Grey's Fort? We lacked cannon. Our major painted a few logs black. I told Beckly, but Beckly said some of his cannons were for show, anyway. They were no better than logs. Suppose the Russian ship sails into Kailua? What if her captain saw those fortifications above the bay and saw cannons there, big cannons, sixteen-pounders, waiting to blow his damned ship out of the water?"

After Jeffery's proposal had been explained, the king called for silence. He wanted three such cannons of wood, as Kukay had described, to be fashioned tonight and before dawn mounted on the cliffs for him to decide how they appeared.

Then Jeffery felt himself being lifted and a nose grated against his nose and he had a confused impression of being told in a high reedy voice, all punctuated through by whistling sounds, that he was a good omen for the islands. His coming had been seen for many years. Makoa! Makoa! Makoa, Kukay!

Sam said, "Write Susan a note and say we both are stuck down here all night on war business for the king. Maybe we won't even git there for breakfast. I'll go see if I can hunt up a runner in all this mob of heathens. Did you ever seen such a hooraw? How can they ever git logs shaped and made to look like cannons by sunup?"

It became a very long night. Sam and Jeffery scratched a pattern in sand by the light of flares and the makaainanas hauled three big koa-wood logs up on the beach. A head priest from the temple was in charge. He was a kahuna-kalaiwaa, one who was accustomed to directing the building of the native ships and Sam had worked before with him.

Sam said while Tamehameha was king this old priest had the whole spiritual galaxy at his command. Merely pointing a finger at you and wishing it, so the makaainana artisans believed, he could condemn you to shrivel and die instantly.

An hour before dawn, in the company of nearly two hundred makaainanas and a score of aliis and kahunas, Jeffery and Sam trudged wearily inland, up the slope, toward the cliffs. The logs, now black and gleaming like polished iron from being painted with charcoal mixed with kukui-nut oil, were being carried over the barren plains, up through the fields, up higher through slippery grass, higher still, under the green sky of very early morning. The artisans fitted the first log into position. Sam went to help place the remaining two logs but Jeffery was too exhausted to budge. He stayed by the first log where he was soon joined by Mr. Holmes.

By the time Sam had returned, Mr. Holmes and Jeffery were sighting down the long slope. With a feather cloak of yellow and red flying from his shoulders, Tamehameha came climbing over the crest at full red dawn.

Afterwards, for long minutes he scowled down at the log which lay in its rock embrasure. It was like a ship's cannon mounted on land, the long black muzzle thrusting through pika-kai thickets toward the harbor. He went to the other two logs and came back and stopped in front of Jeffery and asked, suddenly, what Kukay now would say to his chief? Did Kukay believe these logs were enough like cannons to deceive the warship?

It was certainly putting it up to Jeffery. He had a certain grim amusement mingled with admiration for the old giant. Jeffery got himself up without answering. He walked by himself a full hundred yards to the crowd of workers around the second log. It was placed as carefully in the lava embrasure as the first. It just might suffice. Jeffery didn't know. He wished he were on a ship at sea, sailing into the harbor. He wished he had more military experience.

He returned to where they were waiting, having now to decide what he thought of his own suggestion. He would tell Mr. Monroe what had been done. He would say he thought at least the odds had been strengthened by the addition of the false cannons. However, three false cannons were not very many. If the king meant to make a show of them, Jeffery thought there ought to be more.

Tamehameha grunted and nodded. Mr. Holmes remarked in the dry way he could use now and then that Tamehameha was already considering what should be done at Kearakekua Bay, half a day by foot south of Kailua. Jeffery had forgotten there was another bay below Kailua, the large bay, where Captain Cook had landed.

"Aohe nana, he mauu hiro," answered the reedy voice. He pointed toward the sea and said something to Mr. Holmes which Jeffery could not catch.

Again he contemplated the log. He regarded Jeffery. "I go now," he said with a whistle and explosion of breath.

Jeffery took a deep breath. "What did Tamehameha mean by saying the log might be no better than hiro grass?"

"It's a proverb," said Mr. Holmes, troubled. "Hiro grass is worthless. If you thought Tamehameha took your suggestion to impress you, or have you impress Mr. Monroe, I'm afraid you're quite wrong. He's thinking much less of possible help to come next year than of right now and how by all and every means to fight or frighten off the Russian ship."

He raised an arm, pointing to the sea. "We'll see what Governor Young has to say about our cannons. There's the Taamana bearing around the point. See it? Tamehameha saw it first, quarter of an hour ago."

The bark had anchored out in the bay, Young landing by small boat. Tamehameha had met him, the two going on to the residence, where within a quarter of an hour Mr. Holmes, Sam, and Jeffery joined them.

Governor Young said he had departed Monday evening to bring urgent intelligence to Kailua. The Traveller of Philadelphia had sailed into Honoruru early Monday morning! If Captain Tolamy had delayed by one day he would have been at Honoruru to see the ship come in.

Furthermore, Young said, the ship would remain until early December somewhere on the archipelago. Wilcox, her master, wanted to beach her long enough to replace rotten stern timbers with sound wood before continuing around the Horn to the east coast of America. Wilcox had sent his compliments and would be very pleased to have Captain Tolamy sail with him when the *Traveller* could make way again.

Young also said that the *Traveller* had carried in her cargo the king's military uniforms which had been ordered two years ago. Even as Young was speaking, Jeffery watched crewmen from the bark's small boats going into the residence, each man carrying a large wooden box in his arms. There was a crowding of chiefs to see the new uniforms when the boxes were broken open. Tamehameha had gone inside and as Young followed him he called over his shoulder, "Tolamy, we'll want Sam and ye to 'ear the rest of this . . ."

In the throne room, Young was speaking in the native language to Tamehameha and the chiefs. Four years ago, Young reminded them, Tamehameha had ordered a letter written to the great King of England to ask when the warship promised to him by Captain Vancouver might come. Now, an answer had at last come from around the world, prepared by the king's own prime ministers. He was unfolding a dispatch which Jeffery saw had been wrapped in oiled silk. There were even red seals on the dispatch. Tamehameha was smiling. The uniforms had arrived. The King of England had answered.

Young told Jeffery, "Ye 'ad best see it, captain. Ye can say to Mr. Monroe ye 'ave read it." He pushed the crinkling heavy paper into Jeffery's hands. " 'Twas prepared by the Foreign Office which is 'ard to explain to Tamehameha, for it might give 'im ideas of 'aving such an office 'ere. W'en ye see Mr. Monroe, ye can tell 'im we 'ave the assurance that England'll not stand for the Russians taking our island."

Jeffery went to one of the windows and began by reading a line in which the name of the Prince Regent had caught his eye:

> The Prince Regent expresses Confidence that the complete Success which He has gained over His Enemies in every Quarter of the Globe will have the Effect of securing your Dominion from any Attack or Molestation on their Part . . ..

He read the promise given to defend the islands, read the letter which the British Foreign Office had sent to a barbaric king halfway around the world. The British government had hedged about the warship which Captain Vancouver had once rashly offered Tamehameha. But as if in return for such diplomatic hedging, here was the firm assurance that the British government under the person of the Prince Regent would take it as a violation of existing agreements and treaties in the Pacific were any foreign power to claim dominion or special rights from the Sandwich Islands.

Jeffery asked, "Governor Young, I should like to have a copy of this to carry back to Mr. Monroe."

"Ay. That ye can 'ave."

"I don't suppose you've heard what luck your emissaries to Atooie have had?" Jeffery now asked Governor Young quietly.

"Not yet," Young replied. " 'Olmes 'as been asking me the same. We'll want four or five days more till we get any sort of reply. 'Ow's Susan?"

"She's very comfortable with Mrs. Adams."

"I cannot stay for the marriage. I must leave by noon."

Jeffery did not try to hide his surprise. "You're sailing as soon for Honoruru?"

"Ay. I am more needed in Honoruru than 'ere. Ye can expect to be sailing very soon, yerself, captain. It don't appear as like we'd 'ave the enemy on our backs till atter ye've gone. For our sake I wish ye could delay till ye know the outcome and could tell Mr. Monroe, but seldom can anyone 'ave what 'e'd like to 'ave. I 'ope ye'll assure Mr. Monroe that we mean to fight the Russians as long as we 'ave men alive to fight. Now, sir, because I 'ave still much to do—would ye send a runner for Susan? I want to see 'er afore I sail."

"Yes. I'll send a runner at once."

Jeffery started across the room toward the yard, but he halted when he heard Young booming at Holmes, "Oliver, w'en did Tamehameha get those three sixteen-pounders I saw w'en sailing into the bay? I want all cannons ye can give me. Beckly will be in desp'rate need of them. 'Ow soon can we get those cannons loaded upon the bark?"

Mr. Holmes turned his cherubic face toward Jeffery, blinked an instant through his spectacles, and turned back to his old friend. "Bless me! Were you taken in so easily? You a boatswain from the old days?"

"Taken in? W'at are ye saying, ye old muckle-'eaded Yankee?"

"I'm saying those cannons are no more than three logs we shaped and painted and put up there on the cliffs this morning to make a show if a Russian ship sighted them."

Young's eyes seemed to bulge. "I was took by three logs? Oliver, w'en this business with the Russians is finished, will ye kindly remind me to send ye ten piculs of sandalwood from my next cuttings?"

"Pay up to young Tolamy and Sam Crowell. It was their idea, not mine."

Sam stepped forward. "Mark it down all for Jeff. He's the engineer, not me. But I'm satisfied, gentlemen. If Mr. Young figgered they was cannons, them Russians ain't going to be any smarter than he was."

---

20. Instead of sending a runner, Jeffery had decided to go himself for Susan. He had gone as far as the warriors guarding the entrance to the west road when he stopped short. Coming down from the north, and passing south before him toward the noisy beach, was the great dusty highway with pilgrims marching in to join the thousands who had already arrived for the ending of the Muckahitee.

He heard someone cry, "Noho! Noho!" A palanquin bearing some wild chieftain from the north stopped, allowing Susan and Kala to cross in front and come toward Jeffery. Then Susan ran to him and kissed him and it required a great effort of will for Jeffery to remember he had no right to return the kiss. In a single breath she demanded what he had been doing last night and this morning. Even Mrs. Adams had worried. All of them had waited breakfast. Not long ago they had heard from some of the makaainanas that Olohana had sailed in at dawn. Was it true? Was Governor Young here? Susan had not known what could be happening. So she had decided to come down with Kala and find out for herself.

Jeffery remembered to greet Kala. "Aroha, oe," he said.

Susan now tucked her arm in his. With massive grace, Kala marched on his other side. On their way along the road running west upon the king's point of land, Jeffery explained the activities of yesterday evening with Tamehameha.

Susan was wearing one of Mrs. Adams's pretty gowns of golden silk, and this morning her hair was braided into a coronet of shining brown.

As Jeffery gazed upon her, a small unruly part of his mind began forming a thought. How he wanted her!

Susan regarded him candidly, her eyes pleased by whatever she saw in his. "Have you had time to speak to Tamehameha about marrying us?"

Jeffery stiffened. "No."

"Can't you ask him today?"

"Susan, I'm not going to ask him."

"You'd better. Mr. Holmes may forget with so much else now."

"We're not going to have a wedding here."

"But, Jeffery—"

"What would your father say to a native marriage?" he asked.

"Jeffery," she said, exasperated, "we've gone over all that before when we were sailing down from Honoruru. Mr. Young approves. Even Mr. Holmes approves."

Kala's voice said, "Ike-ware oe, haole kapene Ammay?" and Jeffery had completely forgotten that Kala had stopped behind them. He saw Kala was pointing in the direction of the yard showing through the banana trees. As Kala had asked if he had, he saw Captain Ammay approaching. Captain Sam Crowell had been running. Now Sam stopped and walked forward with a lurch. "When did you git here, Susan?"

"Just now. Kala and I came down from the kuleana and Jeffery met us. Sam, Jeffery's afraid Tamehameha can't spare time to marry us right now."

Sam slowly opened his hands. "Jeff's right, Susan. Jeff, you can both decide better what to do when you git back next Sunday."

"Get back from where?"

Susan cried, "Where's Jeffery going?"

Sam said Tamehameha had decided to send the two of them along with the kahuna-kalai to Kearakekua Bay as quickly as they could leave. Tamehameha wanted twenty-five log cannons placed on the cliffs above Kearakekua in the next three days. John Adams would take over here at Kailua with the makaainanas who had worked last night on the three logs. As they continued into the yard, Sam started telling Susan all over again about last night.

Mr. Young and Mr. Holmes came away from a circle of aliis to greet Susan. Jeffery had not told her he had been the one to think of the idea of using the logs. For a third time she heard the events of last night from Mr. Young and now in complete detail. She listened. She gave Jeffery a quick glance of pride when Mr. Young said young Tolamy had done very well for himself last night. Young even added that both the king and he would want to keep Tolamy here to help them with the defense of the islands if it wasn't so important to get him off to America to carry a statement of the situation to Mr. Monroe in a hurry.

It pleased Jeffery to see Susan so pleased; and it was very pleasant to be praised by Governor Young. Susan had thrown back her head, with color in her cheeks. She said quickly if Jeffery could help by going with Sam for three days to Kearakekua, she did very much want him to go. Three days would be a very long time, though.

When Sam, the kahuna-kalai, and Jeffery sailed the next morning the wind was wrong. Instead of arriving in two hours, it was nearly dark when the peleloo came into Kearakekua Bay, poking slowly toward the northwest shore.

That night they stopped at the house of the headman of the village of Kaavaroa. It was raining early Friday morning when the kahuna-kalai called together the headmen from the villages of Kiloa, Waipunaula, and Kalana, and told them what was wanted.

By midday a small camp was rising inland from the bay on the cliffs. A hundred woodchoppers had gone in small gangs up the great slope of Mauna Roa to cut twenty-five of the largest available trees. With a sharpened stick Jeffery carefully drew a full-scale pattern for the artisans to follow. These keune-hales were men expert at building houses and working with wood; as soon as Jeffery had drawn them what was wanted they set to work.

The men had brought their families with them from the villages and by evening there were a hundred or more rough houses of poles and grass built, a whole little village on the cliffs, with cook fires burning. Jeffery ate and went back to the big cleared space where a new gang of keune-hales were chopping and carving with their stone adzes at the six logs sent down from the upper forests at Mauna Roa a few hours earlier.

Sam grumbled that they weren't getting on as fast as he had hoped. It was the woodchoppers. Most of the trees the woodchoppers had got down this afternoon were too small to be used.

"At this rate we ain't going to be finished by Sunday, either. I want to git back. I been worrying about all those canoes we got hauled down along the shore below the king's court. Them canoes are our fire canoes. They ought to be sailed around to the north side of the king's point of land and hid there if there's any chance of the Russian ship coming in our direction these next couple of weeks."

Jeffery had an inspiration. "Well, look, Sam," he said. "The keunes here understand what to do with the logs once they're brought down here. You'll be busy tomorrow having the parapets dug but I won't have much on my hands. Suppose I go up into the forests with a headman and the woodchoppers?"

Two hours after sunrise, Saturday, the twenty-third, in the company of the headman of Kaavaroa and twenty or thirty makaainanas, Jeffery had climbed high on the west slope of Mauna Roa to the camp of the woodchoppers under the gloomy canopy of wide-spreading trees. He estimated he must have gone at least twelve miles inland since awakening before sunrise and eating.

The air up here was cool and sharp. By noon he had covered perhaps another six miles through the forests, marking trees to be felled. That afternoon a dozen trimmed logs were on their way down the slope.

He had forgotten how early it started to become dark at this time of year and when he saw the woodchoppers light fires for the evening meal, he realized that if he did not hurry he would be caught here on the slope until morning. The headman offered to accompany Jeffery to the camp off Kearakekua, but Jeffery wanted the headman to stay to be certain the woodchoppers finished felling the rest of the marked trees tomorrow. The trail from the bay, he remembered, had been easy to follow.

But at an elevation of three or four thousand feet, a cold rain began to fall. Although Jeffery could not believe it was much after five o'clock in the evening, the sky darkened rapidly. He went downward through the trees, his feet sinking deeply into the wet ancient accumulation of rotted leaves and humus.

The land began to ascend instead of sloping downward. He realized he must have strayed off the path onto a ridge which formed one side of a valley cutting lengthwise across the volcano's slope.

Very soon he discovered he did not have the remotest idea where he was. It was dark as pitch under the trees, the rain coming down in a steady dismal leaking through the leaves. He came across a stream and followed along its bank and finally trudged out into what appeared to be a highland meadow, all gray and luminous under the pale light of the stars showing through more of a heavy mist than a real rain.

Presently he stumbled upon a descending path. He soon heard pigs grunting and kicked out sharply when a hard shape struck his legs. He knew the pigs were used as watchdogs by these village people, the dogs being good for nothing except eating. He stopped at the first dwelling he saw, the square of yellow light shining dimly at the low entrance. Fortunately, it was the house belonging to the headman of this small remote mountain village; a broad-shouldered man, with a flat nose and not many teeth in his head, Jeffery saw, when the kapa cloth covering the entrance was thrown back and a lighted flare was shoved forth.

The headman bowed and stammered that his name was Mauae. At first he was so awed he had trouble speaking. Never before, Mauae admitted, had he seen a white alii, although he and everyone else in the village had heard such a great one was in the forests today with the woodchoppers.

Mauae begged Jeffery to enter. When Jeffery stooped and made his way in, all the other people inside promptly fell to their knees, bending their heads to the hard-packed floor. "Noho me au," Mauae said, dwell with me, be here in my abode; and he also went to his knees.

For the moment, Jeffery merely tried to see where he was without replying. He saw Mauae had two wives, one of whom evidently soon would present him with a third child. There was a chubby son of two or three years. And Jeffery also saw that Mauae's kneeling daughter had red hair. As she knelt, he saw her smooth neck and shoulders and back.

The headman arose when Jeffery questioned him. Jeffery learned he had badly strayed to the northwest. The path to the bay was on the other side of the long ridge. He offered to conduct Jeffery to the bay. But he paused. He bowed again very low. He said timidly for the rest of their lives the inhabitants of his village would never cease talking of such an event if only the white lord would consent to stay here for the night.

As Jeffery reckoned time, it was not very late. He could not believe he had been more than an hour trying to find his way after losing it. It could not be more than seven or seven-thirty and if he hurried he should be able to reach the bay within another hour. He thought of crowding into the lean-to where Sam would be. It was warm and dry here under the tightly thatched roof. He saw the girl peer curiously up at him, holding her hair from her eyes by a hand. The big sturdy woman next to her promptly pinched her to remind her of her manners before the white lord. The girl wriggled, the dark-red hair folding and unfolding over the naked shoulders.

Jeffery found himself wanting to laugh. He said he would be very pleased to stay here for the night if it was no inconvenience.

One woman pulled down a chicken roosting upon a rafter pole and had its neck twisted off before it had uttered a single squawk. The second wife cleared a space for Jeffery near the stone umi in the center of the single room, replenishing the fire with sticks. The father commanded his daughter to attend the lord while food was cooked. Did she not see the lord was wet through? Did this lazy household have no new kapa cloth to supply an honored guest with fresh wearing material?

Jeffery retreated to the stone umi while the girl fetched him a strip of new kapa cloth for the man's malo and a longer and heavier length to throw around his shoulders like a shawl. He gave his dripping jacket and trousers to her and she hung them up to dry on the center ridgepole, stretching on her toes, the firelight playing over her.

He learned her name was Polena. She lost all shyness when he questioned her and she said she'd been born here and had lived here all her life with her family.

Jeffery watched the red gleam of her hair in the firelight and was reminded of the old legend which he had heard from the

kahuna in Atooie. A long time ago, the natives believed, a man
and his sister had been washed ashore upon Atooie. They were of
white skin and red hair. They had been accepted as gods and they
lived together and had redheaded children who voyaged to the
other islands.

Jeffery had thought there might be some truth to the old tale
for every now and then on the islands was born a child with reddish
hair and light-amber skin, such as Polena possessed. They were
called "ehus" and were honored and cherished more than other
children. Perhaps, thought Jeffery, relaxing, warm and dry now—
perhaps in the very early days of exploring the Pacific a Spanish
galleon had foundered and a Spaniard and his sister actually had
survived and managed to float or swim to these unknown islands.

It was pleasant and exciting to watch Polena passing back and
forth and to speculate if she might not have a few drops of ancient
Spanish blood in her. After he had eaten, Polena and the two
wives put away the wooden bowls and eating utensils. The father
dragged the largest sleeping mat toward the end of the house
farthest from the entrance. He approached Jeffery, bowed, and said
the mat there was for the lord.

Jeffery said it was a great kindness. The father said it was nothing.
He was honored. All that was here in his dwelling belonged to his
guest. He bowed again and backed away. He pinched out the burning strings of kukui nuts and there was only the reflection from the
dying fire. The two wives had dragged more mats into the darkness
at the other end of the house. Here they lay down with the son.
The father bowed once more and went to his wives.

Polena remained kneeling before Jeffery. Her hair was like curling
flames and her pale eyes were unreadable. In a low voice, Jeffery
spoke to her. He saw her head turn toward the darkness. Then
she looked back at Jeffery and slowly nodded her head.

Jeffery arose and silently went to the side of the room where
the mat had been spread for him. He lay down and watched Polena
stand before the burning embers and remove the pa'u from around
her hips.

He raised upon an elbow to see why she was delaying and presently her intention struck him in a manner which he never would
have anticipated. He had not thought of her as being so knowing.
It struck him at first with surprise, and finally with a certain grim

humor. He supposed, he thought, he had expected innocence from this beautifully shaped young heathen. Well, he was a fool. He had been here long enough to know better. He was the innocent. No doubt during the past year a great many young kanakas from the neighboring villages one by one in turn had been welcomed and had watched from where Jeffery was watching, while Polena brushed and brushed at the thick red hair, deliberately delaying. Then Jeffery let himself think of making love to her on this same mat and it seemed to him he became aware of smells and odors of which he had not been aware before inside this house of grass.

He caught sight of his jacket and trousers hanging from a roof-pole and when he arose he became consciously aware that his desire had been killed by sudden disgust. He had become completely relaxed. Polena hastily put down her brush of bound olono fibers to embrace him and he thrust her to one side.

"He aha kau noho wale nei?" she demanded angrily.

It seeemed to him he was seeing her clearly for the first time. Because he was not sure he knew the complete answer, he could not reply to her question. When she offered to revive his desire for her he thrust her away less gently, beginning to feel greatly embarrassed, and dressed in haste.

He had been a fool. He had made a wretched mistake. He was deaf to protests. He said stubbornly he was going. The small son bawled. Everyone seemed to be speaking at once. The father offered to beat his daughter if she had been lacking in hospitality. Altogether, Jeffery's escape was a sorry experience.

He said he had forgotten that his companions at Kearakekua would soon be searching for him if he did not return. He had a confused impression of repeating himself and of a pig attempting to bite him and of kicking off the pig. Then there were flares in the wet night and he had got himself at least out of the house but he would not forget how forlorn Polena's voice had become, calling after him as he went up the path with her father.

Her father took him after a half hour of hard climbing to the top of the ridge and showed him the path and paused there, in silence. There was nothing Jeffery could say. The father bowed and vanished very quickly, melting into the darkness. Jeffery followed the path. He did not believe more than a quarter of the night had gone. He should be at the camp well before midnight.

On his way, he somewhat collected himself. He realized now he had not been able to endure having Polena after Susan. He belonged to Susan as much as Susan belonged to him.

About an hour after he had thrust himself in haste and confusion out of the headman's house Jeffery crossed the last ridge, the land falling away before him under the wet dimness from the stars. From where he was he could see perhaps twenty campfires still burning, and the long dark line, a mile or so below him, where during the day parapets had been thrown up. Beyond was the great still expanse of sea.

He climbed over a wall of lava. It had evidently rained heavily here during the day and he made slow progress through the mud of a new taro field. He should have followed the path instead of trying to cut across and arrive more quickly. He went back, getting on the path again, kicking the heavy mud from his sandals.

He descended swiftly toward the nearest fire and was brought up short by a sentinel stationed there with a stone-tipped spear. He had not known that Sam or the kahuna would have posted sentinels. Other warriors came up to cluster around him. Evidently they had arrived during the day, because they were strange to him, and he was told he must wait until the kahuna could be brought. They were polite but they were firm.

The kahuna was apologetic. These sentinels were warriors from the hills who had only been brought down this afternoon with strict orders to keep all strangers away from the fortifications. Sam Crowell was not here. Sam had sailed for Kailua at sunset after sending runners to the forest in search of the other white lord. Jeffery read the message which the kahuna had brought with him.

Jeff—I can't wait longer for you. About an hour ago a runner got here with a note from Oliver Holmes for us to return quick as possible.

Holmes wrote the Russian warship was sighted late yesterday afternoon off Towaihae Bay—that's a night's sailing to the north of Kailua. The wind had failed so the ship was becalmed. But the chiefs at Towaihae Bay couldn't sail their peleloos south, either. They had to send runners. The king didn't receive the first warning until this morning.

The chiefs sent out two dugouts filled with girls, hoping the girls could get aboard and work information from the crew while sweetening the men in the usual style. But the trick didn't work. The girls were all warned off. Five kanakas got aboard, though. But the kanakas were kept aboard. The last king and Holmes heard was the ship was still off Towaihae Bay this morning, still waiting for a wind.

It looks like everybody but Tamehameha again had been foxed by the Russians. But Tamehameha always expected the warship would try for Owhyee, not Honoruru.

The wind's been freshening here the last two hours. It means the warship ought to be getting a share of wind to the north and will be on the way toward Kailua by now. I'm leaving to get back if I can before the ship arrives. I've fixed it to have another peleloo waiting for you. Get to Kailua as fast as you can.

Sam

21. In the very early hours of Sunday morning, the twenty-fourth of November, Jeffery's peleloo carried him to the black shores of Kailua. The light breeze had swept the sky clear of rain clouds. By starlight shining over land and water, Jeffery saw only one ship at anchor beyond the surf. It was a small brig flying an American flag. The sight of it gave him relief. He was not too late. He had arrived before the Russian warship.

Before he jumped to the hard sand, in a last sweeping glance he saw all the flares and torches shining from the north curve of the bay to the south. He had to force himself through the excited crowd gathered along the beach. When he came to the great road he was held back as warriors passed by at a dogtrot, all shadows and moving darkness. Like white ghosts, two kahunas appeared, every minute or so shouting orders at the top of their lungs. All children, women with children, the infirm, and the old were commanded to return to the villages from whence they came. All others, kanakas and wahines, were to collect in the fields above

Kailua and wait until their own headmen or chiefs sought them to give further commands.

In the king's yard it was nearly bright as morning from the many fires and torches. Jeffery ran by aliis in their feathered regalia who were drawing up ranks of fighting men under the ohia and banana trees. Pushing through a throng gathered around the king's two stone residences, he saw Sam Crowell.

Sam was speaking to a young tattooed alii, with shoulders the size of a bull's, who was a good head taller than Sam, almost seven feet high.

"Sam—" Jeffery had been running so hard the past fifteen minutes that he was out of breath. "*Sam!*"

Sam swung around. "Damn if I wasn't scared you wouldn't git here in time."

"I got lost on my way down to the bay. What about the Russian ship?"

"All I know, the ship's somewhere between Towaihae Bay and here. John Adams was jist telling me."

"Is Cap Adams back from Mowee?"

"Yes, Cap got back," Sam said impatiently, "but don't mix up Cap Adams with John Adams, here," and nodded to the tall alii. "This one's *John Adams*. His real name's Prince Kukini and he's one of Tamehameha's favorites."

Jeffery turned to the alii with shoulders the size of a bull's. He did remember now. Last week he had first seen this alii being taught by Tamehameha how to eat with iron forks and knives.

"Aroha, Kukay," gravely said Prince Kukini.

Jeffery replied, "Aroha, John Adams," and then turned back to Sam. "Where's Susan?"

"Safe. Holmes took her and Mrs. Adams and a crowd of alii women and kids two miles north to the lava caves at Kahi."

"You saw her?"

"Saw and talked to her, both. She's safe as anybody can be at present. The warship's expected soon after sunrise. Nobody's sure whether Tamehameha'll git his chance to parley or von Kotzebue'll send an ultimatum to surrender."

"Who's von Kotzebue?"

"Otto von Kotzebue, captain of the Russian ship *Rurick*. The bastard signed the dispatch he sent to Tamehameha yesterday from

Towaihae Bay where the wind becalmed the ship. The dispatch ordered Tamehameha to stay put till the *Rurick* arrived, like the Russians already figgered they could give orders. But don't make no mistake. Tamehameha'll swallow any insult to git von Kotzebue and his main officers ashore, away from the ship."

"I'd better get to Susan—"

Sam's hand shot out. "No, you're needed here. Tamehameha wants you as his interpreter. Now—git set for something. Tamehameha wants to tell the Russians you're Captain Cook's nephew."

Jeffery felt himself jump. "You're not serious?"

"Dead serious. It explains why Tamehameha started calling you 'Kukay.'"

"It doesn't make sense."

"It does if you use your head a minute. The Russians have let Scheffer grab Atooie but it's been done, so to speak, in a left-handed way. Here's the warship arriving. If her captain decides it's a safe bet to announce this has become Russian territory, he'll do it even if he has to set fire to a few native villages. But suppose the Russian captain maybe finds more than he expected? The king's depending on the sight of them cannons above Kailua to convince the captain of the warship it might be wiser to ask for a parley."

"Did they get the logs mounted?"

"John Adams, here, and his crowd beat us. They got twenty-eight mounted on the cliffs. But with the British failing to deliver their warship, all Tamehameha has got is the sight of those logs looking like cannons. If he gits a parley, he'll have his aliis in military uniforms or cheap clothes bought from the traders. It might make a man laugh but at the same time the Russians can at least see the natives are learning fast. Tamehameha can show the Russians that letter from the British Foreign Office. He'll trot you out as Captain Cook's nephew, as another straw in the wind."

"It's a hell of a long bluff."

"You told me Ben Partridge figgered there was two factions at St. Petersburg, with only one faction ready to go at all costs in the Pacific. And it was what you told Tamehameha."

"My God," said Jeffery. "That's only Ben's guess."

"Anyway, it gives Tamehameha's bluff a chance. You're too young, but I ain't forgot how General Greene lost Fort Washington during the Revolution because he was jealous of General

Washington and held back sending troops against Howe. It'll depend on what sort of feller the Russians picked, if Tamehameha's gamble works. If it don't, we attack. Before I forget—Tamehameha's offering the Russians consecrated pig. Nobody on our side's supposed to eat it."

"It's not poisoned?" exclaimed Jeffery.

"No. They're figgering on sacrificing the scraps touched by the Russians. After they eat, Tamehameha'll ask if it's war or peace. If it's war, he'll throw an iron dagger at the Russians' feet. If it's peace, he'll drape a feather collar around von Kotzebue's neck. If it's the dagger, we'll git a signal to launch the fire canoes. The chiefs'll try to kill every Russian ashore like they tried to kill Cook's men forty years ago. I know it's a violation of civilized fighting rules but I don't give a damn," Sam said violently. "Ain't the Russians violating all decent rules, too? Tamehameha can count on you, can't he?"

Jeffery had a hollow sensation. "All right."

"You didn't bring any weapons down from Honoruru, did you? Here—" He pulled two pistols from his belt. He shoved them at Jeffery. "Go on. Take 'em, damn it. I'm sailing one of the fire canoes, myself. Once I git my canoe lit and headed for the warship, I got to start swimming for shore. I won't need any pistols."

The alarm was given a little before dawn. Jeffery had his first view of the warship not long after sunrise when he went down to the beach with a hundred or so high-ranking chiefs and kahunas following Tamehameha.

At the last minute, Tamehameha had split out of his military uniform and had changed, cursing reedily, into a large clean white shirt, his red waistcoat, and the big blue pantaloons. He had tied a colored cloth around his neck and had pulled on a pair of English military shoes which had been made to fit by slitting the leather along the sides and cutting off the toes. Jeffery had wished in his heart that Tamehameha could greet the Russians in one of the flaming feather robes of the proud old days.

In the pale light, the *Rurick* appeared to be about a mile to a mile and a quarter from shore. The wind was slight and the ship was tacking slowly. Although he never knew the actual cause of the long delay before the *Rurick* finally engaged in a decisive act,

Jeffery always believed it must have been the unexpected sight of the cannons showing above Kailua which was responsible.

There was an intolerable wait. Tamehameha was like a rock. Five hundred warriors, naked except for loincloths and cartridge boxes strapped around them, had wheeled into position behind the ranking chiefs and Tamehameha. When Jeffery looked inland he saw the whole road, as far north as the king's point and to the far southern curving of the bay, filled with a double line of armed warriors.

The ship had ceased her tacking. She had come closer in and was swinging around for her portside cannons to cover Kailua. Jeffery had a dreadful instant of wanting to run for it. He heard one of the kahunas pleading with the king to retire to a more protected position. But Tamehameha shook his grizzled head and pointed toward the sea. The Rurick at last had dropped her anchor. Now a small boat was being lowered.

It took perhaps a quarter of an hour for the small boat to come ashore. Jeffery had time to count a dozen men at the oars, rowing steadily, each man in rhythm with the others. At the stern were two officers, very obviously officers by their uniforms. But where was the captain of the Rurick? The man at the prow was in civilian clothes. One was a lean fellow of thirty or thirty-five, with a bold smiling face. The one behind him had a wild shock of hair and appeared to be sketching as he braced himself at the bow with a pad balanced on one knee.

The small boat's keel grated on the coral. The lean fellow jumped lightly to the beach, ran to Tamehameha, knelt, and more astonishingly was lifted up to have his nose rubbed. Jeffery heard Tamehameha exclaim, pleased, "Na'ha. No hea oe?" Jeffery was not very certain what "na'ha" meant, because it could mean either a very good friend or it could mean an adviser. But Tamehameha had asked his friend or adviser from whence he had come. There was a great crowding of chiefs around the na'ha, greeting him, laughing, all the tension breaking.

Jeffery had a glimpse of the artist scrambling upon the shore and gazing in the utmost astonishment at the sight of Tamehameha towering above all the other chiefs. Jeffery thought he knew how that artist felt in that moment. It was how Jeffery, too, had felt the first time he had seen Tamehameha. He saw the seamen and the two officers seemingly rooted at the water's edge. Of them all, only the lean fellow was completely at home.

Then Tamehameha called for Kukay, and Jeffery found himself being presented to the king's na'ha. This na'ha was Mr. Elliot Decastro, who had been the king's physician until some two years ago. Decastro was delighted, indeed, to meet Mr. Cook. He shook Jeffery's hand. Jeffery felt as if he had been struck in the stomach. He had first heard of Decastro from Scheffer on Atooie. Decastro was the one man in the world Jeffery had never expected to come ashore from the warship.

Decastro studied him intently for a moment. Now he was again smiling. He introduced his companion as Monsieur Louis Choris. He was a distinguished French artist, accompanying Captain von Kotzebue on an exploring and scientific expedition into the South Seas. Decastro assured Tamehameha that the Russians were here with only friendly intentions. Even the distinguished German naturalist, Dr. Adelbert von Chamisso, was aboard. Jeffery did not know who Dr. Adelbert von Chamisso was. But he recalled that Scheffer also was a German, and also had pretensions of being a naturalist as well as of being a physician. Here was Decastro, a physician. It was the same pattern, endlessly repeated with minor variations, all harmless and worthy and friendly on the surface.

It gave him a stab of envy to hear Decastro speaking so fluently in the native language. His proficiency greatly exceeded Jeffery's. Decastro was informing Tamehameha how he had gone on to New Archangel, had then traveled to the far lands, and felt at last a wish to rejoin his good friends in Owhyee once more. He had spoken to friends in Russia. They had offered to sail him to the Pacific with them. His good friend, Captain von Kotzebue, was now waiting aboard the great ship to welcome and honor King Tamehameha and to greet him with fine gifts sent him by Alexander I, Czar of Russia, greatest of all nations.

Jeffery listened to this proposal with alarm. Did the Russians expect to get Tamehameha aboard and, once there, keep him there, perhaps carrying him off to Russia? He looked to the old giant and held his peace. Tamehameha would never be taken in so easily.

The king answered with dignity but with bluntness. He had been warned of the coming of a hostile ship. As his na'ha could see, soldiers here were armed and now stationed all along the coast.

Tamehameha's flat thick lips curved in a wide smile. He was sorry he could not visit aboard the ship but his mistrustful people would not suffer him to do so. However, after listening to his na'ha's assurances he now had a better opinion of the Russians. He invited the chief of the Russian ship, along with his two principal underchiefs, to give proof of their friendly intentions by coming ashore. Here Tamehameha would entertain them with a feast and great honors and gifts.

Jeffery thought no prince in the world could have done better. He watched Decastro, who merely stood there a moment or so in silence, as if reflecting, nothing at all showing on the bold smiling face. Then, very courteously, Decastro said he would discuss Tamehameha's invitation with Captain von Kotzebue, and inform the king of what the decision was. He did not say how he would inform the king, nor did the king ask. In less than five minutes the men had embarked and were rowing out from shore.

None of the chiefs or kahunas about the king spoke for a few minutes. Jeffery saw Decastro, now at the stern of the small boat, lift his head to scan the fortifications on the cliffs.

It was well after ten in the morning when the beach echoed with shouts from one end to the other. One by one four boats were being lowered from the *Rurick*. The four boats came directly for the landing, arriving within a quarter of an hour. The three longboats were packed with armed marines, their muskets flashing brightly.

As before, Decastro was at the prow of the small boat. He leaped lightly ashore and deferentially assisted a young, very elegant officer to the hard sand, whom he presented immediately to Tamehameha as Captain Otto von Kotzebue, commanding officer of the expedition. Tamehameha promptly seized von Kotzebue's hand to shake it in the English fashion which he had learned from Governor Young.

For that moment Jeffery had eyes only for Captain von Kotzebue. Jeffery had expected a burly, bearded naval officer, not someone who looked as if he had arrived directly from the court of St. Petersburg. The Russian captain was slight, not more than thirty, Jeffery decided, with narrow eyes, hollow temples where the veins showed, a proud nose, and a mouth and chin which had dropped slackly when the captain had sighted up at Tamehameha.

The marines flowed ashore from their longboats. Sergeants quickly drew them up in double columns on the beach. A dozen officers landed from the small boat along with the French artist, Louis Choris, and two other men in ordinary dress. Jeffery, obeying his orders in the excitement, remained close to Tamehameha's side. Decastro next introduced him to Captain von Kotzebue, who inclined his proud head slightly, giving him an incurious glance. Evidently Decastro had previously informed his commanding officer that young Mr. Cook was acting as the king's interpreter. Jeffery thought he had been accepted without question. At least that was a small hurdle got over with no cracked shins. Louis Choris was presented a second time. The middle-aged civilian with the pepper-and-salt hair and shrewd eyes was presented as Dr. Adelbert von Chamisso, and the second was introduced as his assistant.

Then Tamehameha spoke briefly in the native language. After learning yesterday, he said, of the Russians arriving, he had ordered the erection of two pavilions on the beach where he could make his new friends welcome. A feast was now awaiting them if they would honor him by accepting.

When Tamehameha had finished, Jeffery did his best to translate accurately. Decastro gave him a friendly nod as if to say Jeffery had acquitted himself well.

Jeffery now waited for Decastro to translate the invitation into Russian. But Captain von Kotzebue at once spoke in heavily accented English. He first said he and his officers knew enough of English to have understood Mr. Cook's words. Because on board ship Mr. Decastro had assured him a number of the Sandwich Island chiefs also were conversant with English, he had determined to try to express himself in a language which was common to so many of all who were here. For the chiefs who did not understand, Mr. Decastro would translate afterwards.

At that he paused, as if to question Tamehameha. Decastro must also have informed him that Tamehameha understood English. But Tamehameha said nothing. Jeffery saw Tamehameha was not going to risk exposing himself to a parley in a language in which he had never been completely at ease.

Captain von Kotzebue continued. He said he now had the honor of standing before the celebrated King Tamehameha who had attracted the attention of all Europe through the writings of Captain Cook and Captain Vancouver. For his officers, the gentlemen with him, and his men, Captain von Kotzebue was pleased to accept the king's invitation. He would accompany the king to the pavilion where they could eat and afterwards talk on matters of importance to them both.

It was a stirring sight for Jeffery when they had all gathered on the great road to march to the king's point of land. The five hundred muskets of the king's guard had assembled ahead of the others in columns. Jeffery was at Tamehameha's left, Captain von Kotzebue at Tamehameha's right, and Decastro at von Kotzebue's right. Behind came the officers and gentlemen and the king's advisers. When Jeffery looked behind he saw the two drummer boys beating on the drums, the Russian flag flying behind them. Following came the hundred marines, rather small and diminished in comparison with the warriors bringing up the rear. The great war spears were like a moving forest.

He wondered how the Russians liked this show of strength. Their surprise and curiosity had been evident when they had their first sight of the old king of the islands. Although the officers were quietly looking around while marching along the road, they seemed to have themselves well in hand by now. Jeffery noticed each officer was heavily armed, some of them carrying four and five pistols as well as swords. Probably most of them, if not all, had campaigned against Napoleon. Despite their small numbers, they might manage to fight their way to their boats exactly as Cook's officers had done nearly forty years ago, if an attempt were made to take them by surprise.

During the night a great number of artisans had cleared a space near the temple where two large pavilions of grass and poles had been erected. Through Jeffery, Tamehameha said the pavilion to the west was reserved for Captain von Kotzebue's marines, where food was waiting and servants to serve them. The second pavilion, the larger one, was for themselves. The marines broke ranks and, led by two junior officers, went to the pavilion at the west. It was during this halt that Jeffery first noticed a slender column of black smoke lifting into the sky to the north.

He saw Tamehameha glance at the line of smoke and after that take no more interest in it. Jeffery decided priests at one of the temples on the other side of the point of land had started burning sacrifices to the war gods.

Captain von Kotzebue, Decastro, and the others were going in. Tamehameha had delayed a moment to speak to John Adams. Jeffery saw John Adams nod. Instead of going in with the others, he turned and walked rapidly toward the king's courtyard. Jeffery followed Tamehameha into the pavilion, going past the two sentinels at the entrance who were completely naked except for cartridge boxes and pistols tied around their waists. Inside, Captain von Kotzebue and his officers were looking around with unconcealed curiosity.

The pavilion was a single room of tightly thatched grass and poles, all the light coming from the entrance and from small openings at the floor level whose primary purpose was to allow the air to circulate. Jeffery saw Tamehameha must have brought all his imported chairs for his guests. The only other piece of furniture was a long mahogany table which Jeffery had never seen before.

The aliis and kahunas all looked very hot and uncomfortable in their badly fitted garments. One old white-haired chamberlain of Tamehameha's had his waistcoat halfway up his enormous back and by some miracle had managed to compress himself enough to button the coat over his huge chest. Sweat was streaming down him in rivers. Because he had been ordered by the king to wear this coat, he could not remove it. But he was in such obvious distress that he attracted von Kotzebue's attention, who now unbent slightly and remarked to Jeffery how singular it was that savages surpassed Europeans in bearing the inconveniences which the power of fashion imposed upon them.

Servants carried in wine which Jeffery assumed must have been brought from Honoruru and Señor Marin's vineyard by Governor Young on his hasty voyage last week. After the Russians and the aliis had seated themselves around the table, Tamehameha poured the wine ceremoniously into Chinese goblets which the servants then carried around the table, serving each man sitting there.

Tamehameha arose to propose a toast to his guests, another custom which perhaps he had learned from Governor Young. Jeffery stood, translated, and sat down again.

Von Kotzebue was sitting at Tamehameha's right. The next chair on the right-hand side of the table was Decastro's and next to

Decastro sat the white-haired chamberlain, who looked as if he might soon expire if he could not open his coat to take at least one deep breath. Von Kotzebue answered the toast, Decastro promptly translating. When the ceremonies were ended, Captain von Kotzebue did not wait until food was brought in but began the discussion at once by asking for supplies for his ship. He was in need of fresh water, of food, and of firewood. He told of the quantities he required.

Because Jeffery was leaning forward to listen, he did not see John Adams come in. John Adams had gone quietly around the table. Jeffery now became aware of him, as he pressed against Jeffery when bending down and rapidly whispering to the king. It was very quick. Tamehameha nodded, answered with a few whispered words, then John Adams quietly moved on out into the yard, and Tamehameha continued listening as Decastro now was translating von Kotzebue's request.

If Jeffery had not been sitting close enough to have heard some of John Adams's whispered words he doubted if he would have given any more attention to the slight interruption than the Russians had. Tamehameha's expression had not even changed. But John Adams had told him a runner had arrived from the other side of the point of land. Two of the fire canoes had caught fire. Everything was being done to move the other canoes before the blaze spread and the entire lot went up in flames. Jeffery's first agonized thought had been for Sam. He hoped all the canoes had not been moored close together or Sam would be in the middle of it. His next thought was, what would Tamehameha do now? His heart sank.

Captain von Kotzebue had opened shrewdly, by asking for supplies for his ship. Decastro finished with the translation and sat. Tamehameha's hand had been forced. He had not been given a chance to bring the discussion around to the Russians' seizure of Atooie. He had to either refuse or agree to supply the Russian ship.

Suppose all the fire canoes went up in smoke and flames during the next half hour? It would be three days before Tamehameha could expect his fleet of peleloos to sail around from the eastern side of Owhyee. At first Jeffery thought Tamehameha was remaining silent while trying to decide what to do. Then Jeffery saw a small crowd had rapidly gathered before the entrance, with more

women in the crowd than men. John Adams was there among
them. Instead of replying to von Kotzebue's request or even directing the servants to bring in food, Tamehameha good-naturedly
called to someone at the entrance. All the Russians looked around
to see who it was. Even Decastro's bold head swung with the
others.

A large handsome woman of fifty or so had thrust in her shaved
head and said she too wished to welcome the king's guests. Jeffery
jumped to his feet, not knowing whether he was supposed to translate or not. With an air of great pride, Tamehameha explained this
was his queen, Taamana. He paused, while Jeffery hastily repeated
after him in English. Jeffery had nearly forgotten the king had
ordered, several hours ago, the return of his wives and their women
from the lava caves.

Tamehameha continued. Because it was against the religious
kapus for women to enter a dwelling erected for men, his queen
could do no more than look in. However, she had invited all the
king's guests to visit her and the king's other two wives at their own
palace. Benevolently and kindly, Tamehameha suggested his guests
might enjoy making the visit now. They had refreshed themselves
with wine. They should be a little restored from their passage
ashore. After seeing his queens, his guests could take a short walk—
a short walk was precisely what Tamehameha said, Jeffery always
remembered. When the sun was at the top of the sky, the king
would be in his own palace to welcome his guests. It would then
be time for eating and after eating he would give his answer to
Captain von Kotzebue's request for supplies.

Jeffery finished translating. The king told him to take John
Adams with him and go with the Russians and interpret for the
queen. Not once had the king forgotten Decastro was listening and
understanding every word said. He said he would now go to the
temple where he was required at this time of day to offer prayers
for the Muckahitee. For another moment he looked down from his
height upon everyone at the table with something unfathomable in
his expression. Then he strode out of the pavilion. In his imagination, Jeffery could see Tamehameha going on and on, not to the
temple, but across to the other side of the point where his canoes
were burning.

22.   Because there was nothing else for Captain von
Kotzebue to do but to comply, he and his officers
and gentlemen departed with Jeffery, with John Adams, and with a
small guard of honor which consisted of five warriors, to visit the
second stone house, where the king's wives lived.

If Jeffery failed to have as distinct a recollection of the next hour
and a half as he had of everything else during that day, it was
because for a little while he seemed to have been unexpectedly
whirled away from the main current of events. Because he still
thought of himself as being an observer for Mr. Monroe, he had
remained detached enough to know he was observing an isolated
fragment of historic importance to the islands, the Pacific, and his
own nation. But the reality was so different from what he had
expected a historic fragment to be that he found himself foundering
in the raw events. If some day in the future Mr. Monroe ever
should ask him why one course of action went careening without
very much design from another, nothing consecutively finished, all
he ever could reply, Jeffery knew, was that he had been here. This
was how he had seen it happen.

Decastro had even remarked, "Nothing has much improved since
I departed three years ago, has it, Mr. Cook?"

"How's that?"

Decastro had shrugged. "As usual, Tamehameha has to scamper
to the temple to burn a few chicken feathers with his priests before
he can give an answer to a straight request."

Despite himself, Jeffery's confidence in Tamehameha was shaken.
He was not certain that Tamehameha had gone striding across the
point to the burning canoes. Exactly as Decastro had contemptu-
ously believed, it was possible Tamehameha was now abjectly kneeling in some fetid corner of the temple after sending John Adams in
haste to have Queen Taamana relieve him of his guests.

Although the first time he had seen Queen Taamana was when
she had poked her shaved head into the pavilion, Jeffery had been

previously informed about Queen Taamana from one of the two sources which had also informed him in advance about Tamehameha. Twenty-two years ago Captain Vancouver had met Queen Taamana when he had returned to the islands in command of his own expedition. She had been young then, the king's favorite wife, and when writing of her, Captain Vancouver had implied she was very beautiful.

Now she was at least fifty but evidently she still remained Tamehameha's favorite because he had turned to her when he needed someone to help him with the Russians. When Jeffery arrived with the Russians he saw she was in the center, the two older queens on either side of her, all of them sitting on mats in the hall of the stone house and all decently wrapped in garments of kapa cloth. Captain von Kotzebue entered dubiously but managed to execute a handsome reverence to all three of them. An awkward pause followed, as if no one quite knew what should be done next.

Before the door, in a cradle, was the king's youngest son. Captain von Kotzebue looked down at the baby and announced it was a very pretty girl, mistaking the sex. Decastro covered his commanding officer's error by changing the sex when translating. The queen smiled, pleased by the compliment.

Behind the baby's cradle was a small makaainana boy of ten or twelve, holding a Chinese umbrella. Two other servants drove flies away from the baby and the three queens by poles with the usual tufts of red feathers attached.

Jeffery had more and more of the feeling of everything eddying from him. He heard himself translating for the queens. He heard Captain von Kotzebue's accented English and Decastro's fluent interpretations. The queens had invited the Russian captain to sit near them, which he did, the other officers and two naturalists standing rather uncomfortably by the door as if somehow they had become merely brightly painted figures against a brightly painted canvas. Only the artist, Choris, was real, his sketching pad on one green-trousered knee, a hand moving swiftly.

The queens served watermelons to their guests. There was something childish and incredibly prosaic about it all to Jeffery. Through Jeffery the queens asked questions which very young girls might have asked of visitors. How did the Russian women look? What did they wear? Was their palace as large as this palace of stone?

The two older queens were taking turns smoking a large brass-bound cherry-wood pipe which Jeffery expected they had purchased from one of the Honoruru traders. They had discarded the bone stem and sucked smoke directly through the opening in the bowl. Apparently at a loss for what to say, von Kotzebue inquired about the pipe. One of the queens explained she wanted the pipe bowl, not the stem, because she could hang the pipe bowl around her neck as an ornament after finishing smoking.

One of the two incidents to remain fresh in Jeffery's mind, afterwards, was connected with the pipe. Evidently Queen Taamana did not smoke, because one of the queens chided her, laughing, and thrust the pipe at her. Queen Taamana politely took a few whiffs, swallowed the smoke, and choked. She then promptly handed the pipe to von Kotzebue, who jerked away, promptly refusing. The three queens candidly commented to each other upon the Russian officer's lack of manners. Jeffery looked at Decastro, whose bold face grinned back at him. Neither of them translated the queens' comments to Captain von Kotzebue.

The second incident followed upon the first. As Captain von Kotzebue rose, Queen Taamana extended a plump smooth hand to detain him, asking through Jeffery if he had any news to give her of Captain Vancouver. It gave Jeffery a curiously poignant sensation of having something briefly revealed to him about which he never would know the entire truth when he heard Queen Taamana explain she had met Captain George Vancouver and had never forgotten him. Captain von Kotzebue said coldly that Captain Vancouver had died eighteen years ago, not very long after having returned to England from the Sandwich Islands; and he nodded to his officers and began walking away.

Jeffery had to follow but when he looked back over his shoulder he saw Queen Taamana had burst into tears. All these years Captain Vancouver had been dead. In his Voyages he had written a few lines about a young and beautiful girl who was the favorite wife of King Tamehameha. Now, in the stone house, a fat, heavy-featured heathen woman was crying as if between one instant and another her heart had broken.

In the yard, Jeffery saw a great scurrying of women servants who must have returned from the caves with their mistresses. The young

Russian officers around Captain von Kotzebue were casting more and more appreciative glances at the young makaainanas who went past them. The second pavilion was some hundred yards to the south, near the water. From it Jeffery heard the shouts and snatches of Russian songs where very evidently the hundred marines and the two junior officers were being entertained more to their liking than von Kotzebue and his staff were having it here. Tamehameha was still absent. When Jeffery risked a quick glance to the north he was relieved to see only a faint grayish line of smoke lifting. But where was Tamehameha keeping himself?

He glanced at John Adams but it was impossible to ask questions in front of Decastro. Captain von Kotzebue was demanding where they now were supposed to go. Dr. von Chamisso advanced, his salt-and-pepper hair like an untidy mop in the sunlight. What of Prince Riho-Riho? Was that not the name of the king's son? On board ship, Mr. Decastro had explained to them that the king had this older son who would inherit the throne and the kingdom. Was it possible to see Prince Riho-Riho now?

Jeffery did not know what reply should be made. For some days he had casually understood that Prince Riho-Riho lived with a few friends and confidants by themselves in an enclosure a quarter of a mile east of the king's yard. He was now abruptly reminded he had given very little thought to Prince Riho-Riho. He recalled that, in Honoruru, Governor Young had mentioned the prince as being a womanish creature. But in Kailua he had heard no one mention the prince. It was odd, too. You would have assumed the prince would have been active in preparations to defend Kailua and to invade Atooie.

At least, it was not Jeffery's responsibility to answer. He looked again toward John Adams, who understood enough English to have understood the questions. John Adams scowled down at his big legs. Finally, he said yes, they could visit the prince, who lived secluded from the king's court while undergoing sacred rituals to prepare him to inherit the throne. It was by this path, here.

John Adams led them to the enclosure and to the largest grass house in the center of the enclosure. When they crowded inside they found Riho-Riho on his stomach, completely naked. He lifted his head sluggishly to look at his guests. Near him, Jeffery saw, were four or five naked warriors, guarding the monster. A slim young makaainana male with a tuft of red feathers was driving away the flies from the prince. It was hot in here, dim, with a smell of human sweat and urine and ordure, and Jeffery saw von Kotzebue's face swim palely in the faint light. The ship's captain said in his awkward English, "I should have taken that one as the king's son from his interesting countenance," and pointed to the slim makaainana.

There was nothing for Jeffery to say. He wished now they had not come but it had not been for him to decide. A memory came to him of George Hoomehoome, huge and strong and lively. George Hoomehoome should have been the inheritor of King Tamehameha instead of this gross sluggish thing lying inertly on the hard-packed ground with his friend waving the flies from him. He was sorry for King Tamehameha. Von Kotzebue asked Riho-Riho's age, but Jeffery did not know. He would have guessed between twenty and twenty-two. John Adams was stiffly explaining in the native language, for Jeffery to translate, that Riho-Riho's enormous corpulence was caused by his constant lying on the ground. To be prepared to succeed his father he was under a religious kapu. Common people were not permitted to see him by day. If they did, they would be killed. To prevent such deaths by mischance, Tamehameha had ordered his son to remain here, secluded, away from the inhabitants of Owhyee.

Riho-Riho had managed to get himself off the ground and was gaping at his visitors with a stupid, vacant look. He lurched toward von Kotzebue, picked curiously at the gold braid, and went back to his naked guards and began telling them he wished such a garment as that. Decastro said, very pleasantly, "I believe, gentlemen, the prince has dismissed us."

They were on their way to the yard when a runner arrived, with the information the king was now awaiting them at his palace. It was well past noon. When Jeffery looked to the north, the sky was all blue. There was not a trace of smoke from burning canoes.

When a week or so afterwards Jeffery had to try to remember everything to begin writing his report to Mr. Monroe, he found it impossible to describe how all of a sudden the day began to plunge forward as if a great tide had flowed in more strongly than ever.

When Jeffery entered the throne room he saw that Tamehameha was no longer dressed in the shapeless ludicrous garments of white men. Tamehameha was waiting, in the royal robes of his ancestor, and in that interval somehow he seemed to have become larger. Jeffery went straight to him. He did not dare ask questions because Decastro was behind him. But all his anxiety must have shown in his face because for that instant Tamehameha looked down upon him and seemed to take notice of Jeffery's concern and he laid a huge hand on Jeffery's shoulder. That was all. He turned to welcome his guests, raising his hand slowly in greeting.

While it did not make sense at all, it was as if for a very brief interval Jeffery had had a tiller thrust into his hands and had found the task was more than he could endure; but now the tiller had been taken back by the giant.

While the Russians and the aliis who had returned with the king seated themselves in the same order they had sat around the other table in the pavilion, Jeffery had perhaps a minute, perhaps a little longer, to watch Tamehameha, who was waiting for the noise to subside. From his huge shoulders was draped a cloak of molten gold formed from thousands of tiny golden feathers. From what Jeffery had learned about the weaving on these feather robes, he knew vaguely such a cloak must be rare and of incalculable price, for the feathers, Jeffery had recognized, were from the mamo bird. Each mamo bird had only two or three golden feathers in its brown plumage. The bird was nearly extinct. A cloak such as Tamehameha had put on might have taken five or six generations of weavers, living and dying, to collect the feathers and fashion them into the sturdy olono fibers.

Over the golden robe Tamehameha had placed the scarlet collar of feathers. Around Tamehameha's middle, under the cloak, over the malo, was wrapped a long feather cordon which was composed of a multitude of brilliant red feathers, edged with bright yellow feathers, and the ends of the cordon which hung between the massive royal legs were fitted with rows of human teeth and fish teeth. In the malo, Tamehameha had remembered to stick his iron dagger.

When he began to speak, with a start Jeffery was brought back to his duties. Tamehameha said this meal was only for his honored guests. On such a day, pork was forbidden to him and his ministers. He looked toward Decastro and smiled benignly, as if he expected Decastro to bear him out. Jeffery felt his skin prickle. But Tamehameha had judged Decastro better than Jeffery had. Decastro was not willing to admit before these Russians that this was a ceremony new to him. He bent toward Captain von Kotzebue, assured and easy in his pride as a mercenary, quite obviously explaining this was merely another piece of heathenish superstition.

The mahogany table had been set with imported china cups and plates, as well as coconut cups and ladles, bowls of larch wood of assorted sizes, and iron knives and spoons. Jeffery was surprised at the number of makaainanas who came in with food. He counted at least fifty. They passed baked pig on palm branches, yams, and baked taro roots.

Through Decastro, Captain von Kotzebue again repeated his request for supplies for his ship. Tamehameha answered they would eat first and afterwards he would explain what he had decided to do about supplying the ship. He was very talkative during the meal. Through Jeffery he asked Captain von Kotzebue a number of questions concerning Russia and the customs and habits in Russia. But Jeffery noticed even in his questions Tamehameha said nothing at all to give Captain von Kotzebue the opportunity to lead the talk back to whether or not supplies would be furnished.

At intervals Tamehameha joked with his advisers, commenting pointedly that his guests appeared to become as hot and uncomfortable in their uniforms as everyone else was in haole dress. Decastro whispered translations, and Captain von Kotzebue joined in with the laughter but it seemed to Jeffery that the Russian captain's laughter was forced. Servants snatched away larch bowls still containing pieces of pork, immediately supplying freshly filled bowls. Jeffery assumed the scraps of pork were being carried to the temple on the shore to be burnt at once to the heathen gods.

It was close to two in the afternoon when, without any previous warning, Tamehameha faced Captain von Kotzebue and started speaking with the utmost solemnity. He said, "I learn you are the commander of a ship-of-war and are engaged in a voyage similar to those of Cook and Vancouver and consequently do not engage in trade. It is therefore my intention not to carry on any trade with you but to provide you freely with everything my islands produce. This matter of provisions is now settled. No further mention need be made of it . . ."

Jeffery had to collect himself and translate. As he spoke, he saw Captain von Kotzebue throw up his head in astonishment. Tamehameha had caught him completely off guard.

Tamehameha continued, "I shall now ask you to inform me if it is with the consent of your emperor that his subjects begin to disturb me in my old age. Since I have been king of these islands, no European has had cause to complain of having suffered injustices here. I have made my island an asylum for all nations and have honestly supplied with provisions every ship desiring them."

He rested one hand on the table. "Some time ago there came from the settlement of Sitka men from Russia, a nation with whom I never had intercourse before. They were kindly received and supplied with everything necessary. But they have ill rewarded me, for they have behaved in a hostile manner to my subjects and threatened us with ships-of-war which were to conquer these islands. But this, I tell you," said Tamehameha with nothing reedy or whistling at all in the implacable voice, "this shall not happen as long as I live."

He drew breath and pressed hard after Jeffery's interpretation. "A Russian physician," he stated, saying "Russian" Jeffery always remembered, "by the name of Scheffer, who came here some months ago, pretended he had been sent by your Emperor Alexander to botanize my islands. As I had heard much good of the Emperor Alexander, and was particularly pleased with his bravery, I not only permitted Mr. Scheffer to botanize but promised him every assistance, making him a present of a piece of land, with servants, so that he never would want for provisions. In short, I tried to make Mr. Scheffer's stay as agreeable as possible and refused none of his demands.

"But what," he said, "was the consequence of my hospitality? Settled in the fruitful island of Woahoo, there Mr. Scheffer proved himself my most inveterate enemy, destroying our sanctuary, the temple of Honoruru. On the island of Atooie, this past year, Mr. Scheffer has excited against me the king of Atooie, who submitted to my power years ago. Mr. Scheffer is there at this very moment, threatening my islands. Does your emperor allow this? Does your emperor make war on me?"

While speaking, he had given a sign to the old chamberlain in the tightly buttoned coat. The chamberlain walked as though walk-

ing on eggs to the commode, drew out a bamboo tube from one of
the pigeonholes, and walked all the distance back to the king, who
had paused while waiting for Jeffery to finish interpreting. Captain
von Kotzebue was on his feet, flushed an angry red. Tamehameha
removed a roll of parchment from the bamboo tube handed him
by the old chamberlain. The instant Jeffery completed the translation, before Captain von Kotzebue could answer, Tamehameha
unrolled the parchment. Without a word, he placed it on the table
before the commander of the Russian ship. Jeffery recognized the
parchment as being the letter which had come all around the world
from the British Foreign Office.

Tamehameha returned to the head of the table and deliberately
dropped his hand to the handle of the iron dagger. There was such
a silence that Jeffery heard the beating of his own blood in his ears.
He had never imagined it would be done as simply and directly as
King Tamehameha had now done it. He had thought Tamehameha
would take longer and be less blunt about it. Instead, it had been
like one blow after another from a stone ax, ending in a final crush-
ing thud—and a silence.

Jeffery watched Captain von Kotzebue read the letter. Several
senior officers rose and came hastily to their commanding officer.
Von Kotzebue held the letter out for his officers to read. One of
the senior officers slowly translated it aloud in Russian for the
officers who were unfamiliar with English. Decastro was there,
coolly reading the letter over Captain von Kotzebue's shoulder. He
made a comment in Russian, laughing lightly, as if the letter did
not strike him as anything of importance. Captain von Kotzebue
pointed to a phrase in the letter and answered sourly. The discussion became general.

Jeffery would have given a great deal to have been able to understand Russian during those four or five minutes. Captain von
Kotzebue's voice became increasingly waspish. Decastro argued
with all his fluency. At first there appeared to be a teetering of
opinions among the other officers, until one of the senior officers
said a few gruff words, repeatedly jabbing a hairy finger toward the
parchment. Although Decastro's eyes blazed, he still argued per-
suasively. Now the other officers seemed to join in with Captain
von Kotzebue and the senior officer. A young officer had his say.
Decastro answered derisively as if he knew by now the judgment

had swung against him. The young officer went pale and reached for his sword. Captain von Kotzebue spoke sharply. Then he silenced them all by giving the letter to the young officer, who returned it to Tamehameha, bowing, formally clicking his heels.

As everyone waited, von Kotzebue seemed to gather himself together before announcing his decision. He moistened his lips. Jeffery's heart stood still.

Although Captain von Kotzebue spoke in English, his first words were delivered in so low a tone Jeffery had to strain to hear them. He said he was not personally acquainted with Mr. Scheffer. Now something jealous and spiteful entered his voice as more forcefully he said that Governor Baranov, however, was known to have a character which at best was indifferent. If Governor Baranov had taken Mr. Scheffer under his protection, it was for intentions which he, Captain von Kotzebue, had not been informed. The Rurick, he added, had sailed directly to Owhyee without stopping at Atooie. Consequently, he had not known of the situation on Atooie as described by King Tamehameha until now . . .

He broke off, half turning, waiting for Decastro to translate that much before continuing. Of a sudden, Jeffery felt completely drained. Tamehameha had taken a long chance and he had succeeded. Because Jeffery had not been able to understand Russian, he had no way of knowing exactly why Captain von Kotzebue was standing up there and perjuring himself. Perhaps Captain von Kotzebue had never expected to find more than a few savages here, hopelessly unprepared, instead of a nation of warriors. Perhaps the sight of what he must have believed were sixteen-pounders above Kailua had helped him decide not to risk his reputation and his single warship against overwhelming odds. Perhaps it was the letter from England.

But Decastro still had not spoken. In astonishment, Captain von Kotzebue turned to his interpreter, giving a curt order in Russian. Decastro's face had gone yellowish under its swarthy color. Jeffery almost had sympathy for Decastro, who now looked all around as if seeking at least one man who would stand with him against this betrayal.

Captain von Kotzebue spoke a second time to his mercenary, but now very softly. He put his hand to the butt of one of his pistols. His upper lip stretched like a red string over his white even teeth and his proud nose appeared very thin. Decastro's face became even more yellowish and the bold look changed into something ravaged and helpless. He bowed slightly to his commanding officer, faced Tamehameha, and translated in a voice like ice. Captain von Kotzebue continued. The wicked conduct of the Russians on Atooie should not be ascribed to the will of the Emperor of Russia. The Emperor had never commanded any of his subjects to do an unjust act. However, the extent of the Emperor's empire often prevented him from being immediately informed of evil actions which, nevertheless, would not remain unpunished when they came to his attention.

Captain von Kotzebue sat down, piece by piece, as if his bones had become very brittle. With a silk handkerchief he wiped at his tall shining forehead. Decastro finished, flinging himself into his chair. As far as Jeffery was concerned, it had ended. He thought of Susan. He thought of Sam. He wanted to get away, but he had to remain while he watched Tamehameha place the feather collar around Captain von Kotzebue's slim shoulders. He had to translate what Tamehameha said:

"I have heard that your monarch is a great hero. I love him for it because I am one, myself. I send him this collar as a testimony of my regard."

Jeffery wished Tamehameha would hold his tongue and not ruin the effect of his speech by boasting of being a hero as if he were no more than a savage island chieftain. The speech had been eloquent and simple, of grave dignity, and of immense strength. It was a speech, Jeffery thought, which had been made by the last living giant in the world.

The shouts from the throne room were picked up by the crowd massed in the yard. Servants ran in, carrying pigskins of wine. The old chamberlain rent his coat, taking deep breaths. Russian officers found themselves hugged by exuberant pagans a head taller than they were. In that uproar, Jeffery stubbornly repeated Tamehameha's speech to himself in order to fix it in his memory. It was a speech someday the whole world should know of because after Tamehameha was gone there would be no more giants in the world to give voice against small men who carried fear with them.

Jeffery gave thought briefly to the dark-green island to the north, of the huge fort upon it, and in his mind he seemed to view

Scheffer's calm gray face with the silvery eyes. And Jeffery knew it was not really done with at all today. Only a little had been done, a long bluff which had succeeded for reasons foreseen and not foreseen. Now a race would begin between forces stretching all the way around the world while Scheffer did his utmost to maintain what he had and Tamehameha did his utmost to dislodge him from the fort and from Atooie.

When Jeffery next remembered to look toward Decastro he saw only an empty chair. Decastro had quietly taken himself out of the room during the uproar. Jeffery had a start of alarm. He got as far as the door when Tamehameha ordered him to return to translate more compliments to the Russians. Everything was still continuing. Captain von Kotzebue was harking back to the supplies, now wanting to list what was required. John Adams and a number of other aliis who had some knowledge of English were booming away at the Russian officers. Tamehameha disappeared for a few minutes and returned, having discarded his robes of state. Pulling on his blue pantaloons, he announced they would now visit his temple.

Jeffery was unable to escape. He found himself wedged between great moving masses of flesh. The sunlight reflected on the bay was intensely bright. There was a great hotness. Jeffery watched Tamehameha go to one of the colossal idols of wood which was hung around more than others with fruits and flowers and palm branches and pieces of burnt pig meat. Tamehameha embraced the idol and, through Jeffery, said, "These are our gods whom I worship. Whether I do right or wrong I do not know, but I follow my faith which cannot be wicked as it commands me never to do wrong."

After explaining his guests were not allowed to follow into the deeper mysteries, with his priests Tamehameha entered one of the wooden huts at the far corner of the temple's floor. During this wait, Captain von Kotzebue and his three senior officers examined the idols, commenting on them in Russian. From where Jeffery stood he could look down upon the pavilion in which the marines had been welcomed. Now a great many of the marines, red faced with wine, had come out with young makaainana girls, all tipsy and laughing, to watch the dancing. Five tattooed musicians had seated themselves in a line, facing their audience. Each musician held an instrument which consisted of two calabashes joined together with holes in their tops. They placed these double calabash drums between their naked knees, striking with fingers and the palms of their hands to produce a varying rhythm which at first was in time with the beating of a man's heart. A dozen hura dancers now came through the crowd gathered all along the road and lava wall as well as under the palm trees hiding the king's yard. The hura dancers were immensely corpulent, wearing only necklaces of braided human hair or ferns or flowers and their kapa-cloth aprons. In the hot afternoon air the rich scent of flowers mingled with the steaming animal smells from so many hundreds of bodies and arose from the beach to mingle with the fetid odors from the temple floor. Jeffery felt stifled.

As he watched, he caught a glimpse of Decastro, who was leaning on one corner of the pavilion, gnawing at his lips. Decastro turned his back to the dancers and walked to the water's edge like a man at a loss what to do with himself. He passed by the stone steps of the temple and went eastward, losing himself in the crowd.

Tamehameha was still within the holy enclosure. Jeffery looked toward the north, where more natives had gathered under the ohia trees. It had almost become like a fair again. He felt himself start up, for he had caught sight of Kala. He looked more intently. It was Kala. Behind Kala he saw Susan and Mrs. Adams! What the hell was Susan doing here? She should have known better. He had assumed she was still safely in one of the lava caves.

He heard one of the chiefs call to him but he plunged unheedingly down the steps and slammed his small wiry body through the crowd, leaping over the lava wall which ran parallel to the road going east, came around through the trees, and stopped. Susan had turned, seeing him.

He said angrily, "Don't you know you don't belong here?" and reached for her.

To his immense consternation, she struck him hard on the face with the flat of her hand. In furious silence she swung around and took herself through the trees. There was a shattered instant. Jeffery gave his head a shake. When he started to follow, Kala deliberately put herself before him. Mrs. Adams gathered up her golden skirts to run lightly after Susan.

He could not understand why Susan had struck him. He tried to go past Kala. He called, "Susan—" But John Adams and two warriors had thrust between him and Kala. John Adams told him the

king and the Russian officers had returned to the pavilion. Tamehameha had sent for Kukay. It was not wise to go against the king's
wishes. For Jeffery it had become like a nightmare in the hot,
bright sunlight. He still felt the sting of Susan's hand.

In the pavilion of straw and poles where early this morning
Tamehameha had planned to feast his guests, food was now being
placed on banana leaves laid on the ground. Jeffery approached the
king and spoke urgently in the native language. He believed he had
done his share today and asked to be excused.

Tamehameha told Jeffery he was to stay. Jeffery felt his face become hot. He looked around and silently decided to get away the
first chance that came.

Tamehameha was speaking to Captain von Kotzebue. "I have
seen how the Russians eat," he said. "Now you may satisfy your
curiosity and see how Tamehameha eats." He sat cross-legged while
makaainanas brought him boiled fish, yams, taro root, and a roasted
bird which was no larger than a sparrow.

Jeffery cautiously retreated along one side of the pavilion. John
Adams was doing well enough with the Russians to translate anything more Tamehameha might have to say. If they had to, let
them send for Decastro. Jeffery passed swiftly to the entrance.

He had reached the east road when he came upon Sam Crowell
at the edge of the crowd surrounding the hura dancers. "Sam, how
long have you been here?"

"About five minutes. Ain't Tamehameha and the Russians
through in there yet? I heard how von Kotzebue backed down."

"Yes. Perhaps the Russians will put up a monument to him like
the one we've got of General Greene in Germantown." He looked
at Sam. "You had a rough time of it with the canoes," he said, and
added, "Here, I won't need these any longer," handing Sam the
two heavy pistols.

Sam took the pistols and explained, "It was the fault of a damn
chief who kept smoking his pipe every time I wasn't looking. It
took just one shred of burning tobacco to set off the first canoe.
We lost two. We had to sink a third canoe off the shore but we can
recover it. Tamehameha came running out of the trees looking like
the wrath of God although we had things mostly under control by
the time he got there. I guess he's pleased. This is a great day for

him. It's too bad you can't stay till the first of the year and sail with us when we sail for Atooie."

Jeffery said shortly, "If you know what's good for you, Sam, you'll sail home with me on the *Traveller*," and with no break at all, "I saw Susan half an hour ago."

"One of the queen's women told me jist now she was here somewhere. I was going to look for her, myself. Holmes sprained his ankle and had to be carried to his place from the cave. I don't know what Susan come here for."

"I don't either—" Jeffery hesitated. "I think I scared her when I saw her."

"Scared her?"

"Well, I startled her. She—went off toward the Adams kuleana with Mrs. Adams and Kala. Sam, I've got to see Susan but I'm supposed to be in the pavilion with Tamehameha. Take over for me if anyone looks for me, will you? I'm going to the Adams kuleana."

"Jeff, before you see her there's something . . ."

Jeffery did not wait to hear what Sam had to say. He darted in and out of the crowd and came upon the road leading east to the great highway, the palm trees to his left, the lava wall, the black beach, the curving bay all to his right. Five minutes later, far down on the road he saw Mrs. Adams walking in his direction.

He ran to her. "Where's Susan, Mrs. Adams?"

Her eyes were very black in her pointed porcelain face. She hesitated before replying as if she had to decide whether or not to tell him. While still at the cave, she said finally, from one of the servants bringing news of the landing, Susan had heard that the king's na'ha had returned with the Russians. Susan had not forgotten from three years ago that Elliot Decastro had been called the king's na'ha. Because she believed the warship had stopped at Atooie before sailing to Owhyee, she was determined to find Decastro and ask him for news of her father.

Susan, Mrs. Adams, and Kala had not been able to force their way through the dense crowds on the north road and had not arrived at the king's yard until a little before Jeffery had noticed them. After striking Jeffery on the face, Susan had started almost blindly toward the Adams kuleana. When Mrs. Adams caught up with her, Susan said she was going to the kuleana and would send servants down to hunt for Mr. Decastro.

However, they encountered Decastro near the yard's entrance, where guards had been posted. Decastro was with a chiefess whom, Mrs. Adams said, he must have known when he lived here three years ago. The two were trying to persuade the guards to allow them to pass. But the guards had received orders to allow no one from the warship to leave the point of land.

Mrs. Adams told Jeffery that Susan had run toward Mr. Decastro. The two spoke rapidly for a few minutes, the chiefess leaving them and going to the beach. Then Susan had called to Mrs. Adams, saying Mr. Decastro had talked to her father and had something urgent to say to her. As he did not want the Russians to see him with Susan, he would meet her at the little cove a quarter of a mile beyond the temple. Kala could accompany her.

Afterwards, Mrs. Adams had crossed the great highway. She had gone halfway to her kuleana when she had begun to worry. She had returned, wanting to find Sam or one of the aliis whom she trusted, because she was not certain how safe it would be for Susan to go with Mr. Decastro, whom she had always disliked, even if Kala were with her.

Jeffery asked, "They went east, toward the temple?"

Mrs. Adams said she had last seen them going in that direction, Susan and Kala taking the road, and Decastro going along the beach. It couldn't have been much more than twenty minutes ago.

Jeffery realized that either Captain von Kotzebue had lied when he had told Tamehameha the *Rurick* had not touched at Atooie or Decastro had been lying to Susan. Of the two, he believed Captain von Kotzebue. Twenty minutes ago! Jeffery began running with all his strength.

---

23.   That afternoon there must have been at least a thousand common natives packed densely around the second pavilion and in front of the temple where the musicians and hura dancers were entertaining the marines. The crowd extended back from the shore, beyond the lava wall and road, to the palm

and ohia trees sheltering the king's yard. The road west, toward the dunes and scrub hala trees and lava rocks at the far end of the point of land, was blocked by this jostling excited throng.

Jeffery plunged into the throng and thought he would never get through. He caught glimpses of the red-faced marines. He saw a few young Russian officers with girls on their arms. But he saw nothing at all of Sam. He tried shouting for Sam but his voice was lost in the clamor. He battered his way forward. It was impossible for him to guess how long it took him to work to the outer edge of the throng where once more he could start running. It might have been five minutes. It had seemed three times as long.

After half a mile the road narrowed to a path which wound through the edge of the palm grove above the rocky beach. In another ten minutes he passed out of the grove and on to a narrow spit of land covered with brush. Scrub hala trees to his right screened the shore and sea at the north. To the south a long bare shoulder of lava lifted so high it hid the view of the bay.

He planned to search through the hala trees. But before doing so, he decided to climb to the ridge for a quick look along the south shore. Halfway up he slipped in the coarse lava rubble, falling to his hands and knees. He crawled to the top and looked down. The far side of the cove was ringed by grass shacks of a fishing hamlet and by a few tattered palms. The outlook toward the bay was partially hidden by two great spires of rock with a narrow passage between them—a keavaiti, the natives would have called it—for small boats to pass through. Drawn up on the beach of wet coral and lava fragments were four small dugouts.

All this Jeffery had seen in one embracing glance. But he saw something more. He saw Decastro, Susan, and Kala. Decastro had backed toward one of the dugouts and was facing the lava ridge from which Jeffery was sighting. He had caught Susan around the throat by the crook of his left arm, pinning her head and shoulders against the hollow of his left shoulder. Her hands were tearing at the brown fingers hooking into her. As Decastro backed toward the dugouts, dragging Susan, he menaced Kala with the pistol in his right hand.

Jeffery shouted, gave a leap, landed some fifteen feet lower on the slope, pitched forward, and went tumbling head over heels in a slide of lava fragments until he struck the upper end of the cove. As he thrust himself to his knees he saw Decastro aiming the pistol.

There was a flash. Jeffery fell flat. When he sprang up, he saw Susan had caught Decastro's right arm, spoiling his aim. Jeffery was running at them. Kala had tried to close in on Decastro, who flailed at her with his pistol barrel. Susan wrenched free.

Decastro gave a great leap, cast down his empty pistol, and drew his rapier. Jeffery swerved to one side in time to save himself from being spitted. He heard Susan catch her breath. Decastro, she hastily said, had learned from one of the chiefesses that the cannons were of wood. Decastro planned to take a dugout and get to the warship to warn the officers there instead of returning to the pavilion to warn Captain von Kotzebue.

Not looking around, Jeffery told her, "You and Kala get help. I'll try to hold him."

From behind him Jeffery heard a drumming of footsteps as Susan and Kala ran and began climbing toward the ridge. He saw Decastro cast a thoughtful glance toward the canoes. One of the dugouts had to be shoved into the water. Having missed with the pistol, Decastro had only his rapier. Jeffery doubted if Decastro could budge a heavy dugout with one hand and guard himself at the same time with the rapier.

Jeffery turned his head over his shoulder. Kala had already disappeared down the other side of the lava ridge. Susan was at the top, her hair flying. She cried fiercely, "Watch out!"

All at once Decastro had come at him with a rush. Jeffery was saved by the fact that Decastro was wearing heavy Russian sea boots. He had flung himself back at Susan's cry of warning. The rapier glittered. Decastro tried to wheel to thrust a second time but the leather soles of his boots slipped on the wet coral and lava sand and he went down to one knee, swearing mightily.

He was up in a second. But Jeffery's grass sandals were as good as being barefoot on the shirting hard mixture of coral and lava granules. Jeffery put six or seven yards safely between Decastro and himself and stopped. He cast another quick glance across his shoulder. Now Susan also had gone. He had never felt quite so much alone as he was now. Even if Decastro had to use both hands to shove one of the dugouts, Jeffery was not nearly as certain as he had been that he would have a chance in the short interval to jump Decastro and bear him down before the man could protect himself with his sword.

Jeffery became aware of something happening to him. His chest had tightened. He might get himself run through and killed. His hands felt sticky. How the hell could you go against a man who had a sword?

But Decastro had lowered his blade. "Why make it necessary for me to kill you?" he said very reasonably. "Come along with me to the warship. I'll vouch for you. I'll admit von Kotzebue's the wrong man to command such an expedition but even he won't be afraid to fight wooden cannons. We'll have Kailua in ashes by morning and the island pacified in a week with good interpreters needed."

Jeffery had retreated to the edge of the lava slope. Instead of replying, he squatted, carefully stretching out his hands on each side of him to support himself. He waited.

Decastro turned his back carelessly on Jeffery and humming to himself, swaggered cheerfully toward the dugouts. Although Jeffery was not an old hand at the game, he did not think it would be very safe to try to jump Decastro even if Decastro's back was turned. He felt several fragments of lava under his fingers. He grasped one to hurl at that jaunty back, but caught himself. He felt the thinking and reasoning part of his mind take hold. Deliberately he selected two sharp lava fragments of a size to fit snugly in his hands, stood up, and rather methodically paced after Decastro, his hands thrust into his pockets.

Decastro stopped before the dugouts. Jeffery stopped three or four yards away and waited, hands still in his pockets. It seemed very hot and still in the little cove. He heard a bird shriek loudly and swoop out to sea.

Decastro scratched his neck, eying Jeffery. All at once, Decastro thrust his rapier under his left armpit, stooped, thrust both hands vigorously at the nearest dugout, and swung around at Jeffery again. The dugout had gone perhaps two feet over the squeaking sand during those two seconds. Decastro grinned wordlessly at Jeffery. Again he stooped swiftly, thrusting, whirling around. This time the dugout had advanced a good yard. The next thrust should float the prow into the water. Decastro blinked sweat from his eyes. He hesitated. He filled his lungs and darted around to thrust a third time—and Jeffery gave a loud shout. Decastro sprang up, whipped out his rapier, and pointed it at Jeffery.

Jeffery had prepared himself. When he threw the sharp piece of lava straight at Decastro's face, instinctively Decastro bent his sword arm to save his face. The rapier flashed to one side. Jeffery followed after his throw with a leap. Decastro staggered as Jeffery crashed into him. Jeffery grasped Decastro's bent sword arm by the wrist, forcing it back by the momentum of his leap. Clutching the second sharp fragment in his left hand, he pounded one side of Decastro's face. The sharp lava cut like a razor. It was over almost before it began.

Jeffery got up slowly. The sky seemed to reel violently. A flight of red birds streamed through space. He prodded Decastro with his foot and got no response. Then he heard Decastro's ragged breathing and began to come a little back into himself. He bathed his face and arms from a pool of salt water, then dragged Decastro higher on the beach and stared somberly down at him.

Flies were black over the bleeding gashes. The sun shone hotly on the swollen face. Decastro looked shrunken and small as if minute by minute the body was withering under the bright hard light. Jeffery recalled his stabs of envy because Decastro had been so accomplished and assured. He had thought Decastro might be about thirty-five. Now the spring inside Decastro was all unwound, the smiling boldness gone. At Jeffery's feet was only the used body of a man of fifty, perhaps more, whose hair had been dyed black.

Jeffery found himself wondering, as he waited upon the silent beach with a man who breathed slowly and raggedly, how it would be if you were approaching fifty and were becoming an old hand at the game and still had to continue selling yourself to whosoever would buy. You would be a long ways off, he thought, from everything else when a time finally came for you to be struck down. Jeffery did not quite understand how a few minutes ago he had so greatly wanted to kill this small used man.

Using a corner of his jacket to wipe off the gashed face, he rolled Decastro on his side, away from the direct glare of the sun. He sat beside the unconscious man, waving the flies away. He remembered how Susan had stared down at him from the black ledge and he remembered how she had struck him in the face. He did not feel very happy about anything that had happened. It was not long after that Sam and John Adams came running across the crest of the lava and down to the cove. In running, John Adams had torn off his black frock coat, throwing it away.

John Adams knelt, rolled Decastro on his back, and said the man's jaw was broken but a kahuna would have to look at him to tell how badly injured he was. Sam was asking if Jeffery was hurt. When he was satisfied Jeffery had got off with only a few scratches, he wanted to know how Jeffery had managed to smash up Decastro so badly.

"We went at each other when he slipped on the wet beach," Jeffery said. "I broke his jaw with a lump of lava. What are we going to do with him? Von Kotzebue won't like having one of his men turn up in that shape."

"We maybe could say he had an accident?"

Jeffery found himself grinning back at Sam. "If Decastro became conscious aboard that warship he might say something else, too. I'd hate to have von Kotzebue sail back because he'd learned we only had wooden cannons."

John Adams suggested slitting Decastro's throat and hiding the body. Sam said it was a good suggestion but damn if he could quite bring himself to that. Right now, probably everybody would be marching to the landing place at the beach. Nobody knew for certain if von Kotzebue was sailing to attack Honoruru or would keep his word and anchor there peacefully.

The best thing, as Sam saw it, would be for John Adams to hike off fast to tell the king the reason why they had to hide Decastro and keep him from going off with the Russians. Tamehameha would have to figure how to handle it with von Kotzebue. Then John Adams could bring back a litter and kahunas to carry Decastro off somewhere and keep him out of sight until the ship sailed. Sam and Jeffery would stay here and keep an eye on Decastro until John Adams returned. Jeffery agreed that made good sense. John Adams said, "Makoa!" and went running up the lava ridge and out of sight.

Sam turned Decastro on one side so his face again was turned from the sun. "If this son of a bitch had been in charge of the expedition instead of that popinjay von Kotzebue, maybe Tamehameha wouldn't be so full of beans right now."

Jeffery had been thinking the same thing. Now he said, "You

won't need me any longer. Suppose I go on up to the Adams kuleana?"

"That ain't necessary. Mrs. Adams and Kala'll take care of Susan."

"Susan might," said Jeffery, "like to know that Decastro didn't get away."

"John Adams'll send a runner to the kuleana. Just don't bother her."

Jeffery had started to go, but something in Sam's hoarse voice stopped him. "I want to see her, Sam."

"Leave her be." Sam had stood. "It's what you wanted, isn't it?"

Jeffery had forgotten that he had not yet told Sam. "Not any longer. While I was away from her at Kearakekua I found I was making the greatest mistake I'd ever made in my life. I'm sorry, Sam, but I won't give her up."

"You want to marry her? You'll throw over Rebecca?"

"Rebecca and I were never in love. I'll explain to Susan—"

"It's too late to explain to Susan."

"Why should it be too late?"

"It's too late because I already told her. Last evening when I got in from Kearakekua I walked part way with her to the caves. She was talking about you and all her plans and I couldn't stand listening any more. So I told her you meant to marry Rebecca Koch as soon as you got to Philadelphia."

"My God, Sam!"

"Because she didn't believe me at first, I had to come straight out with everything, Jeff. I had to tell her you brought her down here like you'd do with any native girl—" Sam broke off, his face shiny and contorted in the yellow light. "Go on, damn you," he mumbled. "Why don't you hit me like you did that feller there? I ain't going to stop you."

Without a word Jeffery turned. He heard Sam calling to him. He did not look back. He had once believed Sam was his best friend.

It was perhaps half an hour before sunset when Jeffery passed through the deep cool palm grove to the north of the king's yard and pavilions in order to escape being seen by Tamehameha or his aliis. He crossed the great road, circled around the village of Kailua after being halted by guards who recognized him as the king's

Kukay and allowed him to go on. He came upon the path to the Adams kuleana, now running at a dogtrot, weaving a little from fatigue, his heart and lungs straining.

Now and then he had to slow to a walk because his endurance was failing. It was no good telling himself that Sam had betrayed him. His anger had burnt out against Sam. Jeffery was conscious of having been the one to betray himself by having had the intention of betraying Susan. He had believed you could not go very far on love alone. Sam had been trying only to spare Susan. Jeffery started running again.

Already the shadows were lengthening. A fair breeze had sprung up toward the end of the day. From far away he heard a distant sound of a cannon firing. Upon that, he stopped, looking back down the great descent. A crowd had gathered around the landing place at the beach. Beyond the reef, the Rurick's sails were crimson in the sunset.

Jeffery filled his lungs and continued higher, all else going from his mind but the need to see Susan and tell her Sam had been wrong. He followed the path into the pleasant green valley where a space had been cleared for the big house of the Adamses and the scattered huts around it for the servants. It was very close to the eating hour. Fires were burning in the stone ovens. The maka-ainanas stared curiously at Jeffery. He went straight to the big house and saw the koa-wood door was closed and had the curious and uncomfortable impression of someone inside secretly peering at him.

He rapped on the door. Presently, he pounded harder, calling for Susan. He heard the sound of the door being unbarred from within and Mrs. Adams's triangle of porcelain face looked out at him from a crack where the door had opened. Her voice tinkled like the tinkling of water over round pebbles. He was to go away. He was disturbing everyone. She would have her servants take his sea chest to Captain Crowell's place on the king's point of land. The door closed. It was like having cold water dashed in his face.

He turned and started down the path. By now the sun had set in a purple sky, and when Jeffery looked to the west he saw only a twinkling of lights off the shore. The Russian warship had set her sea lamps and was bound north for Honoruru.

The path veered a little to the southwest before turning to

plunge straight down past the village into the great north-and-south highway. Here, at this turning, Jeffery encountered the shadowy shapes of Sam Crowell, John Adams, and two aliis whom he did not recognize.

Sam said hastily, "Jeff, the king sent us for you. I ain't—busting in on what don't concern me?"

Jeffery said, "What does Tamehameha want?"

"We got fixed with Decastro. John Adams reached Tamehameha in time to git a few words in before von Kotzebue started asking where Decastro was. The king took over quick. He said if he was going to supply the ship at Honoruru, he'd like a favor in return. He reminded von Kotzebue that Decastro used to be his physician. He said he wanted to keep Decastro with him. Maybe von Kotzebue was glad to git rid of the feller. Anyhow, von Kotzebue agreed. Tonight, the king's shipping Decastro off to Mowee to keep him there safe till after the ship's gone and we've started invading Atooie . . ." Sam hesitated. He rubbed his jaw. "We did fine that far," he said, "but von Kotzebue wanted to know who'd interpret for him at Honoruru. The king said Young and George Beckly'd be there. Von Kotzebue asked if Mr. Cook couldn't sail there with him."

"He wanted me?"

"The king would've sent you aboard if he could have found you. You know how Tamehameha is. You can do him a hundred favors and he can make you feel you're the best man he's got on the whole island. But if anything slips and you ain't there when he takes a notion he wants you—he can git that ugly look on his ugly face damn quick. After von Kotzebue got aboard, Tamehameha began remembering he hadn't told Young or anybody at Honoruru why he'd planned to call you 'Kukay' and claim you were Captain Cook's nephew. So he grabbed John Adams and said you had to be found quick. He's got the peleloo you and Susan came here on ready to sail. We're to git you aboard and headed for Honoruru and he's hoping the peleloo can beat the *Rurick* there. You'll stay in Honoruru till they know what the *Rurick's* going to do, and then you can git aboard the *Traveller* and go on to Philadelphy. There ain't anything I can say, Jeff. There jist ain't. I'm jist telling you what Tamehameha ordered."

Jeffery asked, "What about Susan?"

"She'll have to stay with the Adamses till the *Bordeaux* gits in. That won't be very long." Sam hesitated. "You got your sea chest up there at the Adamses', ain't you? You go on up there and git it. Me and John Adams and the rest of us'll stay here till you git back."

Jeffery said, "That won't be necessary."

"Don't you want your chest?"

"Mrs. Adams is having her servants send the chest to your place."

"You ain't going to say goodbye to Susan?"

"She wouldn't see me."

"You ain't letting it end like that?"

"Yes," Jeffery told Sam.

It was dark when they arrived at the great road and waited a few minutes. Mrs. Adams had done exactly as she had said she would do. Two makaainanas came, bearing Jeffery's sea chest between them. Sam never said a word or asked what had passed between Susan and Jeffery. They continued on to the landing place, where men were holding flares. The crewmen had already shoved the peleloo into the water on her flat double keels. Jeffery looked around as if he expected to see someone and realized he had been half expecting to see Tamehameha. It made him understand how unimportant, actually, he had been to Tamehameha. He was a very small piece in a very large design, no more. Tamehameha had remembered him long enough to remember Kukay must be sent to Honoruru. The order was given. John Adams would attend to it. The old savage, whose expression was only from time to time as savage now as any man ever had seen, had then dismissed Kukay. Jeffery thought it must be something like that. He was so close to complete collapse from fatigue and all else happening today that possibly he was moved unreasonably by this casual dismissal from Tamehameha. It was small thanks. It left him very sore.

He asked Sam, "You won't change your mind and sail home with me?"

"Jeff, I got an account to settle with Scheffer. When you see Mr. Monroe tell him for Christ's sake to git young Hoomehoome and ships and men out to us quick, won't you?"

"I'll ask Uncle Jonathan to help me raise up a cry. Write me."

"I'll write you. Jeff—" Sam had stepped into the water as Jeffery climbed up into one of the hulls. He stuck his hand up to touch Jeffery's shoulder. "Jeff, I'm sorry for what I did. I can't ever tell you."

"Don't feel that way. I made a damn fool of myself . . . Take care of yourself. Goodbye Sam. Aroha, John Adams. Aroha!"

"Goodbye, Jeff."

"Aroha, Kukay."

As the peleloo was paddled into deeper water and the big triangular sail lifted to the wind, Jeffery heard the voices coming fainter and fainter from the shore. Well, it was done. It was finished. He never wanted to see Susan again. Tamehameha had not even come down to see him depart. They were gone. They were all gone. And Sam had gone with them. He crawled from the port hull to the platform of poles. The Rurick had two hours' start. But the kahuna at the tiller said he would hug close to the shore and try to catch the sea current off Upolu to pass the warship before daybreak.

----

24. Twenty-two days after sailing from Kailua, late Monday night, December 16, 1816, Jeffery was sitting at a table in the same stone sleeping chamber which he had first occupied when he had landed last May at Honoruru. The stone lamp was lit, the light shining palely upon the letter to his uncle which Jeffery had been trying to write for the past three hours. He put down his quill pen, listening a moment to the rain falling outside, before taking up the letter to see how it read as far as he had written. It had been a difficult letter to write. It began:

Honoruru, December 16, 1816

Dear Uncle Jonathan—

I have completed my report to Mr. Monroe & in the same packet will send this letter to you because I have decided not to sail tomorrow morning with the *Traveller* for home but to stay and see this through.

I am sending you the report for you to read it before delivering it to Mr. Monroe. In the report I have tried to give a complete account of everything that happened since Sam Crowell and I arrived last May. I hope you will urge Mr. Monroe to do all that can be done to locate Prince George Hoomehoome and have him shipped to Kailua, on Owhyee, where King Tamehameha will give him every honor due him and help restore him to his proper position on Atooie.

The Russian warship sailed from Honoruru two days ago, Saturday morning, after being detained longer than anticipated by the severe storm which struck us last week. By all accounts from the two sailing canoes which followed the *Rurick*, she cleared Atooie and is well off on her long voyage for home.

This represents a minor triumph for King Tamehameha and the islands but I am afraid it may only prove a temporary setback to Governor Baranov on New Archangel and his agent, Anton Scheffer, unless the Sandwich Islands receive assistance from England and United States within the next twelve months or sooner.

In less than thirty days King Tamehameha will invade Atooie with a force of ten thousand men carried by a fleet of double sailing canoes and small sloops. Sam Crowell is one of the captains of the invasion.

King Tamehameha is forced to make this attack. The longer he delays, the more time Governor Baranov will have to reinforce Scheffer from New Archangel. Once Scheffer is solidly entrenched on Atooie, he need only stay behind his fort, on an island already given over to the Czar, and wait until the Czar is finally brought around by the war faction in St. Petersburg to commit Russia entirely to this adventure in the Pacific.

I had hoped the news of his son being alive would persuade King Kaumuualii to withdraw from at least actively supporting the Russians against us in the invasion. But since the middle of last month, King Tamehameha and Governor Young have sent three peleloos containing high-ranking chiefs as emissaries to the king of Atooie. Either our chiefs were captured by the Russians before they got to the king of Atooie or they failed to persuade the king that his son is alive—and were held prisoners, or killed.

As a consequence, we shall have to go against both the Russians and the king of Atooie's warriors when we invade next month. In this last week, Governor Young has appeared very discouraged. Three times he asked me if I would not reconsider and stay because they are in want of white men to go as officers on the invasion.

During the past two weeks I have been debating with myself what I ought to do, follow my military orders and depart, or stay. As probably you know even better than I do, I am slow at arriving at decisions. The only hasty decision I believe I ever made, of any importance to me, was when I was with you now over a year ago and listened to Mr. Monroe explain why he wanted me to act as his agent in the islands. Sometimes I still am not very certain if the decision I made that day was a good one. Certainly, the longer I remain here the more I know how inept I am as an intelligence agent. Now I have decided to disobey my military orders I expect Mr. Monroe will regret having sent me.

I won't pretend the decision I have at last fully come to has not been influenced by my strong feeling for Mr. Ben Partridge's daughter, Susan Partridge. I am so much in love with Susan . . .

Jeffery thoughtfully tickled his nose with the quill. Presently he dipped the quill's point into Captain Beckly's ink, and scratched out two lines describing his feelings before continuing his reading:

Susan is a Connecticut girl, going on twenty. Having been now away from her for three weeks and one day I know entirely I would not want to live without her.

I have written Rebecca a short letter, also enclosed in the packet addressed to you. I shall have to ask you to deliver Rebecca's letter for me. No doubt she will be relieved and pleased to have discovered in time what a sorry husband I would have made for her.

As I have written in the report to Mr. Monroe, Susan's father was a prisoner with me on Atooie, helped me to escape, and failed at the last minute to escape, himself. I owe being here now to Ben Partridge. Susan is sailing for Australia to stay there with relatives. She leaves on the *Bordeaux* which by this week may even have stopped at Kailua to take her aboard.

In addition to all my other reasons for wanting to remain and see the invasion through, it seems to me I owe it to Susan and even more to her father, to do all I can to help rescue Ben or to negotiate for his release.

It is now close to midnight. Captain Wilcox of the *Traveller* is asleep in the chamber next to mine. He plans to sail tomorrow at dawn when the wind usually drops and it is calm enough for the native canoes to haul the ships out through the reef. I shall give him this letter to wrap in the packet for you which I gave him earlier this evening while at dinner in the fort with Governor Young, Prince Krimoko ("Billy Pitt" in my report), Captain Alex Adams who came in a few days ago on the king's bark, and George Beckly, one of the best men who ever lived next to Sam Crowell.

If I cannot marry Susan, I will never marry anyone. Knowing there is no other girl for me has helped clear my thinking and feelings about remaining. If we succeed with the invasion and free her father, I shall go on to Australia and stay there until she agrees to sail for home with me. It is a chance which will never come again to go on the invasion, to do what I can do, to be along with Sam, and to try to release Susan's father.

Furthermore, I want the Russians defeated. I want them driven out of the Pacific before they can spread to the shores of our own continent. I hope you can persuade Mr. Monroe to see that I can do more here, by staying, even though I had orders . . .

Jeffery yawned. He stuck his feet under the Chinese table to rest a minute before beginning again. The light in the stone lamp flickered palely. He pulled the lamp closer and saw it was dry of oil. The light flickered a moment or so longer and went out. Moist blackness instantly rushed into the chamber. Jeffery got up in the dark and tried to think how at this hour he could awaken someone to get more kukui-nut oil for the lamp. He had to finish the letter in time to give it to Captain Wilcox before daybreak.

He remembered the Chinese candles in the big room. He could get one of them without having to awaken Beckly and ask for a new lamp. He felt his way to the door, opening it, hearing the door squeak loudly on its wooden pinions. When he entered the narrow stone hall he halted, thinking someone was near him. He felt his neck hairs bristle. He half turned. Before he could shout, a rough cloth was thrown over his head. Huge hands seized him. The cloth was wrapped tighter, nearly suffocating him.

He felt himself being taken up as he struggled. He was carried a distance outside the fort, he knew, because he felt the rain beating on his body. The thick cloth around his head muffled his cries and it became all he could do to breathe and fill his lungs with air. He was thrown briefly to the wet ground, bound tightly, and once more lifted by many hands.

He was paddled out into the bay in a dugout. He knew that. He was at the bottom of the dugout and could feel the smooth inner curving with his arms and legs and could feel the movement of the dugout. Then he was lifted up and heard muffled native voices. When he was brought out of the rain and laid upon a mat he realized he was in the deckhouse of a peleloo. Somehow, he thought, Scheffer had sent men secretly to Woahoo to capture him and transport him back to Atooie.

He did not know how long he remained there with the wet cloth around his head. Perhaps for a time he lost consciousness. Then the cords were cut. The cloth was removed from around his head. He sat up slowly. Daylight came through the triangular opening at the aft of the deckhouse of poles and pandanus mats, and Governor Young squatted not far from Jeffery.

Jeffery asked, "You planned this?"

"Captain Tolamy," said Governor Young formally, "Tamehameha told me to 'ave ye stay to 'elp us. I tried my best. When ye would not come willingly, I 'ad nothing else to do afore ye went aboard the *Traveller* tomorrow morning."

"God damn it to hell—"

"Will ye listen, because if ye are in mind of cursing, ye can curse 'ere by yerself. We are in a desp'rate and dire way. We 'ave done our best to convince Kaumuualii 'tis no trick or lie when we say Hoomehoome is alive. Ye're the man w'at saw Hoomehoome. If anyone can convince Kaumuualii, ye can. We 'ave got ten thousand men ready to invade. We want ye to go afore the invasion. We'll send white men with ye, Sam Crowell if 'e's not too sick, Cap Adams, maybe Tony Allan or one of the Winship brothers. We 'ave worked out 'ow ye can get into the island without being seen. Ye know what a keavaiti is? 'Tis an opening in rocks along a shore where a small boat can pass through to the land. At the northwest end of Atooie there's a twenty-mile stretch of cliffs rising 'alf a mile or so, straight up from the sea. 'Tis the Na Pali coast. Tamehameha 'as learned of a keavaiti where a small boat can land. 'Tis a two days' march eastwards through forests to get to the king's village at Whymea River. But ye can get to the village from round behind the Russian fort and ye should 'ave a chance to speak direct to Kaumuualii afore Scheffer 'ears of it and tries to stop you."

After a little reflection it seemed to Jeffery that he could have asked for nothing better. Such an expedition was within his capabilities, he thought. He had convinced everyone with whom he had talked that George Hoomehoome existed and he saw no reason why he should fear failing with George's father. As a matter of fact he was beginning to feel quite excited. There had been no need to kidnap him for a task of this nature.

Servants had brought in food and calabashes of fresh water. Jeffery was beginning to feel better. He sat across from the old man and found he was hungry and ate and asked how soon he was expected to sail for Atooie. Immediately?

Tamehameha did not want him to sail until after the end of the Muckahitee, two weeks from now. There was this final rite. Jeffery was to see it to be the first to report its outcome to King Kaumuualii on Atooie. Jeffery blinked. He asked what the final Muckahitee rite had to do with his going to Atooie. How could that affect the success of the invasion or the impression to be made upon King Kaumuualii?

From Governor Young, that morning, the peleloo sailing south under strong winds, Jeffery learned that at the end of the Muckahitee there was the annual religious ritual of King Tamehameha's symbolic death and return to life, a ritual which harked back thousands of years. In the old days every chief and kinglet on the archipelago had to undergo this annual ritual. After Tamehameha had conquered the islands, he alone submitted to this final rite. On the last morning of the Muckahitee, before dawn, he would paddle to sea and at sunrise paddle back and walk upon the beach at Kailua, naked and unarmed, while five of his greatest warriors hurled spears at him. Afterwards, when Tamehameha was seen to be still alive, all the thousands congregated for the spectacle would be convinced they had seen nothing less than a testing of a god. Furthermore, the news of the king's successful passing of this ritual

204 THE MISSION OF JEFFERY TOLAMY

would travel all over the archipelago. Even on Atooie the inhabitants were waiting to hear if Tamehameha lived after the ritual or had died.

"Ye don't understand 'ow superstitious these natives are," Governor Young said. "Just 'aving Tamehameha go through that ceremony two weeks from now will 'elp our cause on Atooie more than ye might suspect. 'Tis why 'e wants ye to be the one to carry the news to King Kaumuualii."

Uneasily, Jeffery said, "I hope Tamehameha picks friends he trusts two weeks from now."

The flaky eyes opened wide. "W'at do ye mean?"

"Suppose one of those warriors actually tries to kill him?"

"One? They all 'ave to try to kill 'im. There's no 'umbug about it. But Tamehameha's been dodging those spears every year since 'e got to be a chief. 'E'll do it this time, same as always 'e 'as done. 'Tis not yer concern."

Then Jeffery thought of the four peleloos sent to Atooie by Young and Tamehameha. Three had not returned. One had returned with one chief in it, half-alive, and a woman who was dead. Had they tried to land by the keavaiti on those high cliffs at the north of Atooie?

Governor Young said Tamehameha had not known of the keavaiti until last week. Susan Partridge had told him. Susan had learned of the failure of the emissaries and she had gone to Tamehameha, saying she knew of a landing place at the north of Atooie where a small boat could reach shore without being seen. She had discovered it two years ago when she had been with her father on Atooie and they had been exploring the island for sandalwood.

Jeffery said, "Has Susan sailed yet?"

"She's not sailing. The Bordeaux put in last week and put out again." Governor Young leaned forward, the old parrot face pinched and fierce. "She traded 'er information about the landing place for permission from Tamehameha to wait at Kailua till atter the invasion. I know 'ow ye 'ave broken with 'er. Jade Adams was on the march to the lava caves, and she 'eard Sam Crowell telling Susan ye were promised to a Philadelphy girl. 'Twas a shameful thing ye planned, to 'ave Susan to yerself at Kailua a few days afore ye sailed off. Now she thinks only of waiting to be 'ere when 'er

father's released. And Tamehameha 'as said she could. I 'old ye
responsible. 'Twas all arranged to 'ave 'er safe away. 'Tis your doing.
I 'ave no sympathy for ye. As far as it concerns me, y'ere a prisoner.
Ye'll stay with Sam Crowell on the point when we land at Kailua,
if 'e'll take ye in. If ye try to escape, God 'elp ye. If Sam won't make
ye march to King Kaumuualii, I'll send ye with Beckly and Cap
Adams and Allan, who will. Ye'll speak up to Kaumuualii and say
w'at ye 'ave told us about Hoomehoome and ye'll do w'at ye can
to 'ave 'im get Susan's father released afore we invade."

Jeffery was thunderstruck. When he told Governor Young he
had already decided to volunteer, he was not believed.

"Ye'll not take me in with yer lies like ye did Susan," said the
old man as he crawled out to the platform. Jeffery was left alone in
the deckhouse of poles and pandanus leaves. The storm had increased. The sky became dark at midday, the wind roaring hugely.

***

25.   They landed at Kailua an hour before noon, Wednesday, December 18. Accompanied by a small guard,
Governor Young marched Jeffery to the king's point and north
across it to the opposite shore where Sam had been given a kuleana
of perhaps two acres of cleared space above the beach. Sam had a
grass house for himself and in the rear were four smaller houses for
the family of makaainanas given by the king to him as servants.

After delivering Jeffery and his sea chest, which had been taken
from Honoruru with him, Governor Young politely declined Sam's
invitation to stay for the noon meal. He departed, dry and spare,
teetering as if from age, but the dozen warriors had to trot to keep
up with him.

Sam had a grayish look to him, Jeffery thought. But Sam said
he was all right. The nine sloops whose building he had supervised
had been assembled at Towaihae Bay. He had been loafing the past
couple of days and guessed he was beginning to have a cramped
feeling like everybody else, waiting for the Muckahitee to come to
an end. Then he gave Jeffery a long shrewd look, dropped on a pile

of lahala mats, removed his boots, wriggled his toes comfortably, and said, "Git it off your chest."

"You knew they were going to kidnap me?"

"Jeff, I didn't know nothing. When Holmes left for Honoruru last week he told me he was going to git Young to ask you to stay on. I told him you could be bullheaded but if a feller didn't crowd you too hard you'd usually come around to seeing what ought to be done."

Jeffery heatedly explained he had made up his mind to volunteer. It had not been necessary for Governor Young to kidnap him the night before the Traveller sailed, giving instructions to George Beckly to lie to Captain Wilcox next morning and say Captain Tolamy at the last minute had agreed to return to Kailua. Instead of allowing him to volunteer, he had been dragged down here like a reluctant conscript. Now he expected everyone in Kailua would hear he had been brought back forcibly.

When he finished Sam was sympathetic. Jeffery thought Sam believed him, but he was not entirely certain. Finally, he asked about Susan. Sam said every time he thought of what he'd done it made him sick. That evening when the Russians were arriving and he had accompanied Susan part way to the lava caves, he had never had it come to his mind that Jade Adams was in the crowd behind and probably could catch most of what was being said.

"Have you seen her?" Jeffery asked.

"Seen her? Sure. I been up there two or three times going over charts with her and Cap Adams."

"How does she look?"

"She looks pretty as ever. But all she thinks and talks of is to git her old man out of those dungeons."

"What about that landing place she told Tamehameha she knew of on Atooie?"

"It's there, all right. She's got it marked on Cap Adams's sea chart." He slouched to the door and leaned on one of the poles to stare across the beach to the sea. "Jeff, I ain't got a chance with her. I know that now. Did you write her from Honoruru?"

"Three letters."

"She never answered?"

"She never got them. I tore them up." Jeffery was unable to tell Sam how stiff and wooden his three attempts had sounded when he had read them back to himself. "Anyway, I'm here. I'll see her now," he added.

"You ain't going to be able to."

Jeffery stiffened. "Like hell I won't."

"It's all spread around how you brought Susan down here jist like she was any makaainana girl. Do you think Cap Adams is going to let you walk into his kuleana and maybe cause her more grief? Why, it even," Sam said thickly, "still takes me by the throat when I let myself think about it."

Hearing that from Sam hit Jeffery hard.

There was a meeting in the throne room next afternoon, so that Jeffery might be told officially what was planned. Tamehameha was naked except for his malo and he had an oldness about him which Jeffery had not previously noticed. He had arrived from the temple where he was offering sacrifices to his gods and he was in a surly temper as if he regretted the time he was giving to this meeting and wished to get back to the temple as quickly as possible. He was curt to Jeffery. But he was equally curt to Cap Adams and Mr. Young and Sam.

Cap Adams unrolled a chart and spread it on the floor of koawood planks. On the chart Atooie had the rough outline of a stone spearhead, the base slightly curved. The narrow point of the island lay due west, the broad base to the east. Whymea Bay was at the south, the river running north from the sea midway to the center of the island. Cap Adams said the Na Pali cliffs were around the sharp point of the island, extending twenty-some miles to the northeast. For these twenty miles the cliffs lifted up sheer from the sea. Very few natives ever sailed around by the cliffs because of the dangerous currents and rocks and fewer natives passed through the forests extending inland from the Na Pali coast because they believed ghosts and demons inhabited the rainy misty islands. Because the cliffs were considered impregnable, it was extremely doubtful if the Russians would have placed any of their men or auxiliaries to guard it.

As Jeffery heard it now from Cap Adams, two years ago Susan and her father had explored the highlands while hunting for virgin sandalwood. They had camped one night on the edge of the cliffs. The next morning had been one of the rare mornings without mist or rain. Thousands of feet below them, they had sighted a small keavaiti, or opening, large enough to allow a ship's boat to enter and gain the shore. Susan had never forgotten it, and Cap Adams showed Jeffery where last week she had marked the keavaiti on the chart for the king to see.

For the first time, as Jeffery looked at the chart, he began to have the sense of having committed himself to the islands. He was no longer a spectator, an observer; he was a participant now. But Cap Adams was rolling up his chart, and everyone was very matter-of-fact. Tamehameha asked Jeffery if he had understood what was wanted, and when Jeffery nodded no one pressed around Jeffery or reminded him of how important to the success of the invasion his journey to Atooie would be. Tamehameha grunted, dismissing them, looking toward his waiting priests, nodded, got up, and left the throne room. Jeffery heard Governor Young tell Sam that Tamehameha was supposed to remain out of sight at the temple for these last two weeks.

The room looked dingy and disheveled. Jeffery heard the soft gnawing of a rat somewhere at the foundations under the floor. Instead of waiting for Sam, he went out through the yard and down to the lava wall and looked toward the swarming beach. The crowds had increased in the past three weeks. He looked toward the slopes. The green valley where Susan was staying was somewhere up there, now hidden by a golden mist. He should have written her. But he had taken her love too lightly at first. He should have known. He heard footsteps on the coarse lava path and turned his head, standing straighter.

Governor Young was approaching him, regarding him out of his parrot's eyes. "Are ye satisfied we can get ye to King Kaumuualii safely?"

"It looks like a good chance," said Jeffery. "But I'd like to ask you a question, Mr. Young. Even before I departed three weeks ago, didn't Tamehameha have it in mind to send me to King Kaumuualii?"

"'Ow do ye mean, 'ave it in mind?"

"For one thing, Tamehameha never saw me off when I sailed for Honoruru. I remember thinking I was too far down in the ranks for Tamehameha to give a damn about seeing me off. But I'm not so sure now. It makes me wonder if all along he didn't know he'd see me again. By God," Jeffery burst out suddenly, "I don't like it that way, Mr. Young."

That was Thursday, December the nineteenth. Early Friday morning, Sam returned from a meeting with Mr. Young at the king's residence. Mr. Young had wanted Sam to go to Towaihae Bay for a few days as soon as George Beckly shipped cannons down from Honoruru. The sloops were to be armed.

Sam told Jeffery the priests had definitely set the final morning of the Muckahitee thirteen days from now, the second of January of the new year by the Christian calendar. That meant everyone had thirteen more days to stuff themselves, to get fat, to twiddle thumbs, for Jeffery to plan what he was going to say to King Kaumuualii, and to wait.

Sam said hoarsely, "By Jesus God, wouldn't you think these damned heathens'd know better than to risk the only feller what they've got who can save 'em? I got a notion to git drunk. What are you going to do today?" Sam examined him. "You got shaved, didn't you?"

"Yes, I shaved," Jeffery said.

"You ain't going to have a chance to see her, if that's what you're figgering to do."

"I'll see her."

"Cap Adams won't let you inside his kuleana."

"Didn't you tell me Susan swam every afternoon in that pool behind the kuleana?"

Sam squatted on one of the mats. He looked himself over for any lice he might have collected this morning. Finally he said very deliberately, "I stuck my nose into Susan's and your business once. I ain't saying nothing any more."

That afternoon Jeffery still could not understand why Sam had believed it would be difficult for him to see Susan. He had gone through the taro fields, several miles to the north of the path which ran to the Adams kuleana. When Jeffery was above the crumbling cliffs he turned south until he arrived at the stream which came from the dark line of forest higher on the slope. The cliffs had so weathered and crumbled they were not much more than six or seven feet high in many places and did, very much, resemble fortifications.

As he waited he imagined Susan very soon coming through the trees. He would go to her, telling her humbly how very much in the wrong he had been. Even if she answered him coldly, as she had the last time he had seen her, he would persist. He would tell her he could not live without her as his wife and continue to tell her until she had to believe him.

Within fifteen or twenty minutes he heard someone approaching through the trees. He had believed this time he would be very sure of himself, but suddenly he was not at all sure. Forgetting he had decided to remain quietly where he was, he took a step forward. But he halted as a large makaainana woman appeared on the other side of the pool. Following her came three more. One carried a folded yellow holoku which evidently was meant for Susan to change into after her swim. Two carried soft mats for Susan to lie upon. The fourth carried a large bowl filled with anapanapa leaves. The smallest woman among the four was at least a head taller than Jeffery. They were huge, broad of face, glistening. One gave a great shout as if of warning to anyone in the trees.

Because they were women he made the mistake of standing his ground. They fastened boisterously upon him and threw him to the ground. His breath was knocked out of him. He gasped. He struggled. He was helpless.

It was dark when he limped into Sam's kuleana. Before saying a word, Sam filled a calabash from a barrel of the potent native okolehau. It was one of the barrels he had borrowed from the king's store.

Sam said, "It was no use trying to warn you, Jeff. Jade Adams has got all her makaainana women watching for you."

"I'm supposed to rank as an alii."

"John Adams once told me what happened to him last year when he was trying to git a north Kohala chiefess who didn't take a notion to him right then. Did them makaainana women squat on you?"

"Next time—"

"You ain't going to try a next time?"

"Did you think I was giving up?"

The day before Christmas Jeffery boldly entered the Adams yard and he had stumbled more than once on the way because his silk trousers were torn and one knee was bloody and hurt. He had been shaken enough by his falls to be conscious of where he was and of what he was doing. Now he was this far he was determined to go the rest of the way, and he got as far as the yard. Through a blur he saw the makaainana women gathering to rush at him but a man's voice called to them, flat and hard, like a whiplash.

Cap Adams walked to him and looked him up and down and then took off his sea cap and very politely said, "Captain Tolamy, I'll tell yew as one man to another, Susan don't want to see yew. She and my wife took off half an hour ago to collect kukui nuts as soon as the women came running to say yew were coming."

"I'll wait until Susan gets back."

"She won't talk to yew, sir. But here yew are, stinking of okolehau what Sam Crowell stole most likely from the king's stores. Are yew proud of yerself? I ask yew. I don't want Susan to think she has to go into hiding to prevent my women servants from taking after yew the way they done the other time. I won't hev my women servants doing that twice to a white man. I won't hev Susan and my wife thinking they hev to run from yew, either. I'm asking will yew kindly turn around and get back to Kailua and not try to cause more trouble and grief at my place."

It was one of the most painful moments of Jeffery's life. He had had to learn through this solid little sea captain how very final it was. He hated Susan. He hated them all. He hated the islands.

"I won't," Jeffery said, "bother anyone up here again . . ."

He was almost sober from the shock and from his walk down to Kailua in the heat by the time he reached the great road where he was jostled by the crowd. Angry at himself, defeated, he let himself be swept to one side under a row of palm trees where he stumbled into a girl who saved him from falling by grasping his arm.

They looked at each other for a moment without speaking. At first he thought he was seeing Polena, but it was another ehu, not Polena, although this tall girl had the same flaming hair, pale eyes, and light amber-colored skin. This one, though, he saw, was taller than Polena with strong shoulders and smooth flanks and she had adorned her wrists and ankles with flowers and a wreath of ferns was green against the smooth throat. She smiled and told him her name was Pihikula. She was a young chiefess from north Kohala, here with her family on her first visit to Kailua. For a little time they spoke idly to each other under the shade of the palms, and then not so idly and much more directly.

Pihikula accompanied Jeffery to Sam's empty house and stayed with Jeffery that night and made love once more with him on Christmas morning and afterwards he fell into a deep sleep with her head upon his shoulder.

She was gone when Sam returned late that afternoon from Towaihae Bay. If Sam ever learned from the servants that Jeffery had had a young chiefess with him overnight, Sam never mentioned it.

Twice that afternoon Jeffery washed in the surf, having the servants pour fresh water over him. Because he discovered lice were still on him from the lice Pihikula evidently had collected from the crowds at Kailua, the second time he had the servants scrub him with handfuls of crushed sandalwood chips. After all his bathing and being scrubbed he did not understand why he should feel unclean; but he did.

Sam watched silently while he shaved for the first time in days. Then he borrowed a clean jacket which was too big and he borrowed trousers which he made fit by rolling them at the bottoms and tightening them around his lean belly with a pigskin thong. That evening he ate very little.

Sam said, "It ain't been much of a Christmas, has it?"

"Not much," Jeffery said. He could not understand why he should still be thinking of Susan, wondering how she had passed Christmas day with Jade and Cap Adams.

It was a bright moonlight night when he went down to the beach by himself. For a long time he watched the rollers coming in, one after the other, each third roller bigger than the others. Once he had thought he wanted only a girl but he had learned from last night that the nature of one experience was not the nature of another.

He found himself casting back to those days of the long voyage on the *Clymestre* when he had read through all of the twenty-two volumes of *Polexandre* which Rebecca had given him as a farewell gift. He remembered the dreams which he had dreamt aboard the *Clymestre* after closing a volume of *Polexandre* and thinking forward to the day when he would arrive at the Sandwich Islands so far around the curve of earth. Suddenly he threw a stone into the waves and rose to his feet. He had loved Susan and had lost her. Now he knew how much he had lost. He had also learned that he could never replace her by trying to surfeit himself and stifle the empty feeling in his heart with another.

On the second of January, eight days later, Sam and Jeffery squatted on their heels in an empty nook above the road and waited. It was the final morning of the Muckahitee, and in the strange greenish light which showed in these latitudes before dawn, Jeffery estimated there must be nearly seven thousand islanders gathered around the bay, all waiting, as the shape of King Tamehameha came down the steps of the temple and around the circle of beach, followed by white-clad kahunas.

It was happening. It was being done, Jeffery had to tell himself as if he might be dreaming. Alone, Tamehameha walked to the landing place in measured strides. Slowly he divested himself of his royal feather cloak which fell from his hands to the black sand like liquid gold. Slowly he kicked off one sandal of bullock hide and then the other. Slowly he took from his grizzled head a helmet of feathers shaped something like the helmets the Spanish conquistadores wore centuries ago, with a great flaming crest of scarlet feathers at the top. This he laid beside the feather cloak and the sandals. He removed his loincloth of dyed brown kapa cloth decorated with black designs and dropped it on the pile. Unclothed, he pushed a small dugout into the surf, boarded it expertly, and paddled swiftly toward the reefs.

Jeffery watched the dugout grow smaller and smaller. As he waited it was as if he went drifting back in time to long-ago evenings in Philadelphia, perched high on the library ladder with one of the chronicles of ancient days open on his knees. The words of the pages were lifting upwards into a haze, forming shapes and figures of their own. This was done in those times. That was done. A lamb was slaughtered. A pig was sacrificed. A king was strangled —or a mock-king was strangled at the end of the winter solstice.

It had been done in ancient Rome, in ancient Greece, in Egypt, Babylon, Nineveh, back further in time, further still, to an antique plain on which lifted a village of huts. The tribal leader died in fact, in effigy, or by proxy, or he submitted his life to a test. In actuality or in symbol, or in the person of another, the king returned for a new cycle of ruling.

He watched while five alii warriors, among whom towered John Adams, arrived in even and regular steps upon the beach. One by one they planted the tall spears in the hard sand, as a moaning rose from the assembled throng.

When again Jeffery looked to the sea he was surprised to find Tamehameha's dugout already had gained the line of reefs. The dugout was turning, disappearing, and lifting in the rise and fall of waves. Now it was caught by the third wave, which of every three ran the strongest. The strong surf carried the dugout and its solitary occupant toward the shore, rushing faster and faster.

The greenish cast of the sky slowly changed to a pale mauve, shot through with streaks the color of blood. The silence became intense. When Jeffery looked to his left he saw that Sam had become rigid, staring out at the man who was to fulfill the ancient ritual of the death and possible rebirth of a tribal leader.

Looking in the unearthly light as if he were cast of bronze, John Adams advanced ten paces before the other warriors. Before the sun lifted entirely from the sea the thing had to be done. Either the king would rule another year—or he would be slain. John Adams was watching the dugout approach upon the running wave of white. He raised a spear almost twenty feet in length and as huge around as Jeffery's wrist, tipped with sharpened bone.

Tamehameha landed about a hundred paces distant from John Adams. He stepped from the dugout, agile and light for all his great size, advanced in a short rush and stopped, shaking his huge head like a bull about to charge. Jeffery saw him. Thousands saw him come forward, and then it happened very quickly. John Adams drew back his arm and hurled the first spear. Even after seeing it Jeffery could sometimes not quite believe the scene he now watched.

Tamehameha seized the first spear in mid-air. Immediately he spun it and used it to parry the other spears flung at him by the four remaining warriors. When Tamehameha had finished, the shattered spears were at his naked feet. The sun was edging a red rim above the sea.

Afterwards—afterwards, Jeffery never had heard such a roaring in all his lifetime as came from those thousands of throats. It was a noise like thunder. It was a noise like thunder and waves crashing.

Men and women set fire to strips of bark and burnt their flesh. They flung away their malos and aprons and ran around naked, screeching at the top of their lungs. In their frenzy they coupled publicly like pigs or dogs on the beach, along the side of the road, and in the fields. Tamehameha had been led back to the temple and was gone from sight. A stench filled the air from the sacrificial fires.

In his mind Jeffery still had a vision of something huge rushing across the beach, more like a dark angry bull than a human being, snatching at that first spear and all in the same motion striking this way and that against the flight of other spears, smashing them down to the sand, and raising a triumphant head toward the red rim of morning sun.

"Sometimes," said Mr. Holmes, with an absent look on his pink face, "I think Boston never existed."

Sam and Jeffery climbed slowly down toward the road. Halfway to the road they caught sight of a shiny black face, struggling through the crowd to get to them. Sam cupped his hands around his mouth and shouted, "Tony! Tony Allan!" Jeffery had not known Allan was anywhere within a hundred miles of Kailua.

The black man pushed through the crowd to them, wiped sweat from his neck and arms, and said he had arrived last night. He had stayed all night with Governor Young and had watched the ritual from the north shore. "Gov'nor Young said to hunt you two up. We're sailing soon as we can."

The *Taamana* had come around to about a mile off the north point. Not very far from Sam's beach she let down a sea anchor to hold her against a stiff offshore breeze while she sent in a longboat for the three men. Governor Young, Mr. Holmes, and John Adams had arrived from the king's yard to see them off. Governor Young said the king had gone directly back to the temple and for the next three days would have to remain there, fasting; otherwise he would have been here, too.

"It was a brave thing he did," Sam said. "Tell him so for me. Tell him Tony and me'll git Jeff to King Kaumuualii, too. We ain't going to fail."

"Ay, ye won't fail. There are three things I want ye all to remember. W'ile 'tis not likely ye'll see Scheffer, if ye do, 'e's to know 'e's to be under the king's maru.''

It was a new word to Jeffery. He saw Sam did not understand it either. Jeffery asked, "What's that, sir? Maru?"

"The natives say it, 'under the king's shade.' I come direct from the king. 'Tis 'is word to ye. Scheffer is to 'ave 'is maru and to know of it," Young said almost defiantly.

Sam's face seemed to go blank. "You don't mean the king'll let that bastard go free if ever we git hold of him?"

"Ay."

Sam growled from his throat, "If I get my hands on Scheffer, he'll wish he had a maru. Damn me if he won't.''

"By God!" said Jeffery passionately.

"Are ye too young to understand that if ye offer the enemy 'is life, at a last ditch, and the balance comes near equal betwixt 'im and ye, 'twill sap 'is strength? 'Ow," asked the old man's booming voice, "d'ye believe Tamehameha conquered the archipelago in the years gone so long? 'E didn't do it by driving all 'is enemies in rats' 'oles for each of 'em to fight to the death. Besides, don't ye see? If Scheffer's kilt, 'twill make a martyr of 'im with the Russians."

Tony Allan said, "I'll talk to Sam and Jeff, Mr. Young. What else was it you had?"

Jeffery shaded his eyes against the sun. The ocean was dazzling. He saw something small and black far out near the larger blackness of the brig. The longboat was being rowed in. In another fifteen minutes the longboat would be grating its keel on the harsh beach.

" 'Tis this," Governor Young said, with a glance at Sam's stiff face and another at Jeffery. "Cap Adams and I 'ave gone over the schedule, but I'll give it to ye 'ere again. Cap will git ye close to Atooie as 'e can 'thout being sighted. Ye should be ten to twelve leagues off the coast, three days 'ence, next Sunday. 'E'll drop the longboat for ye to set sail and make a course for the Na Pali coast and the keavaiti there. Ye should land at the Na Pali the fourth day, Monday. I'll give ye two days to 'ead east to Whymea River—ye'll arrive at the king's village Wednesday. We'll say three days for ye to reach an agreement with Kaumuualii or to 'ave it come to nothing."

"Saturday," said Jeffery, holding the dates in his head.

"Saturday," repeated the big deep voice against the wind. "Ye'll need a few more days to commun'cate with Adams, who'll stand off to sea near the Na Pali. We'll say the deadline's the twentieth of January. If we 'aven't 'eard from ye by then, we'll sail with the fleet for Atooie. 'Ave ye questions?"

Sam looked at Jeffery. It was clear enough. In eighteen days, Tamehameha would launch the invasion. Again Jeffery sighted toward the longboat, which had been rowed in half the distance from the brig to the shore. He heard Sam asking about making the landing on Atooie. Sam said Susan had told him the passage through the rocks was hidden from sight when you approached by sea. Although she had marked it plainly on the chart, Sam said they still might miss it. They might have to turn the longboat around and sail back to the brig for water and provisions before making a second attempt. It would throw off Mr. Young's time schedule by several days.

Jeffery had shaded his eyes against the glare. He could see Cap Adams at the tiller and six kanakas at the oars but there was no one else in the longboat. He knew Susan and Mrs. Adams had been placed overnight on the brig to prevent them from being caught up in this morning's frenzy. Jeffery was seized by a keen disappointment. He had hoped to see Susan before sailing for Atooie. She and Mrs. Adams had evidently been landed to return to the Adams kuleana before the brig had come around the point to take on new passengers. He was angry. Governor Young had deliberately arranged it to prevent him from seeing Susan.

He turned as Sam finished and asked hotly, "You ordered Susan taken off?"

"Captain, ye anticipate me." Governor Young turned to Sam. "I 'ad one more thing to tell ye. Ye'll 'ave no difficulty to reach the landing for the reason that Susan will be with ye in the longboat atter ye sail from the brig and 'ead for Atooie."

"She ain't going?" Sam said hoarsely.

"Ay, she goes with ye to Atooie. She is a friend of King Kaumuu-alii and even more a friend of Kaumuualii's wives. She knows the island better than any of us 'ere on Owhyee. She can 'elp Mr. Tolamy. Kaumuualii will be more likely to listen to 'er than any-one else Tamehameha could send."

Jeffery said to Sam, "To hell with this, Sam. Tamehameha's taken us in. She can't go."

218 THE MISSION OF JEFFERY TOLAMY

"Mr. Young, git Susan off that brig," Sam said.

"Take 'er off? Damn ye both!" the old man roared. "She wants to get near 'er father. Tamehameha saw she would be as good or better than Tolamy to send to Kaumuualii. D'ye think 'e cares w'at danger it might be for 'er when in eighteen days 'e will be sailing with every able-bodied man on 'is islands to attack Atooie? I tell ye there's nothing I nor any other can do. What! Will ye two decide ye'll stay? Then 'twill be Susan who goes alone to take the news of 'is son being alive to Kaumuualii and to tell 'im that Tamehameha 'as passed the Muckahitee for another year!"

---

26. Sunday night, some sixteen leagues to the southwest of Atooie by Cap Adams's reckoning, a longboat was lowered from the stern of the brig. Tony Allan climbed down first to help Susan. Jeffery and Sam came afterwards. Susan took the tiller while Sam and Tony Allan set the mast and raised the sail.

Toward morning Jeffery could hear a faraway thunder of surf and, by the shifting of the wind on his face, he knew Susan had changed the longboat's course. On board the Taamana Susan had been with Jade Adams at night and during the day Jeffery had seen very little of her. He could not help hoping that now on this mission the opportunity might at last come for them to be alone together.

As daylight came, fog blew down thinly and presently through its rifts Jeffery saw the Na Pali cliffs, a great line of gray sentinels off toward the coast. Susan held away, waiting for the morning wind to clear the fog but it began to rain. Jeffery no longer had a sense of time. It might have been an hour afterwards that Susan called out sharply, swinging the prow toward land. Jeffery saw through the rain two rocky projections shoring outwards from the gray rise of land which appeared to go straight up and up from the tumble of surf until he could see no ending because the cliffs vanished in gray rain.

He was jarred when a wave crashed against the longboat. Susan must have caught sight of the narrow opening between the two rocky spires and pointed the longboat dead for land, the surf picking them up and hurling them forward with a roaring sound. Jeffery felt the hard shock when the hull struck bottom. It was like being inside a stone grinding mill—then, instantly, it became like being inside a revolving green bottle. Jeffery felt himself go pitching upwards, strangled and grasping for air, and next was aware of sliding along coral in a rush of green water. He clung for his life and presently the green sea was sliding away from him.

He staggered to his feet and saw Susan in front of him. He grabbed her and the two of them ran, as the roaring rose again behind them. Sky and sand and water revolved around Jeffery; he was flung face down. He felt Susan's hand tug hard in his, but he did not let go. They sat up, drenched. Sam bawled from near them, "Where's Tony?"

Tony bawled, "Here."

He had been flung to their left on higher ground. The longboat had been smashed. The four got themselves away from the boiling surf. Sam and Tony retrieved their muskets, cleaned them, and strapped them over their shoulders. Jeffery had lost his musket but his pistols were intact.

Their landing place could scarcely be called a cove. It was a narrow, V-shaped indentation in the rise of gray cliffs, leading back perhaps twenty yards from the shore to a mass of rubble and rotted trees collected at the base of the rocks. For two thousand feet, Jeffery estimated, the rocks rose in jumped peaks and weathered spires, craggy and desolate. Fog and rain hid the land above.

It was at least an hour before they finally found a way up the cliff. Susan was lighter and quicker than the men and had crawled over a boulder as large as a grass hut and now only her head was visible. She called excitedly. Behind the boulder a groove ran up at a steep angle. She wasn't sure it was a path but she thought they could get higher by crawling along the groove.

After perhaps a quarter of an hour of slow going, they came to a shallow cup of rock about two rods in area and possibly a hundred feet or more above the cove. There was a covering of earth mold and sand filling the shallow depression in the ledge and Tony discovered a few hoofprints where goats must have come down fairly recently from the highlands. Then Jeffery found a sort of path to the right, which seemed to go upwards.

It was well along in the afternoon when at last they reached the top of the barren rugged land which spread inland from the cliffs for a mile or so to the edge of a forest. They stopped to rest and Tony Allan said he was hungry.

Although they had lost their store of provisions in the longboat, all of them had filled the pockets of their coats with salted pig and taro cakes wrapped in oiled silk. Susan's face looked pinched from fatigue. Jeffery was exhausted. Sam said, "We'll take off half an hour and see if we can find some wood which ain't too wet to burn."

When Jeffery started off, Sam said, "Fix a pile of leaves for Susan to rest herself on. Me and Tony'll git wood."

It was the first time Jeffery and Susan had been alone together. He said, "These leaves are wet, Susan."

"Everything's wet or damp up here on the Na Pali. Two years ago Pa and I had a miserable time of it."

"How about this log? At least it's something to sit on. Wait a minute." He took off his coat and laid it over the log.

"You'll freeze."

"We'll soon have a fire."

There was so much he had wanted to tell her. She huddled on the log, wrapping her cloak around her. The mist had thickened. She leaned forward and raised her face to him and said very seriously, "I can guess how you and Sam feel, having to take a woman along. But I can back you up when you tell King Kaumuualii that Prince George is alive. I'll tell him King Tamehameha never knew about Prince George until he heard it from you. It'll be another reason, too, to have Pa taken from that damned Russian fort. King Kaumuualii'll want to question Pa and hear what Pa has to say. I don't know why the king's let the Russians hold Pa for so long. If Scheffer's lied to him, you can tell him about Pa."

"I will."

Then she said very steadily, "I'd better tell you something else. I didn't care when Jade's women caught you because you didn't write me from Honoruru. Governor Young told me you'd have sailed if he hadn't stopped you. I might have been with child."

Her voice had changed. It went deep into him. He did look at her but her face was hooded by her cloak and a mist was between them. He felt stricken.

"I would have killed myself if I had been," she said before he could ask. "But you never wrote. You would have sailed."

"No, I was staying," he said.

Before he could say anything more, Sam and Tony came back, carrying armloads of brush and leaves they had scraped from the dry sides of a rock. They got a fire going, warmed themselves and ate. By early evening they had gone five miles deeper into the forest.

Presently a moon of sorts appeared, distorted in shape by the mist which clung like veils to the black branches of the trees and the giant rocks littering the highlands. Semiparasitical sandalwood grew here among the other trees of the forest, and a certain uniformity of spacing resulted from the large and small trees clumping together.

The uniformity created the illusion to Jeffery of advancing through a ghostly park land, cut through by gullies and chasms. The aisles of trees radiated away from him. With every few steps forward, he would find himself in the center of a new radiation of lines receding into a silvery distance.

Sam was ahead; Tony Allan in the rear. Susan was marching alongside of Jeffery, answering the questions he put to her from time to time about King Kaumuualii. He had a sense of her carefully considering every question and trying to answer completely. It was not as difficult as it had been to speak with her. Outwardly, at least, she had completely become a member of the little group of four and was trying to help and prepare Jeffery for the time when he must stand before Kaumuualii.

She said Kaumuualii spoke excellent English for an islander. He was vain, she thought, and very different from Tamehameha. "He isn't such a heathenish mixture of wickedness and goodness. Kaumuualii's advanced closer to our times. He's learned enough about foreigners to want to be like them."

There was no sign at all of human beings in the misty depths of forest. The cold moonlight, the twisting and writhing of the mist, the twitterings of unseen birds disturbed in the black tree branches above—all of it began to wear on Jeffery's nerves. He was stumbling more, too, from fatigue. Susan had long since ceased speaking, trudging along silently. When Jeffery helped her over fallen logs or through a tangled ravine, she accepted his hand without a word.

Jeffery thought it must be midnight when he spoke to Sam. They had gone far enough for one night. Susan protested faintly. She wanted to continue. They had very little food remaining and they were not likely to get more until they reached the king's village. They had not made as good time as they had hoped.

Tony Allan came forward. "Ma'am, we're all ready to drop. I vote we stay here till daylight."

They cut brush with their knives and made a lean-to of sorts for Susan. The men arranged beds of leaves for themselves in a half circle around the lean-to. Jeffery dropped upon the leaves, but he was too exhausted and tense to fall asleep. In a very few minutes he heard Sam's snores and envied Sam. When he lifted his head he could see the shadowy length of Tony Allan on Sam's other side. The moonlight filtered mistily through the trees. Jeffery gazed toward the clump of shadows where the lean-to had been raised by the side of the little gully. He wondered if Susan had fallen asleep. He wanted very much to believe her feelings toward him had changed slightly. If he could retrieve some of her respect for him as a man, by succeeding with Kaumuualii and obtaining her father's release, at least, he told himself, it would be a start.

The next morning, as the sun lifted and warmed the air, they ate the last of their food. By the middle of the day they had rounded the northern flank of the mountain and gone another eight or ten miles. They stopped to pick wild berries and suck the pith of wild sugar cane which they found growing below the forest. Early in the afternoon they arrived at the upper end of Whymea Gorge and stopped. It had not taken them as long as they had thought it would.

Here they held a short conference. Sam believed one of them should remain behind and Jeffery agreed. Tony said, "I can talk the language better than Sam, Jeff. I guess it better be me if one of us ought to hide and see how the rest of you make out. We got to set a place, though."

Susan suggested that Tony make his way to Arrow Rock. It was above the mouth of the river on the west side of the gorge, the same side they were on now. It was the old ceremonial rock and years ago someone had chiseled an arrow in it.

Tony said he could find the rock, all right. He'd go slow and easy toward the river's mouth, staying on this side, above the river, doing his best to avoid Russian sentinels. He could manage for three days. If Sam or Jeff didn't come for him within three days he'd know they'd had grief. After three days, if he saw a chance to slip into the village he'd do it. The main thing, though, would be for him to attempt to reach the *Taamana* and carry word back to Kailua that something had gone wrong. If he had to, he could roll one of the half-rotten tree trunks into the surf from that cove where they'd landed. If it wasn't smashed against the rocks he considered he'd have a fair chance of being picked up by the brig. If not, he could try to swim and float across the channel to the little island of Niihau.

They said goodbye and watched Tony go. When Tony reached the trees he turned and waved to them. Then he was gone, and Jeffery wondered if Susan and Sam were asking themselves if they would ever see Tony again.

Susan led the two men nearly a mile due north along the rim of the gorge until she located a trail downwards. They began the slow descent to the river, a blue thread winding far below among green fields. The steep rocky walls were streaked with color, with lava blues, oranges, and vivid scarlets.

It rained. Afterwards a rainbow arched across the gorge and then sunshine filtered through a mist. Jeffery noticed the air was becoming warmer and softer as they got closer and closer to the floor of the gorge.

They crossed an ancient twenty-foot causeway of stone and hard-packed earth to the riverbank. When Jeffery asked about it, Susan said it probably had been built centuries and centuries ago. She broke off suddenly, pointing silently ahead.

Near the river several makaainanas had been digging at their field of taro. They were looking up at the strangers. "We'd better call them," Jeffery said. "We can't escape being seen any longer. Besides we'll need help to get across the river."

He felt her hand lightly on his arm as she stood on her toes to look across toward the river. He did not move. "They'll be less afraid of you," he told her. "Can you ask them to take us across the river in their dugout?"

Susan nodded. Her hand lifted as Sam's bellow sounded across the field. The makaainanas approached, kneeling while Susan spoke.

The two men poled them to the other side, shoving their dugout back into the river as soon as Susan and Sam and Jeffery had climbed to the eastern bank. On this side a road or wide path followed along the river. There was a village around the bend where Jeffery asked to be directed to the village headman. Instead, with much clamoring and shouting, they were led by a rapidly gathering crowd to the leafy pavilion of one of the local aliis, who was the chief of this region. They saw no Russians or Kodiaks.

Susan and Jeffery both spoke to the alii, a man of medium size as aliis grew, gray haired, scarred, and tattooed. The alii listened and was polite, very polite. Jeffery said they had brought a message for the king and asked to be taken to Kaumuualii for him to decide if the message was worth listening to, rather than to inform the Russians first of their coming.

The alii asked how and where they had landed without being seen. Susan raised her head proudly and said that, too, was a matter for the king. The alii looked down at Susan and gave her a grave, rather grim, smile. He told the guards to watch the three haoles and departed.

Sam said suddenly, "There ain't no reason why we can't make ourselves comfortable till we're wanted." He looked at Susan and he looked at Jeffery. He scratched one elbow reflectively. He stretched on the mats near the entrance and clasped his hands under his head and remarked that he was plumb beat; and he shut his eyes.

It was very warm. Susan had removed her cloak and appeared very small within the dim high pavilion. Flies hummed. A lizard crawled across the earthen floor. Jeffery became very much aware of her and of the sudden awkward silence between them. Sam's determined action could not have been any more obvious. Jeffery risked a glance to see how she had taken it. Her eyes lifted to his. Jeffery had a troubled sensation. Susan's color increased. He was afraid she had become angry at both Sam and him. But something amused stole over her lips. Her eyes flickered toward Sam as if they could not help themselves. He was still resolutely sprawled on the mats, his eyes squeezed shut.

Susan went silently into the shadowy rear of the pavilion, coolly turning her back on both Sam and Jeffery. He remembered how headlong he once had been with her and now found he did not even know if he dared go the distance of two yards to intrude upon her silence. For the briefest instant her head turned, and she looked at him curiously. He was by her side the next instant, and the instant afterwards he had his arms around her.

At first she was merely unresisting, as if she were still unsure of both herself and him. But he felt her arms slowly tighten. All at once she yielded and responded with a sudden fierceness, then pulled her lips away, throwing back her head to study him intently. Her face was an oval whiteness in the shadows. He heard her long sigh.

"What an awful rake you must have been in Philadelphia," she whispered. "But I can't help it, Jeffery. I do love you."

He was about to assure her he was nothing of the kind in Philadelphia. But just in time he had a restraining flash of wisdom. Instead of speaking, he kissed her. She kissed him back with equal warmth and he was infinitely grateful because she had not ceased loving him after all.

He whispered, "I've been wrong about everything. Three times I tried to write you from Honoruru and tore up the letters because they didn't say what I wanted to say. I couldn't get to you on Owhyee. I wouldn't have sailed away from you. I love you too much. I couldn't have gone."

"I hated you because you didn't write."

"Please marry me."

"I suppose I shall have to," she answered, but she was smiling again.

"Susan—"

She held him away. "We're both being foolish at a time like this. How can we think of what we'll do until we get back to Honoruru?"

"We'll get back to Honoruru. Will you marry me when we do get back?"

She seemed to hesitate, and he whispered violently, "A real marriage this time. Cap Adams can take us to sea and have a marriage at sea."

"Yes. But I want Pa to be there. We've got to get him released."

Jeffery would have said more, but Sam lifted his head sharply in a warning movement. The alii was re-entering his pavilion, with more warriors.

Jeffery and Sam were relieved of their arms. Susan said hastily not to resist. Let the alii see they were here asking for a peaceful parley. Very soon they were conducted outside, where three litters were waiting. The alii ordered them to place themselves upon the litters.

Before getting on his litter Sam gazed hard at Susan and then back to Jeffery. "Have you two made up or not?"

Impulsively Susan kissed Sam on the cheek before the alii could interfere.

Jeffery did not have another chance to speak to Susan. He had to rejoice in silence. She had forgiven him. She would marry him as soon as they returned to Honoruru. He promised himself he would do all he could to make Susan proud of him. He felt a gathering of his forces. He had spoken to the greatest chiefs of Honoruru and of Kailua. He did not see why it should be very different when he spoke to Kaumuualii here at Whymea.

It was almost night when Jeffery first had a view of the harbor and the sea beyond. At least half a mile away was a large village all along one side of the river with the huts extending back to the walls of the cliffs at the east. He lifted himself up in the litter, hanging onto the poles, as the bearers ran smoothly along the pebbled way. Now he could clearly see the huge earthen mounds of the Russian fort which had been raised since his departure.

The path plunged abruptly through large trees and wound along the base of the east cliff among hundreds of rude huts. People thronged the lanes to watch the cavalcade go by. The litters were carried up a long grassy incline to a thick grove of trees, where men were waiting with burning torches. Ahead of him, beyond the crowd, Jeffery saw a large structure of poles and woven grass, with a thatched roof covered with leaves so recently picked they were still green and fresh.

Aliis and kahunas arrived, the twilight deepening. Jeffery was pulled roughly from the litter and pushed straight toward the large house, Sam behind him, Susan still farther in the rear.

---

27. Jeffery found himself inside a room even larger than Tamehameha's throne room in Kailua. A kahuna had ordered him to stand and not move. Sam was next to him. Susan had not yet appeared. The earthen floor was hidden by mats on which were strewn sweet-smelling rushes. Hanging from the hand-hewn rafters were calabashes and gourds, and six or seven stone lamps burning brightly. During the years foreign furniture had been accumulated, sofas and chairs, a vast table which looked as if it might have been designed and fashioned by English craftsmen, French mirrors and pier glasses of a greater number than Tamehameha had ever imported for himself in Kailua.

A score or more of aliis, men and women, were in this room, regarding Sam and Jeffery. On the sofa near the entrance was a stout man of fifty or so. His wide square face was fat around the jowls, and on his iron-gray hair was a coronet of feathers.

It must be King Kaumuualii, Jeffery decided; it couldn't be anyone else. He was wearing a crumpled, crimson, British sea cloak, stained by his sweat. There was no shirt under it, nor were there ornaments on him except for a bit of bamboo as round as a finger and as long, which hung from his swarthy neck. Instead of trousers he wore a decorated brown and black kapa loincloth, his thick legs bare, with heavy European shoes on his feet.

They were all silent, King Kaumuualii as well as everyone else, while Susan was brought in. When the square-jowled alii looked at Susan, she promptly knelt before him, casting an agonized glance at Sam and Jeffery for them to do the same. Belatedly the two men awkwardly got to their knees, Sam's gaunt cheeks turning a dull red. Then the man got himself up from the sofa and walked to Susan and the first words Jeffery heard him speak were, "Miss Paht'idge, my word, you here!" He took her hands, lifting her.

"You haven't forgotten me, King Kaumuualii?"

"My word, you here? W'at a surprise, Miss Paht'idge!"

Jeffery heard that pained, deep, surprised voice; and it was not right. Tamehameha's reedy whistle had been singularly without any show of style or airs, but King Kaumuualii sounded as if he had assumed the manners and speech and exclamations which he'd remembered from an English lord of a long time ago.

Susan was smiling up at the broad face. "Your Highness, I came to ask you why you haven't helped my pa," she said in straightforward fashion, "and—" she indicated Jeffery—"Captain Tolamy came with me on a matter of great importance to you about your son."

King Kaumuualii did not once look at Sam or Jeffery. "How you come here and me not know?" he asked Susan.

"Na Pali," she promptly explained. "We found a keavaiti for landing our boat and climbed the cliffs."

"Bad coming, Na Pali way." King Kaumuualii said. "Bad coming." He was still holding her hands. "Why you come here?" he asked her, the large spaniel eyes suddenly swimming with tears. Jeffery got off his knees. Everyone in the room was watching Susan and the king. Sam also got off the floor and peered anxiously at the king and Susan as if something was happening which alarmed him.

Jeffery heard the king demand, "Why you coming here when your father dead?"

Dead? What was the fool talking about? Ben wasn't dead. Jeffery took a step forward and stopped . . .

"You not know? Tamehameha send me kanaka and wahine to say my son not dead. I send kanaka and wahine to Tamehameha and say it but you to know your father dead. My word, very sorry for you."

Governor Young had known, it flashed through Jeffery's mind. Young had told them that one alii had sailed back from Atooie with a dead chiefess in the peleloo. But Young had said nothing of learning that Ben Partridge had died!

"He dead three months," Kaumuualii told Susan. "Very sorry. My word, he dig hole. Men find him next day. Dead in hole."

"Pa's dead? He died in that tunnel . . ." She stared at Jeffery unbelievingly, and crumpled at the king's feet.

Jeffery and Sam tried to reach her. King Kaumuualii gave a shout, ordering them to stand away. Warriors seized them. The king lifted Susan and called to three of his women chiefs, who took her and carried her slowly toward the women's pavilion. Again Jeffery attempted to go to her and was struck down.

Jeffery was tied to one of the oak chairs. Someone lifted his head by the hair and a calabash of water was dashed in his face. He tried to stand and could not. There was a steady coming and going through the room of chiefs and priests, and a naked servant had tied strings of kukui nuts not far from Jeffery, lighting them. He saw Sam over on the other side of the room, slumped in a chair, similarly tied, blood on his face.

When King Kaumuualii again entered the room, Jeffery would not have been surprised to see either Scheffer or Russian officers from the fort accompanying him. Kaumuualii returned alone, shedding his cloak, which a servant immediately snatched off the floor. The king seated himself sullenly on his red sofa, glancing once at Jeffery. He entered into a discussion with his aliis, the voices low.

He picked up a war club from the floor, absently holding the club between his knees, polishing the wood with the palm of his hands. Presently he stood, approaching Jeffery. "Why you come here? Say quick. Tamehameha make Muckahitee? He sent you tell?"

"Tamehameha's passed it. He wanted you to know. Where's Susan?"

"She bad sick. Woman try fix her. Tamehameha make lie on my son."

Jeffery gathered himself for the effort. His head still reeled from the blow. Ben dead? It was impossible. Jeffery raised his head stupidly. Kaumuualii had shouted at him. "I saw your son," he said. "I was with him."

"Lie!"

"No. I've come here to tell you . . ."

"Say quick," ordered the king. "O kakou ke rohe. We hear."

Jeffery began at the beginning but he found he was leaving out details and having to go back to explain. It was difficult to think because something in his brain was shredding away: Ben dead?

Kaumuualii had returned to the sofa, his head bent, the crown of feathers crooked on his head. He listened. He did not interrupt.

When, finally, Jeffery stopped, he had an instant of panic until he realized he was finished. He had ended. There it was. He tried to lift an arm to wipe the sweat streaming down his forehead and was reminded that his arms were still tightly bound.

Kaumuualii asked, "You pau—no more?"

"Prince George ought to arrive on the island in ten or eleven months—"

"My word! You say talk like Tamehameha make say to my people for long time now." Kaumuualii got himself up from the sofa. "How big my son?"

Jeffery jerked his arm but could not raise it. The king nodded to one of the chiefs, who sliced through the cords with a stone knife. Jeffery shakily lifted a hand as high as it would go above his head. "Bigger than that, I'd say."

"You say big lie. My son *this* big—" Kaumuualii answered. He bent forward, placing his hand about four feet above the mats, tenderly, as he would touch the head of a small boy. His bamboo amulet swung out from the feathered chain around his neck. This thwarted, pompous man, Jeffery realized with a despairing sensation, was still seeing the small son of years ago.

"Prince George has had time to grow, sir."

Tears welled into the brown eyes and Kaumuualii raised his head again. He wagged it slowly back and forth. Yes, a son would be very big now, perhaps, he admitted. But his son was dead. The old man of Kailua had thought of this dreadful lie as a last resort to stir up the subjects of King Kaumuualii against their king and the foreigners. Kaumuualii's Russian friends at the fort had warned him. First, ambassadors from Tamehameha had arrived. Kaumuualii had been forced to kill nearly all of them in a vain attempt to prevent their words from carrying to his subjects. Now this young haole had been dispatched with the same lie and more lies. But the Russians at the fort had truly anticipated Tamehameha's cunning. He paused. He had spoken as much for his aliis to hear as for Jeffery because now, in English, he asked, "How you make speech with my son?"

"At first, as I'm doing now with you, sir."

"He no talk haole-talk. My word, I catch you in big lie!"

"Your son learned haole-talk, sir. George could even write it. Afterwards he tried to teach me your language."

Kaumuualii's face turned darker. "You say lie for Tamehameha. No talk more."

"I will talk more. Your son was alive as I am—"

"I say, no talk. Son dead."

"I say, sir, inside of a year at the most your son will be landed on these islands to demand an accounting from you if you betray Atooie to the Russians."

Tears of rage filled Kaumuualii's eyes. He lifted the war club and struck Jeffery a glancing blow across the face. Jeffery stumbled back in blinding pain, clasping his hands to his face. He fell to one knee. He staggered up and charged dazedly at Kaumuualii and was stopped instantly by two aliis, who threw him against the chair. He crashed into it, going over upon the floor, the chair splintering, fragments of wood striking his legs.

Jeffery never understood why he did not lose complete consciousness instantly. He even knew that Sam had tried to get to him, that Sam had been knocked down.

Jeffery felt himself being raised from the floor and dropped upon soft mats. Pain sheared in waves through his face. He saw through a redness. He had the actual physical impression of an invisible mask of pain being fitted over his face and screwed tighter and tighter. It was excruciating. All about him thrumming noises gradually separating into voices of separate individuals. Kaumuualii raised a stone lamp in his hand to look down at Jeffery.

"My word! My word! Why you so bad?"

When he came to he thought the kahunas were torturing him. He struggled weakly to fight them off. His hands and legs were bound once more while the surgeon-priest skillfully attended to his broken nose. To prevent him from choking, long reeds were inserted through the nostrils. It was like having red-hot nails driven into his face. Again he lost consciousness.

He came to once more, struggling still, his nose a pulpy mass. He had a notion he had been transported elsewhere and was no longer in the big room and he did not particularly care where he was. A string of burning kukui nuts glittered before his inflamed eyes. He seemed to go hurtling into black space, the thread of light vanishing and reappearing, the dim room curving about him.

Scheffer came to see him early the next morning. He was dressed in a Russian military jacket and was smoking his porcelain pipe when he walked in with two aliis.

Dazed with pain, Jeffery looked up at the blunt-featured face and heard the deep voice, so wonderfully articulate, exclaim, "Captain Tolamy, what have these savages done to you!"

Scheffer ordered the aliis to leave the hut, berating them in their own language for having so mistreated a white man. Then he squatted before Jeffery and pulled out a knife. Jeffery jerked back. A big hand grasped him; the voice said, "Come now, sir." The silvery eyes were twinkling. Quickly he sliced the cords, put away his knife, and helped Jeffery to sit up. Gently, the big fingers unwrapped the crude native bandages, and Scheffer shook his head. It was a pity. King Kaumuualii was no better than an idiot child, losing his temper and smashing a man's nose with a war club. At least the kahunas had been skillful. The nose ought to heal. Captain Tolamy eventually could breathe as well or nearly as well as before but nothing could be done to restore the nose to its original shape. It hurt, didn't it? Those savages! They were graceless savages.

Pain was like a haze before Jeffery's eyes, the sympathetic voice coming from the haze. Scheffer replaced the bandages on Jeffery's nose. He said he would bring his regimental surgeon this afternoon to have a look at that nose. He stood now, still shaking his head. With a start of surprise, Jeffery realized the man was waiting for him to speak. When Jeffery did not, Scheffer said easily that Captain Tolamy hadn't asked about Miss Susan.

Jeffery asked how was she? Where was she? It was like being struck at another point. The instant he began asking about her the ache increased. What would become of her?

She was taking it hard because of her father's death. Scheffer said, "My dear friend, you would grieve to see her."

"You killed her father."

It was the first time Jeffery could remember ever seeing Scheffer taken by surprise. Scheffer almost let his pipe drop from his hand.

"That is a strange and silly accusation, Captain Tolamy," Scheffer said after a moment.

"We were blocked away from each other in the tunnel but Ben spoke to me. He told me he was all right."

"His back was broken."

Jeffery sat very still . . .

Finally he echoed, "Ben's back was broken?"

"The day after you escaped my men descended into the tunnel you dug, sir. They found Mr. Partridge not far below his cell. He had crawled that far from the other end, which was blocked. I had nothing to do with his death. My officers can verify it for you when you accompany me to the fort. If Partridge spoke to you, he spoke as a dying man. I eschew all responsibility for his death, sir."

Jeffery could not help but believe him. He had always had a guiltiness, a concern about Ben which he had not wanted to admit even to himself. Ben! Ben! Jeffery turned his head away from Scheffer.

Scheffer waited and presently said, gently and softly, "Do you see now, sir? Miss Susan grieves. She asks for you."

"You've—told her how her father died?"

"My dear friend, I have told her everything."

Susan was asking for him! But there was a look of delicacy on Scheffer's face which for some reason warned Jeffery to hold silent.

"First, before I take you to her, this is a small matter I wish you to settle . . ."

The eyes were all silver. This small matter, the deep voice explained, was this falsehood, this lie Tamehameha had asked young Tolamy to carry to Atooie. Tolamy knew it wasn't true. King Kaumuualii's son had been killed years ago. Why persist with it? What good would such a lie do except to enrage King Kaumuualii? Recant, sir. A small thing, sir, after all. If Tolamy were willing to recant in a short speech to the natives in their own tongue—why, then, explained Dr. Scheffer—why, then, sir, all pain and trouble were ended. An accommodation could be quickly reached. He would have Tolamy at once transported to the fort. The best of attention. Opium tablets to allay the pain. Miss Susan to nurse him if he wished— The silvery eyes seemed to expand and fill the whole room and the voice was whispering and soft, a friend's voice. About the ship, now; about the Clymestre . . .

"What do you say to sixty thousand Russian eagles, gold eagles, sir? Can we come to an accommodation at that price for your ship's cargo and her use until spring? I can afford to be generous. Seventy-five thousand in gold, ship harmed or not. Now, come. Confess Prince George is dead. Say so to the natives like an honest man. In fifteen minutes I will have you reunited with Miss Susan. Come, sir," said Scheffer urgently. "If you will not trust me, at least you will trust Miss Susan? She asks you through me to cease such stupid resistance and to recant."

Scheffer had overreached himself. Susan would be the last person to recant or to ask anyone else to. Jeffery shook his head. "No."

Undisturbed, Dr. Scheffer rose. He called to the aliis, who bound Jeffrey tighter than before. Then Scheffer stuck his pipe between his teeth and departed.

Jeffery was left alone for three or four days—he was not certain how many days had gone by but he knew too many had passed to expect help from Tony Allan. Either Tony had attempted to descend into the gorge, had been caught or perhaps killed, or he was trying to make his way across the headlands west of Atooie.

Jeffery had a sense of complete failure. He had not been able to convince the king. He did not even know what had become of Sam. When he had inquired and had inquired again, the aliis invariably refused to answer.

Susan? In his mind he lived over again the moments with her in the dusty hot shadows of the pavilion by the river. He saw her face, her wide forehead and shadowy eyes, and he seemed to feel her hands slowly lift and gradually press more firmly. He had been very certain of succeeding with Kaumuualii and quickly returning with her to Honoruru for Cap Adams to marry them at sea. Ben dead! Susan taken! If only he could go to her.

It would be very easy to recant. She had believed him to be a rake and still could love him, but if ever she found he was a weakling, with no backbone to resist, he was quite certain Ben Partridge's daughter would lose all regard for him . . .

That night Jeffery was awake when Scheffer once more came to him. Solicitously, as to a man sick in mind as well as in body, Scheffer renewed his promise. Eighty thousand in gold Russian eagles, all paid, no strings, the instant Captain Tolamy entered the fort. It was a fortune! What other young man could hope to gain so much by ten years' adventuring of his ship in all the far places of the world?

He spoke easily and gently, but Jeffery damned him. Scheffer laughed and filled his big pipe bowl with tobacco. Then he said, not quite as easily as before, "Between man and man, Tolamy, you disappoint me."

There came to Jeffery, in his despair, a vision of a shaky old man, an old man with parrot eyes. John Young had said to offer Scheffer Tamehameha's maru—the king's amnesty. He had said it was a way of weakening an enemy. Besides, it would prevent Scheffer from being a martyr to the Russians. It was an old man's wisdom, Jeffery had decided. What would Sam say, Sam who was burning to kill Scheffer? Well, where was Sam now? Where were they all? Where was Tony Allan? Where was Susan? John Young had said King Tamehameha hadn't conquered the archipelago by driving all his enemies into rats' holes for them one by one to fight to the death. Let your enemy escape? It would change the triumph of victory to dust. But where was victory in this mean hut?

Then in desperation Jeffery spoke, and Dr. Scheffer listened and the eyes became like purest silver.

"You are a young fool," he said sharply when Jeffery had finished. "Do I need Tamehameha's maru when in three months to six months he will be begging his old life from me?" The voice thickened, the big pale head bent, and he said, very quickly, all in a breath, like a man starting to run, "Now listen to me, unless you recant—in one hour you will be taken to the ceremonial rock across the river. You know what is to be done to you, sir? Three times—three times you will be asked to recant your lie, your ferocious lie . . ." the voice went trailing off.

The silvery eyes peered at Jeffery's battered face, apparently seeing something which Jeffery was unaware of possessing. "I have no more arguments to persuade you, young man," said Scheffer, and he pulled at his sleeve. He drew out the little derringer hidden up there against his flesh. In the same motion, he had it cocked and was shoving it at Jeffery.

Perhaps it was all a put-up job between Scheffer and King Kaumuualii—Jeffery never did know; he never could decide. But the king was peering through the kapa cloth at the entrance; and in he came, majestic and huge in his royal cloak of feathers.

Like lightning, the king knocked away the derringer as Scheffer pulled the trigger. Put-up job or not, it was close, too close. The explosion filled the hut. Jeffery jerked and fell back, burnt powder streaking his hand like fire. He looked around and saw where the bullet had splintered one of the poles supporting the wall. Scheffer's face began folding over and over upon itself, becoming round

and solid and benevolent, and he stuck the smoking derringer into
his jacket pocket with one hand.

"Young man—at least I have attempted to give you a quick
death. It is not my fault I failed. I am sorry for you. Good night,
sir."

The aliis entered and Jeffery struggled with them. He fought
all the time it took them to carry him down to the river and
transport him by raft to the other bank. When he was there, by
the light of flares, they managed to tie thick ropes of vines around
his waist. Four aliis seized the end of each vine, holding the lines
tight, Jeffrey in the middle. Priests gathered, chanting. Other aliis
pricked Jeffrey with stone- and bone-tipped spears, prodding him
upwards.

---

28. Jeffery was pulled and prodded up a winding trail
which ascended to the top of the cliffs above the
west bank of the river. In the sifting light he saw the bulky shape
of Kaumuualii ahead of him, surrounded by priests and warriors.
Behind him trailed a howling mob, torches flaming and twinkling
redly in the marshes.

Kaumuualii called a command. A priest threw up his arms. There
was a scurrying, while warriors rushed upwards. Jeffery was halted.
Dazedly, he watched a dozen warriors come down from the higher
rocks, a few among them bearing in their arms a long limp object,
like lengths of reeds bound together. They threw this at Jeffery's
feet and lifted burning torches to see his face. Jeffery was looking
down at all that remained of Tony Allan. Tony's black head was
smashed in. A broken spear quivered like a gigantic thorn from his
crushed chest. He was not newly dead, for the blood was like rust
on the black skin.

The warriors waited and were disappointed. They kicked the
body and stuck spears through it. Jeffery paid Tony the only honor
of which he was capable at the moment, forcing something like a
silent laugh as if to inform the warriors he thought they were fools

for further mutilating a body past feeling anything more of earth and air and water.

With more cries, Jeffery was hauled to the top of the cliff, where he was held by spears against his chest. Behind him, Tony Allan's body was roughly shoved off the cliff. Tony was gone, Jeffery thought. Goodbye, Tony. Aroha! Aroha nui!

Jeffery felt the spears prick him harder. A tattooed warrior had advanced with a long spear, lowering it until the stone point exactly touched Jeffery's navel. King Kaumuualii stepped forth. He was frowning and his face was red as brick in the flares. He spoke to the warrior who pushed the spear at Jeffery, forcing him a step back. Jeffery looked around and found himself upon a face of rock whose surface sloped gradually, then slanted rapidly until it shelved off into nothingness.

Warriors filed down on either side, their spears pointed to prevent him from breaking away. Once more he felt himself prodded by the spears as Kaumuualii advanced to question him. Idly, Jeffery noticed a groove in the rock, off toward the left, with worn lines diagonally cut away from it like the head of an arrow. It was a little like a dream, Tony gone, the wind blowing in from the sea on Jeffery's skin, the stone point of spear pricking him.

Kaumuualii paused. There came a silence. He asked if Tolamy would admit it was a lie conceived by Tamehameha that the prince lived. When Jeffery did not answer, the spear thrust him more vigorously.

During the silence Jeffery had been staring at the ancient mark cut in the rock. He saw the mark was an arrow which pointed to the sea. A memory stirred in Jeffery's mind. Susan had told Tony to make a rendezvous at the ceremonial rock above the mouth of Whymea River. She had called it Arrow Rock. He had a clear poignant image in his mind of her face that afternoon, anxiously lifting up to Tony's black face. He tried desperately to get his wits together. Arrow Rock? Yes, there was a whole flowing in his mind. He had forgotten he had known about Arrow Rock long before Susan had mentioned it. He started; the pressure of the spear in his flesh had become sharper.

A second time Kaumuualii spoke in Jeffery's language. "You say lie." The stone spear dug harder into Jeffery. He looked down and he saw the point cutting into his flesh. He wanted to step back and he brought himself up short. Except for the curving space of rock behind him, everything ended. After four or five backward steps, down he would go, tumbling over and over again to smash against the base of the cliff.

Kaumuualii's voice lifted a third time. In the island language he told Jeffery not to refuse or it would cost him his life. He had brought Tolamy here because this rock had a special meaning for Kaumuualii. If he persisted in this lie it was fitting for him to lose his life on this spot.

Jeffery braced himself. He took breath. He said he knew why he had been brought here. "You and your son used to come here!" he pointed toward the arrow cut in the rock. "That's the arrow Captain Cook cut or his men cut for him when they first landed."

"Tamehameha tell you!"

"No, your son told me. George Hoomehoome described this rock."

"You lie. Tamehameha tell you."

The morning sun had climbed above the eastern rim of mountains, illuminating Kaumuualii's tall, square figure, the red light on the broad face, the bamboo amulet dark against the glistening skin.

"Your son told me of you bringing him here as a child." Jeffery's voice was bitter. "I could have told you when you first questioned me after we arrived if you had given me the chance. But I was knocked on the head. I couldn't think. That amulet you're wearing!" He flung out his hand. "By God, I remember George told me how he ran off with that amulet of yours. He even opened it to find what was in it and you beat him. He never forgot. You've got a lock of Captain Vancouver's hair stuffed in it . . . Now, if I'm going to be pushed off this rock, at least I'll have you with me!"

Jeffery had twisted, the stone spear searing along his side. He leaped at Kaumuualii and a warrior knocked him away. He fell and rolled and nearly did go over the rock—and would have, too, if Kaumuualii had not jumped forward, snatching him by an arm and hauling him back. Kaumuualii lifted him up and hugged him. He called, "Aikane! Aikane!"—his friend—and began weeping while all the crowd gathered around.

They carried Jeffery down the path and across the river to a pavilion where Kaumuualii called to his kahunas and women, ordering them to wash Jeffery and to care for him tenderly.

Soon Sam was brought in. When Jeffery told him what had happened, Sam said heavily, "We'll git Tony buried proper on high ground, Jeff. Tony knew what risks he was taking. I figgered both you and Tony was dead. Why didn't you tell the king about that damned arrow and the amulet when you first saw him?"

"That smash on the head dazed me, Sam. I still don't know very much of what I said. I had heard Kaumuualii say Ben was dead. Susan had crumpled. And I'd got a smash on the head."

Sam observed him. "They busted your nose, didn't they? You ain't ever going to look the same again, Jeff, even after your nose gits down to normal." Then he asked, "You didn't know Ben Partridge was dead when you left Atooie?"

"My God, no!"

"I was jist asking. Kaumuualii told Susan he sent word of her father's death back to the south by that chief he let go. Don't you remember?"

Until now, Jeffery had not remembered. "Kaumuualii must have lied. John Young told me the chief had returned with the dead chiefess. But Young never mentioned anything of Ben dying."

"Maybe Tamehameha told him not to. Suppose Tamehameha figgered it was important for Susan to lead you from the Na Pali because she knew more about Atooie than any chiefs he had? If Susan knew her old man was dead, would she've been so eager to go?" Sam spit. "A woman don't make no more difference to that old bastard at Kailua than a man. He used her like he'd use anybody to help him save his damn islands. So he told Young to keep his mouth shut and Young did. You remember how jumpy and worried Young was all that time?"

Jeffery had a convulsion of all his nerves. He could forgive Tamehameha for using him but he could never forgive him for using Susan.

Sam hauled himself to his feet, painfully rubbing with a circular motion at the old wound Scheffer had given him in his belly. "Where's Susan? You haven't said. She's not—"

"She's alive. But Scheffer's holding her in the fort. We've got to get her out, somehow."

"Damn if we won't," Sam said, laying his hands on Jeffery's shoulders. "We ain't licked. She and you made up?"

Jeffery nodded.

"We'll git back, Jeff."

"I'll want you beside us when we're married if ever we do return to Honoruru."

"I'll stand behind you both even if I git so drunk from celebrating," Sam promised, "somebody's got to be behind me . . ."

King Kaumuualii called a meeting of his chiefs, sending for Jeffery. Kaumuualii spoke first. He announced he was not as convinced as he had been that his son had been killed years ago by a Yankee sea captain. He feared he had been badly deceived by the Russians. He asked Jeffery to come forward before the assembly; and now Jeffery said all he should have said the first time and finished by promising that Prince George Hoomehoome was being returned to the islands as soon as a ship could bring him.

He gave them, finally, Tamehameha's offer. If King Kaumuualii would hold his warriors neutral during the invasion, as soon as the Russians were driven off the island the island would be placed once again under King Kaumuualii in vassalship to Tamehameha, the rights going to Prince George upon the king's death. Jeffery was led back to the pavilion, where food was given Sam and him, guards still at the door. The king would send them his answer.

Toward evening King Kaumuualii came, himself, to announce a decision had been reached. His warriors would attack the fort under his leadership if Scheffer refused to withdraw. His chiefs and priests, as well as himself, were strongly opposed to accepting help from Tamehameha. If Tamehameha's warriors landed, they were afraid Tamehameha's warriors would remain.

They would attempt the fight themselves. A message to this effect already had been dispatched by sailing canoe to Kailua. If the king failed and was killed, in return he asked Tamehameha to remember his promise and to restore the island to Prince George.

Jeffery stood in the shadowy glare of the torches and argued, thinking of that strong fort and wondering how Kaumuualii ever expected to conquer it with only three thousand men. He said Tamehameha's ten thousand warriors joined with Kaumuualii's forces might have a fair chance against the fort's cannons and muskets. To throw three thousand warriors against such a force would mean sacrificing them all.

King Kaumuualii's face got an ugly stubborn look on it. He angrily gripped his koa-wood war club and grunted that the decision was made. Then suddenly his face relaxed and he smiled and laid his hand on Jeffery's shoulder. "Much better take island from Russ'ans," he said. "Russ'ans go. Someday my son here. Someday my son fight son of Tamehameha. Someday my son be king all islands."

Later Sam said thoughtfully, "It might happen yet, Jeff. That Prince Riho-Riho ain't much account. If George is strong and has got brains like you say, one of these days when he gits here and rules this island, he ain't going to stand for that fat jackass telling him what to say."

All during the afternoon warriors had established lines around the fort, killing two Kodiaks who had ventured forth to trade with native women. Scheffer, however, had managed to launch a canoe to one of his ships, informing them to stand by and expect trouble; and his cannons were charged and run out, the ships lifting anchor and sailing a mile from the sand bar.

That evening Jeffery helped Kaumuualii prepare a manifesto to be sent to the Russians. It gave Scheffer forty-eight hours to clear out from the island with all his men. It closed with a declaration that, because certain promises had been obtained from H.M. King George Kaumuualii by fraud and deceit, here and now, as of this day, January 14, 1817, these promises were revoked; and all possessions of the said king were to be returned to him, to be held by him, and to be passed on to his lawful heir, Prince George Kaumuualii II, as a dependency of Tamehameha. King Kaumuualii had refused to grant the "H.M." before Tamehameha's name, but Jeffery was indifferent. It was like gall and wormwood whenever he was reminded of how callously Tamehameha had used Susan and himself. He had looked upon Tamehameha as an old hero. His disillusionment was complete.

Along with the manifesto, Jeffery wrote a dispatch to Scheffer, which Kaumuualii signed, asking that Miss Susan Partridge be released from the fort immediately.

Sam and Jeffery had their arms and ammunition restored to

them. Jeffery got back Tony's musket. Bamboo drums beat well into the night, runners going and coming. The priests—the poe-kilo-kahunas, as they were called—those skilled in divining—slaughtered pigs and chickens all during that first night, examining their entrails for signs and predictions. By midnight the older men and women and all the children were traveling north up the river, away from the fort toward places of refuge.

The manifesto and letter had been carried to the fort by an old alii, accompanied by a guard of ten more aliis, all in their feather cloaks, wearing helmets either of gourds or of wickerwork covered with feathers. Some time after midnight, Scheffer replied to the manifesto, sending a smart young Russian lieutenant with a formal invitation to Kaumuualii to meet Scheffer tomorrow at dawn on board the *Ilmen* for a discussion. The implication was that Scheffer was prepared to withdraw gracefully, according to the command, if Kaumuualii was still dissatisfied after the shipboard meeting.

Sam said, "I don't think much of that offer. Suppose Scheffer tries to kidnap Kaumuualii?"

The idea already had occurred to the older priests, who protested at once, and Kaumuualii told the young lieutenant he refused to go near the ship for any discussion. The Russian lieutenant shrugged, unconcerned. He was convinced these heathen would have no chance to storm the fort. He answered that Scheffer refused to hold a parley outside the fort or away from one of the ships.

"He go or we make war," said the king.

The young lieutenant was certainly no more than a year or so older than Jeffery. He smiled in a tranquil, impudent fashion and said a war would not last very long against Russian cannons and muskets, would it? He clicked his heels, preparing to depart.

Jeffery said, "If you please? You have said nothing of Miss Partridge. We asked for her release."

The young lieutenant answered that Mr. Scheffer had decided it was much safer for Miss Partridge to remain inside the fort until this trouble was put down.

Jeffery felt choked. The lieutenant had shrugged. What could he do? He had scarcely veiled his contempt for these two white men here who were siding with the savages against their own kind.

Jeffery perceived it would merely amuse the lieutenant if he lost his head and broke into futile rage. With cold politeness he said,

"Will you give Miss Partridge a message from Captain Crowell and myself?"

"It is not permitted." The lieutenant turned his back to Jeffery and asked Kaumuualii, "One goes now, yes?"

Jeffery felt Sam's hard hand gripping his arm, warning him to hold on to himself.

For the rest of the hours of the night, Kaumuualii remained in the big stone temple at the north of the village. Sam and Jeffery sat with the chiefs hearing the increasing tumult of warriors arriving from nearby hamlets.

Before dawn, Scheffer's cannons started systematically pounding the village into shambles. Already, Kaumuualii had departed from his temple toward an encampment fixed two miles up the river, and the remaining warriors and chiefs were to follow along with the commoners left in the village. As Sam and Jeffery stumbled out in the half-darkness, seeing a red blaze down by the river, the crashes of cannon were like thunder.

Three hundred warriors had formed in a phalanx—a close-ordered marching formation known as a makawalu, comparable to a regiment. This makawalu of warriors marched down the incline in solid style, ranks holding even when a spent cannon ball slammed whirring over their heads like a great bee to crash into a banana tree.

The river road was encumbered by hundreds of commoners carrying on their shoulders calabashes hastily stuffed with cloth and food, saved from their ruined or burning huts. By midmorning they had arrived at a large meadow or plain formed by a bend of the river which was called "Ta'aiu."

A pavilion had been erected in the center of the meadow for King Kaumuualii with smaller pavilions of leaves and poles around it for his principal chiefs and priests, and hundreds of huts and lean-tos were hastily being raised to hold the warriors and camp followers streaming in from all over the island. Jeffery had little time at first to see anything of the encampment, because as soon as he arrived with Sam, they were summoned to the king's pavilion. Here were gathered twoscore of the high-ranking aliis and priests.

The king said they had been discussing a plan of attack. His warriors were in want of muskets and pistols, having no more than sixteen such weapons altogether—gifts from the Russians—with not enough powder to last for more than three or four shots each. He questioned Jeffery, who said that Sam and he had sufficient powder and shot with them to manage for three or four hundred rounds each, perhaps more.

The king and his advisers had more knowledge of the fort than Jeffery had thought. On the ground the king scratched a rough plan of the fort—the five points of the half-star pointing toward the sea, and the four angles of the half-octagon facing the land side. The Whymea River ran from north to south past the fort toward the sand bar, and the channels through the sand bar to the sea. Parallel to the river ran the east walls of the gorge. These walls turned at an angle to go eastward, and the angle or flank of turning was fifty to sixty rods away from the fort. Lacking firearms, the king proposed to send one makawalu of slingshot warriors upon the cliff heights overlooking the fort, giving orders to these men to try to kill or knock out the men at the cannons. He asked if Jeffery and his friend would be willing to join this makawalu and aid them by trying to shoot the cannoneers just before an attack was launched.

Jeffery had Susan constantly in his mind. If Sam and he were stuck high on those cliffs and a breach was made in the fort, there would be little opportunity to get down in time to join the fighting inside the fort. In his mind, Jeffery still had the memory of the trading house of wood which had been erected well up from the river, not far from the fort. You could get that far, he decided, with reasonable safety, using the trading house as protection from the cannon and musket shots. It would be closer, too, and if you dug in there and shot from the trading post and had any luck at all you might be able to kill off or badly harass the gunners manning the dozen or so cannons on that side. He could not conceive of how three thousand natives could manage to smash through the fort's entrance or climb the walls, but if any of them did succeed, he considered he would be close enough to the fighting to go on in with them to hunt for Susan.

He spoke up then; and the king listened to him. The king outlined his plan of the campaign and the chiefs discussed it and they debated where the haoles ought to be stationed, some wanting the two men on the cliffs, others saying the two could better be used along with the makawalu of five hundred men already detailed to creep along the riverbank and rush the fort from the scanty protection of the trading house.

They squatted and smoked their pipes and argued and debated and scratched more plans on the earth and Sam listened and by and by he offered his advice; and it was good advice. The chiefs heard him out. He argued for Jeffery's idea of having the two of them trying to dig in somewhere near the trading post and sniping at the gunners from there. Before going to sleep that night, they learned that the attack was scheduled for Thursday, two days away.

Sam and Jeffery had their own hut, not far from the king's pavilion. They could look out through the slanting entrance and see the hundreds of campfires still burning, hearing the voices, the cries, the wailing notes of priests, and now and then sharp commands from distant sentinels as more warriors arrived from the mountains.

That night Jeffery tossed restlessly. He could not adjust himself to how everything had frayed miserably away from what he had expected. Although he could tell himself he had succeeded in some measure with the mission upon which Tamehameha had sent him, there was no satisfaction to be gained from it. Rather, it was all to the contrary. Susan's father had died. Tamehameha had coldly sacrificed Susan. She was captured. Tony had been killed through a miserable and needless misunderstanding. The Russians and their Kodiaks were safely within a fort which Scheffer would have built to be impregnable against Stone Age weapons.

Jeffery happened to remember once thinking of how he would return to America in a small blaze of glory. Perhaps Mr. Monroe would offer him a medal after being privately prompted by Congressman Jonathan Perkins. He felt a taste of dregs in his mouth. Would a medal, a handshake, a small blaze of glory bring Susan's father to her and return Tony Allan to the cordage yard?

It was as if each day, each week, Jeffery were receiving a new education which was nothing like the education he had received in Philadelphia. It seemed suddenly to Jeffery it would be far more satisfactory to dominate that old heathen, King Tamehameha, just once than to have any of the small blaze of glory which quite possibly would be awaiting him at home if by inconceivable chance the Russians were overturned in the Pacific . . .

The next morning, after seeing to their own weapons and using up all their loose powder and shot in making more paper twists, Sam and Jeffery started on a tour of the camp. At one end were the mountain men from the west and central parts of the island, smaller and hairier than the big warriors who lived along the coast. Two makawalus—regiments of about five hundred each—were camped along the river, the men armed primarily with their slingshots, short javelins and stone knives or clubs. South along the meadow was the principal body of warriors, two thousand perhaps, although it was hard for Jeffery to estimate the exact number.

Of this number, at least half were armed with the tall spear—the pololu—the vaulting and thrusting spear. It was made of the hardest wood, pointed with stone or barbed with goat's horn; and for nearly half an hour Jeffery watched a dozen or so warriors running toward a mound of brush nearly fifteen feet high and then suddenly pitching the point into the ground and flying up over the obstacle like birds.

Sam's eyes were gleaming. "Won't that maybe surprise them Russians?"

Kapa pennants hung from spears stuck in the ground before the larger shelters for chiefs. During the day hundreds of younger women flocked into the camp, caught by the excitement. Now and then Jeffery saw a wailing makaainana being led through the hundreds of huts, a rope tied around the man's waist, his ears bloody from being split as punishment for trying to evade the war summons.

That afternoon Sam and Jeffery were called to the king's pavilion, where they met the alii in charge of the fourth makawalu, a thousand men altogether, who had been assigned to attack the fort from the river after a first feint against the ships and a second against the sea walls of the fort had been ordered.

This alii carried a vaulting spear in one hand and from his middle hung a fearful sort of weapon between a spear and a club, something of the order of an ancient halbert. He towered above Sam by a good head. This chief, Kewalo, would take the foreigners with him in the canoes of his regiment down the river. In effect, then, Jeffery found himself detailed as one of two snipers in a regiment of spearmen.

By sundown King Kaumuualii had repeated orders and instructions to the five principal commanders—actually, each one had the native title of "Kalaimoku," which placed them in rank above the other aliis. Each commander knew what his regiment was to do before or by dawn tomorrow. The fourth regiment, commanded by Kewalo, had the largest number of men, a thousand at least, with another hundred artisans to carry the battering rams in the attempt to make a breach through the fort's gates. The first regiment of slingshot skirmishers amounted to about five hundred. The second regiment of skirmishers, who were expected to descend the south walls of the cliff and crawl along the beach and attack the fort from the sea with slings and javelins and grapples, numbered five hundred. The third regiment of fishermen, who were expected to deploy in their canoes through the sandbank and cause a diversion with the ships, also numbered half a thousand. The fifth regiment to be held in reserve by the village, composed of spearmen, had a thousand men.

The island was not large, and when Jeffery thought about it, it seemed to him the king had done magnificently well to have brought well-nigh four thousand men to this single camp in less than forty-eight hours, moreover, to have them come stocked with arms and provisions for combat. He doubted if Tamehameha could have done any better.

Jeffery's respect had increased for this blunt, brick-faced king whose English was spoken so pompously and so ludicrously. In the native language, King Kaumuualii spoke to the point, drawing diagrams on the ground with a pointed spear for each commander to perceive his position at the time of attack on the morrow. It was solemn and earnest business for them all. Each commander restated his orders. Darkness having come, Kaumuualii said farewell to his five commanders and to Sam and Jeffery; and with his chief priests left his pavilion.

The first regiment of slingshot men already had broken camp and now were marching to the heights. Kaumuualii and his priests planned to accompany the first regiment and by morning be hidden well above the fort. Chief Kewalo told the two haoles to pick up their weapons and ammunition and come along with him to the east side of the meadow where his pavilion was pitched. As Jeffery marched behind Kewalo in the rainy darkness, he heard the sounds of another company of warriors breaking camp. Kewalo said that

248 THE MISSION OF JEFFERY TOLAMY

was the second regiment of skirmishers, preparing also to mount
the cliffs. They would go on in the night and descend the heights
south of the fort, where they were to take positions to attack when
the shell horns sounded at dawn.

---

29. Sleep escaped him. During the night hours Jeffery had
a sense of the whole camp throbbing and murmur-
ing. He heard voices, cries, and often the tramp of feet going by in
the darkness. A cold mist blew down from the mountains. Kewalo
had said a mist would be even better than rain.

Jeffery started up when from outside the pavilion a lesser alii
sounded piercing blasts on a shell horn, the blasts being taken up
by other horns throughout the south and east ends of the meadow.
Sam rose, stretched, and stepped out against the red light of a
torch. More torches flickered. Kewalo came down through a
shadowy line of men, a huge helmet of feathers upon his head. He
said the haoles were to go with him in his canoe and turned and
shouted an order to meet at the riverbank and form there by the
canoes.

Jeffery was crowded well forward into Kewalo's big dugout, Sam
behind him. Twenty men paddled, going softly now; and for at
least an hour they floated along the river, the mist thick.

Somewhere ahead of him, he knew, must be another flotilla of
dugouts belonging to the regiment of fishermen who were charged
with passing by the fort and through the sandbank's channels to
the sea. Behind him, at least sixty more dugouts followed, each one
bearing from twenty to thirty spearmen. Jeffery had never been in
a battle.

He had thought of a battle as something diagramed on a map, all
the details there, one movement and another like chessmen advancing and retreating. In this thick night fog, while floating upon
an invisible river, he had a sense of being lost. Everything was
hurtling away from him. He had no knowledge of what was taking
place or what was going to take place.

Someone in the prow, Kewalo perhaps, passed word back to the men at the paddles. There came a grating as the dugout slid upwards upon sand. Jeffery started—grasping at his musket. Sam whispered, "Jist go easy. Lay low a few yards ahead on the beach."

"Where's the fort?"

"Somewhere beyond. Do like I say."

Jeffery got his feet upon the sand. He had an impression of men floating around him, creeping forward, disappearing in the wreathing darkness. The smell here was different—it was a sea smell. When he listened he heard the faint thunder of surf. He advanced a yard or so and stopped; it was like being lost; he was remote, detached. He jumped when someone touched him. It was Sam. "Kewalo says for us to wait here till they git the signal."

He lay in the sand, Sam crawling ahead a little way. Sam returned and whispered to move on forward. It was safer there. Jeffery crawled forward. The river was at low water with the sandy beach fairly flat on each side of it and a higher embankment on beyond. With Sam he crouched below this embankment and did as Sam did, blowing sand from the lock of his musket. His hands and fingers somehow had become sticky with moisture.

He heard Sam's whisper, "There's the fort."

Jeffery still failed to perceive anything in the darkness. Sam whispered Scheffer was being smart. Scheffer must be ready for an attack; he wasn't showing any lights inside the fort to blind his gunners.

As he waited Jeffery was reminded of Susan, who would also be waiting somewhere inside those walls. Perhaps her apprehension would be even greater than his because she could not know what was gathering. But she would be too proud, he was certain, to reveal her fears.

Jeffery wanted to be hard and cool. But the time dragged. Nothing happened.

He looked to right and left. As salmon-grayness infused the blackness, he could perceive shapes of men gradually forming and becoming substantial. Exactly as he was doing, they were crouching under the protection of the embankment. Now, a slow dawning began.

Not far from Jeffery a spearman lifted his hideous head and showed his teeth in what was meant for a reassuring grimace. At the warrior's side lay his long vaulting spear, ready to be grasped. His left hand held a club to which a heavy stone was lobbed. From his neck dangled a strangling cord. Thrust in his loincloth was a wooden dagger edged with shark teeth.

Now the light increased and the fort began to reveal itself, slowly, one projection of wall and then another, like prows of ships cleaving through the morning mist. A flash of light briefly flickered from the walls. Then what might have been a man's head lifted and disappeared.

The trading house took on shape and pattern. It was a blockhouse of koa logs with the slanting roof, twenty feet square perhaps, formidable by itself in that early light. Not far from his right he saw a sort of pathway leading up the embankment and to the trading house—and then on, going to the great dark gate beyond. He remembered that morning months ago when he and the Pennsylvanians from the Clymestre had been taken up that same pathway. Susan must have been taken through those gates, too. The gates were narrow and tall, at least four feet thick of solid koa, protected on each side by shooting-slits through the stone walls of the fort.

He tried to sight around to see where the artisans were stationed with their battering rams and the mist wreathed in and out with the sea breeze and he could perceive nothing of them. He shivered.

Where were they? Suppose they were lost? He found he was shaking as with a fever. The light seemed to be brighter. Of a sudden, Sam had lifted. "Listen!"

"What is it?" asked Jeffery, hearing his whisper pitched too high.

A flaming arrow streaked high in the air from the cliffs to the east of the fort, and down into the mist. He heard something which at first he thought was thunder. The sound came from the sea. Sam muttered, "There they go!" The cannons thumped once, twice, then again and again from ships invisible beyond the sand bars. The canoemen must be engaging the ships. He tried to stand to see better. Sam calmly pulled him down.

Beyond the banks, scores of swift canoes had put out into the fog and were attacking the ships but Jeffery could not see how the attack was going nor had he any notion of what was happening. He could hear only the rumble of cannons.

Then in a minute or five minutes, time as time beginning to have no meaning, the fort's cannons sounded, and to his ears came a shrill faint shouting, like children's cries, with rattling clacks of ragged musket shots from the fort. The muskets steadied, beginning to volley regularly.

The sea side of the fort had been rushed by the skirmishers according to the schedule. Now dawn came more brightly. As the rising sun changed the mist into transparent red, the outline of the fort became crimson, with the red rock walls of the cliffs rising behind. High above, scarcely visible, was a rustling, a movement like wind blowing across the tops of tufted grass, where the first regiment of slingshot men were raining stones into the fort. A fire spear flashed, another, another, a hundred of them, flaring down, vanishing in mist, appearing again, red and bright like streaks of lightning, plunging directly down and vanishing a final time inside the fort. The childish faraway cries along the sea walls of the fort increased where some of the skirmishers must have managed to grapple the walls with bent bamboo hooks and were attempting to climb upwards. The sound of muskets was louder.

The action began losing shape for Jeffery, time breaking into scattered intervals. Sam again held him down. "Keep cool, will you?" He couldn't keep cool. His heart was pounding like those cannons. Why didn't they charge? What were they waiting for?

Then from out at sea came a larger sound, a puffing and a tearing, followed by a kind of thud which echoed and re-echoed. There was a yellow brightness in the sea mist. The yellow brightness turned to redness. A mile off the river's mouth a ship was aflame.

Sam raised his head. "My God, Jeff, ain't that the *Clymestre?* Damn them Russians. God *damn* them! They've let the heathens git my ship afire."

A sound broke over Jeffery's head like a swift flock of birds in flight. Instantly afterwards, ten yards from him, at the river's edge, a dugout leaped crazily and shattered into pieces. Sam and Jeffery fell flat. They heard a thundering noise from the fort's cannons which had started firing on this side. Next, as if in echo, was a single concussion from far away as the *Clymestre's* powder magazine was touched off. Jeffery felt the air shake.

In the following instant of silence, Jeffery looked at Sam, whose leather face grimaced with rage and grief. "Sam, we'll make them pay for it. Mr. Monroe can demand an indemnity."

"Indemnity? Them bastards! They steal my ship and try to use it 'gainst us. Those sons of bitches. I'll git Scheffer. I'll git an indemnity from him. By God, you'll see. My own ship!"

Sam's face hardened. Shell horns began blowing around them, and Sam touched Jeffery, signaling for him to get up. To the right and left of Jeffery, spearmen were leaping up the embankment, shrieking, running straight toward the fort. Jeffery followed with Sam, who suddenly dropped, Jeffery doing the same. Sam had to shout for Jeffery to hear.

"Crawl for the trading house. Take the right corner!"

Jeffery did as he ordered, separating from Sam. The noise was deafening. He crawled to the right-hand side of the trading house, falling flat on his belly and poking his musket barrel toward the fort's gates. He estimated the distance to be two hundred yards. He fired. He doubted if he had hit any of the Kodiaks firing back from above the wooden gates. He reloaded. Dust and smoke swirled up thickly, hiding the gates from him. He had to wait for the air to clear. To his right, from the river's banks, had swarmed hundreds of men. Their shapes flowed past Jeffery in the dust and smoke. They had charged with two forty-foot koa trunks as battering rams. A cannon flashed from above, the sound following after the flash. Men screamed in pain as grapeshot cut them down.

Jeffery saw a gunner up there who had swung out to swab at the cannon. He fired. The gunner swung back behind the walls. Jeffery had shot his second shot too low. He reached into his pouch for another powder twist, biting the paper with his teeth. Off to the other side of the trading house Sam had knelt when Jeffery looked over his shoulder anxiously to see how Sam was making out. Sam's musket was on the ground. Sam fired one pistol and a second.

He crawled to Jeffery, dragging his musket with one hand. He squatted while he reloaded. "I can't git that bastard."

"I've missed him twice."

The Kodiaks had run along the earthen walls, angling north of the gates, firing short-bore muskets down into the spearmen. Shell horns blew more weakly. The spearmen had rallied, again trying to batter down the fort's gate with the two koa-wood trunks. The twelve-pounder from the point of stone ramp thumped loudly. Sam raised a pistol, aimed, and fired when one of the Kodiaks swabbed at the cannon. He swore. "Them spearmen can't take much more grapeshot."

Jeffery took aim and missed a third time. There was only an instant when the Kodiaks had risen to swab out the cannon. Now Sam had fired. Jeffery reloaded. The Kodiaks manning the nearest twelve-pounder were too well sheltered by the walls. Jeffery wriggled forward, holding his aim. It had been a mistake to select the trading house as a shelter for sniping. Kewalo's spearmen were not receiving the assistance they needed. The twelve-pounder flashed and thumped. Through the smoke, Jeffery saw spearmen falling. He waited. Now!

He heard Sam exclaim, "You got him!"

But as soon as the nearest twelve-pounder was silenced, a second from the next ramp or point of the fort was swung around hastily. The first shot smashed into the side of the trading house. Jeffery was stunned. Burning wood showered around him.

The shell horns screamed. Men were streaming away from the fort, some staggering. Somewhere in the smoky dust Kewalo was shouting to re-form, but the ranks had broken.

Another blast of grapeshot ripped through the trees south of the burning trading house. The dry wood of the trading house walls crackled and blazed. Flames and smoke hid them from the fort. Sam shouted, "We better git out of here while we can."

They crawled to the embankment, their going hidden from the fort by the blazing trading house. Smoke and mist drifted heavily, with spurts of flame flashing at intervals when the fort's cannons sounded. The fourth regiment of spearmen had dug down behind the embankment, nursing their wounds, the more seriously injured warriors being dragged to canoes and taken up the river by women.

Despairingly, Jeffery demanded, "Are we licked already?"

"I don't know any more than you do."

"Are they getting ready to retreat?"

"Nobody close to action ever knows nothing of what's happening. We'll jist sit tight here and wait for orders."

After a time a runner came crawling along the sandy slopes, hunting for the haoles. He said Kewalo was asking for them. Kewalo's quarters had been established half a mile north along the river, well out of range of musket and cannon grapeshot from the fort.

When they arrived at Kewalo's headquarters, they found Kewalo waiting for them. He had been shot above the ankle of his left leg.

He was sitting on a koa log, his leg bandaged and propped in front of him. When Jeffery inquired, Kewalo was contemptuous of his injury. Kewalo quickly explained. He had been expecting orders from King Kaumuualii to regroup and attack again. He had wanted the two haoles to be prepared. However, when orders had arrived from the king, Kewalo had merely been instructed to have his regiment stand fast and repel any sortie from the fort. The two haoles were to remain here at headquarters and eat and rest themselves until the king decided how next to use them.

The sun was high in the sky. It was difficult for Jeffery to realize that time had gone so quickly. It was already past noon. Only a few minutes ago, it seemed to him, the spearmen had been charging the fort's gates. The camp servants brought food and there was an unexpected lull for Jeffery. Everything became very ordinary. Warriors loafed under the palms, ate, sharpened their spears, and a few found women for themselves.

The lull ended when Kewalo limped from his pavilion to join Sam and Jeffery. Kewalo was not as discouraged as might be expected. He informed them that the feint this morning, by the third regiment, against the Russians' ships, had been successful. One ship was destroyed. A second was severely damaged. Nearly half the canoes had returned. Kewalo believed at least fifty or a hundred more men of the third regiment were hiding out on the sand bars, waiting to come ashore at night. The second regiment of skirmishers, though, had been badly hurt. Only a dozen or so had been able to climb the walls. The fourth regiment of spearmen, who'd tried to batter down the gates, had also fallen thickly. The fourth regiment had suffered seriously. But Kewalo still had two hundred fresh troops in reserve. This afternoon he meant to join them with his other troops and prepare for the next attack if King Kaumuualii sent down orders. Over by the ruined village was the fifth regiment, still waiting, not used at all this morning.

Sam growled it had been a mistake for Jeff and him to think they could serve to much purpose by sniping from that trading house. Jeffery saw that Sam had been hit hard by the loss of his ship. He had a ravaged look and his voice was harsh. He said Jeff and he had not been of much damned account this morning. Kewalo said mistakes had been made by everyone, yes. But King Kaumuualii was now satisfied the fort was not as impregnable as the Russians had claimed.

When Jeffery asked if there would be a second try at the fort, the expression on Kewalo's grave, lined face momentarily became savage. He leaned forward. They were not quitting. This was only the beginning.

Sam and Jeffery were ordered to remain at headquarters. Once again, for several hours, it seemed to Jeffery as if everything had stopped. Now and then they heard sudden spurts of musket firing from the fort. In middle afternoon the remaining Russian ships sailed as close to the sand bars as they dared, releasing several broadsides of grapeshot. It rained and ceased raining. An hour before sunset a runner arrived from the eastern heights and said the king wanted the haoles.

King Kaumualii's pavilion was erected among the trees about a quarter of a mile east from the eastern wall of the Whymea Gorge. All around his pavilion were camped men of the first regiment. Kaumuualii was planning a second attack tomorrow morning. The palavering went on into the night.

Jeffery had slumped from fatigue but roused when Sam nudged him and whispered, "You'd better listen to what he's saying, Jeff. You and me might git separated tomorrow."

The king had marked a diagram of the fort in the earth with a spear. The attack tomorrow would begin exactly as it had this morning. What remained of the first and second regiments were ordered to regroup, one feinting once more at Russian ships in the harbor, the other a second time to come from the seaside under the fort's walls. Jeffery saw a young chief's face quiver and instantly become impassive. Jeffery surmised that was the chief selected to lead the regiment ordered to attack the fort's walls. Perhaps for an instant he had wondered how many of his men would be alive by noon tomorrow.

The king ordered Kewalo to attack once more at the gate. Now, however, the king revised his tactics from this morning. Tomorrow's attack was to be only a feint. Kewalo's troops were to strike once at the gate, draw off rapidly, and next charge north along the angle of earthen walls. At the same time the fifth regiment of a thousand spearmen would be signaled to charge out from the village, the whole tide of them attempting to mount the north and northeastern slopes by vaulting with their spears.

The king now turned to Sam and Jeffery. He said his original plan of having the two haoles stationed here on the heights was better—but he said it without rancor. Jeffery saw him in a different light tonight. He had thought of him as being vain and rather pompous, attempting to ape haole ways. Now he seemed to see a big brown-faced man, working phlegmatically but steadily, wearing a feather cloak instead of a military uniform. Jeffery had the impression that Kaumuualii was doing his job and was doing it well. Perhaps Kaumuualii did not measure up to his old huge enemy, Tamehameha, in strategy and foresight. With Tamehameha last November, when the *Rurick* had appeared off Kailua, Jeffery had had a sense of exhilaration. There was nothing of that tonight, merely a sense of a steady and relentless grinding away against obstacles. Where Tamehameha might have improvised brilliantly after the first day's setback, Kaumuualii was hunching his shoulders and planning to take more punishment.

The king said the Russians had mounted twenty cannons on the island side of the fort and reports this afternoon indicated they were making furious attempts to haul more cannons from the sea side around to the north approaches. North from the fort the ground between the river and the cliffs was rocky, covered with outcroppings of lava, with rows of trees growing along the rise to the cliffs. The king believed his troops from the village could get within a fair distance of the fort, and be protected from salvos of grapeshot by the ground cover and by the trees.

He ordered Sam and Jeffery to start sniping at the cannoneers at dawn and to keep firing. He hoped their shots—and much more, the stones and fire arrows from the first regiment—would interrupt enough salvos for the spearmen below to swarm up over the walls. Kaumuualii had great hopes of actually getting into the fort, but if the attack failed tomorrow, he announced, he would lay siege to the fort to try to starve out Scheffer, the Russians, the Kodiaks. That gave Jeffery a coldness. Susan? A siege might last for months.

He listened to Kaumuualii harangue the assembled aliis and kahunas. Kaumuualii was also concerned about having to delay. If he failed to capture the fort and had to besiege it, Tamehameha might arrive with ten thousand warriors from the south.

Not so very long ago Jeffery had had great faith in Tamehameha, but no longer. Tamehameha had used Susan. He had used Jeffery.

If he landed here with his men, Jeffery could understand Kaumuualii's apprehensions.

Before the assembly broke up that night, King Kaumuualii handed Sam and Jeffery two yellow and red feather cloaks. They were short cloaks, not the long cloaks for ceremonial wear. Kaumuualii informed them they were to wear the cloaks tomorrow and not to remove them even if the day became hot. He was stern about it.

Neither of the two haoles was known by the wild mountain men up here. He did not want to lose his two haoles by having his mountain men take them for two Russians foraying from the fort. To make more certain of Sam and Jeffery's safety, Kaumuualii issued orders to the squat dark-skinned chief to have a warning carried to all the mountain men hiding along the top of the gorge that the two haoles wearing the king's feather cloaks were to receive every protection.

Jeffery slept that night. He slept like a log, solid, all the way through. After closing his eyes it seemed to him it was only the next minute when Sam was shaking him awake. They had less than one hour before dawn to get across to the edge of the gorge.

It was different from yesterday morning. Jeffery could look down and see a mist wreathing and forming and re-forming, with the sea out there showing through great ragged gaps of fog or mist. The sun came up, red and gold and amber; the sky streaking and blazing and rainbows arching.

Sam and Jeffery climbed down fifty or sixty feet and found a nook of sorts between crimson rocks, a koa tree growing below them. As dawn spread and turned the mist to fire, Jeffery could see hundreds of the mountain men cautiously edging down and down, trying to get as close to the fort as they dared.

Now the sun was red and round, light spreading fast. Jeffery looked down and down and saw the shape of the fort emerge and it was like resting on the back of a great bird, the fort below him. He could make out the parade grounds, Kodiaks drawn up there—and the barracks and the smaller stone huts which, he remembered, the Russian officer had used. He hoped Susan was safe in one of those huts. The barracks was of wood. It looked—from here—as if the roof had been charred yesterday. He tried not to think of Susan.

If only, he thought, he could have a sight at Scheffer this morning! He prayed silently and violently. Please, God, give me my chance. Give my enemy over to me . . .

Suddenly, two of the mountain men above Jeffery plunged their kapa-wrapped spears in the brush fire, then hurled them down. One spear landed outside the walls. The other carried well inside, landing a few yards to the east of the wooden barracks, burning harmlessly.

Sam said, "You're a better shot than I am with muskets. You take mine as well as Tony's and try to pick off the gunners to the river side. I'll use my pistols for the near side."

"No, look here," Jeffery said. He pointed to a ledge below the tree. "I'm going down there. I'll have a better chance down there."

"Then I'm coming with you," Sam replied.

---

30. Muskets rattled as they lowered themselves to the ledge of rose and crimson streaked lava. There was sweet-smelling grass growing in the grooves and weathered surfaces of rock. Here, on the east side of the gorge's mouth, the fort and the river below, the sea spreading out beyond, the incline downwards was broken by pinnacles and spires and fallen masses of rock. It was more like a steep slope of hills, trees growing here and there upon it, than the precipitous drop of cliffs.

Jeffery, crouching in the grass, cautiously thrust the long barrel of one musket between two rocks. Not far from him, he heard the heavy familiar barking thump as Sam fired a horse pistol.

Like falling comets, a flight of fire arrows streaked downwards. From where Jeffery lay, the fort below him spread in distorted perspective, a great crabbed ugly-looking barnyard, and he saw some Kodiaks and Russians, all appearing about as large as children's dolls, dragging four more ships' cannons to the wooden trestles. Farther on, the men inside the fort, the cannons, and the buildings, all progressively diminished in size.

The mountain men hugged the sides of the cliff, hiding behind pinnacles and rocks. As daylight increased, their stones and burning arrows and fire spears poured well within the northwestern lines of the fort. Even as Jeffery watched he saw three flaming spears strike the roof of the armory, blazing brightly before falling to the ground.

The whole attack from the cliffs was concentrated on this single northeast section of the fort in an attempt to silence the cannons covering the approaches toward the village. Jeffery was firing steadily, no longer very much aware of anything that was happening save in that spot below where struggling Kodiaks were attempting to bring cannons around to get at the men on the cliff.

From somewhere, shell horns were blowing faintly. The tattered remnants of the third regiment of skirmishers set up a howling which came faintly to Jeffery when the warriors charged from the beach and once again tried to throw grappling hooks of bent bamboo over the stone walls, to the south.

Sam had ceased firing to reload his pistols. He shouted, "By God! There they come from the river!"

Jeffery raised his head an instant, seeing very little. The river was a bluish-green smear beyond the fort. Men were now charging, a brownish moving flow like muddy water, the smoke half hiding them. In a minute or so, the fifth regiment of spearmen would come out from those trees at the north.

Jeffery aimed downward. It was different from shooting squirrels off tree branches in a Pennsylvania forest. He felt a wild excitement. His heart was racing like a mill pump in a spring freshet. Around him was a noise like a hundred Fourth of Julys all on the same day. The ships' cannons on the inner edge of the earthen fortifications were mounted on heavily constructed wooden trestles, nothing at all to compare with the finished stonework inner runways along the five points to the south. Scheffer obviously had not anticipated having to stand off an attack from inland.

There came a thin screaming from the gates. Through the smoke, Jeffery caught glimpses of the ragged row of Kodiaks shooting down on the river side at Kewalo's spearmen battering the gates.

What looked like a great bird suddenly went hurling past his eyes, falling, striking a rock and bounding straight up, the shape changing into a naked islander, who crumpled limply.

Jeffery became aware of a pattering near him. At first he thought the mountain men were hurling their stones at him; then, with a start, he realized the squadron of Kodiaks below were firing up at Sam and him in volleys. A little figure down there was waving a sword. Jeffery got that figure in his sights and fired. Sam shot off his pistols again. Now the cluster of Kodiaks was breaking away from the cannon.

Demons began yelling. The fifth makalawu of spearmen had started its charge from the north. Kewalo's men swerved around and away from the gates and a whole furious mob was down there attempting to climb the earth mounds. No longer trying to protect themselves by crouching behind rocks, mountain men slid down from the cliffs. In that brief space of time, the slingshots and Sam and Jeffery's shots temporarily demoralized six cannoneers. Sam was swearing at the top of his lungs. Jeffery saw the shapes of the island warriors as though reduced through the wrong end of a spyglass. They came hurtling out of smoke and mist, leaping upwards on their spears, like jumping frogs more than birds.

The cannons were discharging more raggedly. Jeffery saw a cluster of perhaps a dozen spearmen on top of the earth walls, more climbing up. He heard the yells and shouts of triumph. He felt as if his own throat was splitting and realized that he was yelling encouragement along with all the mountain men clinging up here to the cliff.

"Christ, Sam! Look at them!" Jeffery slung over his shoulder the musket which had belonged to Tony Allan and took up the one Sam had given him. "I'm going down to hunt for Susan. Cover me."

"Not yet. Wait a minute. Make certain, first."

"To hell with making certain. Cover me!"

"Damn me if you'll go down alone."

Jeffery jumped. He landed ten feet below, rolled, and came up with a thump against a tree which all but knocked the breath out of him. Sam followed more warily. Jeffery lowered himself down a slide of rock, held himself flat, and blinked lava dust from his eyes when a musket shot whined and splattered next to him.

The crashing of cannons was louder. To his left a score of wild makaainanas were standing, whirling their slings, loosing stones straight across into the dust and confusion and smoke of the walls.

As he got down lower, Jeffery had the illusion of seeing the massive brown walls of the fort tilt away and become steeper, much steeper than he had realized they were. He was deafened when cannons at the embrasures west of him volleyed grapeshot toward the brown flood still coming in from the north. He crouched behind lava rocks, taking his time to aim, shooting one musket after the other. He saw a Kodiak throw up his hands and stagger before a reddish-brown cloud of dust and smoke hid everything below him. He reloaded both muskets, again slinging one in reserve over his shoulder.

So close to him that he could have touched them with his musket barrel, two enormous spearmen ran below and swerved and vaulted up on the earth walls. Musket firing was incessant. In the emergency, Scheffer or his officers must have deployed all the forces from the south walls in a charge toward the north end. The spearmen broke and fled, streaming back toward the trees; the fort still held.

Jeffery heard Sam calling, telling him for God's sake to get down. Sam squirmed a few yards, rolling to his side while he loaded his pistols. He said, "We're in hell's own pitch down here if they're retreating. See if we can git to that gully. We'll crawl along it till we git north where the trees are."

Halfway along the gully there was an open space. Something fanned air at Jeffery. He put his hand stupidly to his cheek and found his palm was smeared crimson. Sam punched him on the leg. "Hurry, damn it."

Jeffery began crawling faster. He was closer to the trees. He could see knots of men clustering together, chiefs shouting orders for them to re-form for another charge. Jeffery looked back. At first he didn't see Sam at all—and then his heart stopped a beat. It was like having everything inside of him come to a stop. He got himself turned around and went back to Sam. Two islanders slipped forward through the grass to help and an interval came and went. Then, presently, Sam was carried inside a half-burned hut and laid upon lahala mats, sunlight showing through the scorched blackened holes of the roof. Jeffery was standing. Someone had hold of his arm. Across all the years his aunt's voice came to him, saying she hoped he would grow into a big man. His father had been a big man. He remembered that wintery morning when he had gone out upon the wharf in Baltimore and first had met Sam Crowell and

Sam had looked down at him, not saying anything for nearly a minute. He had a detached surprise at the flood of trivialities rushing into his mind as if to blur and shield his mind in this stricken interval.

A kahuna was kneeling over Sam. All his life Jeffery would remember every detail inside this miserable shattered native hut, the poles at all angles, the floor of dirt, the broken calabashes strewn around his feet.

It was raining and the kahuna had tried to wrap thick kapa cloth around Sam's grizzled head. Jeffery could not yet tell whether the musket shot had only grazed his skull or was buried in deep.

"Sam," Jeffery said, and then louder. "Sam. Sam!"

Sam looked up at Jeffery. "Jeff—" he said. "Damn if we'll let that feller Scheffer—"

He stopped speaking abruptly. His eyes filled with astonishment at what was happening to him. Jeffery stooped lower, when a second time Sam tried to speak. Sam cawed wordlessly. Then, a third time, he made the effort. He said, "Jeff, ain't this the beatingest thing yet?" and that was all he said. It was all he ever would say. The eyes still remained open but they were no longer surprised at anything.

Kewalo sent a messenger to bring Jeffery. The runner announced breathlessly that King Kaumuualii was on his way down from the heights. Jeffery picked up Sam's big pistol and thrust it in his belt. The other pistols were scattered along the bloody gully where Sam had fallen after being hit.

Numbly Jeffery pulled the pistol from his belt. He rammed the wooden rod into the barrel. Sam's charge was still in there, ready to be fired. He returned the pistol to his belt, slung Tony Allan's musket over his right shoulder, took Sam's musket in his hands, and without looking back followed after the runner.

He followed the messenger through the trees, hearing the steady thumps of cannons from the fort, half surprised because he had thought the fighting had ceased.

King Kaumuualii was already there, streaked with sweat. He told Jeffery to wait, and finished giving instructions to the chiefs. The wooden timbers supporting the trestles on which the cannons were mounted had caught fire at the north end of the fort. The oily koa timbers were still blazing. Right now was the time to throw a second attack. He gave orders to rally all the spearmen and skirmishers for a final effort. Runners darted away, some to the river, others toward the base of the cliff.

He turned to Jeffery. Jeffery would stay with him during the attack. He asked Jeffery to hold his fire until he got close enough to the walls to kill or disable the gunners, firing the cannons east of where all the trestles were on fire.

Kewalo blew his shell horn and went hobbling through the trees with his men gathering behind him. The king ran like a bear, taking quick heavy steps which covered more ground than Jeffery would have believed possible.

Through rain and mist and smoke came several shattering explosions. Screaming warriors raced along on either side of Jeffery while others converged ahead of their king to protect him. Black smoke gushed. A man next to Jeffery went into the sand, feet kicking upwards, falling limply. The most awful blast in all the world unexpectedly went off somewhere near Jeffery, killing or maiming a dozen warriors behind the king.

When Jeffery half fell against slippery earthen walls he had no coherent idea of how he had arrived. In the instant, he saw a shape rising, all humped and cramped, on a twenty-foot spear. Now groups of four, of six, then dozens of warriors, went flying into red air on their spears, vaulting to the top of the earthen mound, digging their heels and fingers to climb higher, smashing with their clubs or sharks' teeth swords.

The king was hauled up on top. Hands reached for Jeffery. A wave of heat scorched one side of his face. He saw Kaumuualii straight before him, wading in against a pack of little Kodiaks who were desperately attempting to swing a cannon dead around in order to clear away the warriors who had breached the fort's wall.

Jeffery had lost Sam's musket in running. He used Sam's big pistol. He felt the jar of the concussion in his wrist. The Kodiak who had been trying to touch off the cannon staggered, and fell from the wooden trestle to the ground.

Jeffery steadied himself a moment, unslinging the other musket and getting it in the crook of his arm. The island fighting men poured in around their king, thrusting with the shark-toothed swords or smashing with the war clubs. Smoke billowed thickly.

Then the king jumped down, fifteen feet, to lead the fighting there. Jeffery jumped after him. He caught sight of an officer running around the barracks building. The officer stopped short and knelt, supporting his pistol hand with his left fist, coolly trying to get a bead on the king. Jeffery had perhaps six seconds. This one, he thought, is for Sam; and he pulled the trigger. The officer sat down stupidly. When Jeffery ran past him, the officer was still sitting stupidly, his back against the barracks wall, his head slumped on his chest with something like a red third eye in the middle of his forehead.

Off by the gates a cannon suddenly exploded with a sheet of flame and a roar which came echoing back from the cliffs. Jeffery passed between the big barracks and the armory, kneeling while he reloaded. A second wave of islanders was sweeping in from the north walls, driving the Kodiaks before them. Someone careened into Jeffery. A musket was discharged loudly near his face; a gush of hotness poured past his shoulder. He felt the blast through the thick feather cloak.

Immediately afterwards, air and earth shook. Jeffery had a dazed idea his musket had burst its barrel. Then it was like that time years ago at Grey's Fort, when the cannon had exploded. He felt himself flopping to the ground, drafts of heat waves flooding over him from the explosion in the armory.

He staggered to his feet. He went forward, toward the parade grounds. The fighting was at the southeast angle of the fort, and around the gates. To his right, the shattered armory was ablaze now. A Russian bugle sounded thinly.

He shouted, "Susan! Susan!" He ran drunkenly east of the parade grounds in search of her, along stone walls now deserted. He reached the stone house which he remembered Scheffer used to occupy, and with the butt of his rifle knocked open the door. "Susan!"

No one was in here. Chairs and tables were overturned. The rooms were empty, the filing cases smashed, the shelves stripped bare. Around the next angle of the south walls was the second stone house. It was as empty as the first.

Jeffery was like a man demented. He shouted, "Susan!" and ran through the echoing halls to the door. A pall of smoke hung over the parade grounds before him, with fire blazing to the north. To the west, muskets were spitting with snaps like dry sticks cracking, where some Kodiaks were making a determined stand. One square of them had knelt while a second and inner square volleyed over their heads. A cluster of Russian officers remained in the center of the double square. But Scheffer was not among them.

Jeffery halted, wiping his eyes with a ragged arm. He sighted through smoke, catching a glimpse of the big barracks building, bleak and bare in the glare of the burning armory. He loped across the parade grounds, his musket in the crook of his right arm. When he ran past the flagstaff, he saw the Russian flag still waving. He went on. Someone else could pull down the Russian standard.

He heard a steady yelling from outside the gate where the king's skirmishers were evidently still smashing at the gate with a koa log. Shapes ran past him. At the second blow from the musket butt, the barracks door gave way. Jeffery stepped warily within the dimness.

The barracks were empty. The soldiers were gone. Jeffery turned left, going into the guardroom. He pulled open the thick slab of door hinged by iron triangles to the massive corner post and descended the steps cut into lava stone. The cries and shots of the fighting came more faintly.

The dungeon had always been like a great foul stone cellar under the barracks with a kind of half-light, a quarter-light, coming through from cracks in the rough planking above and from the slits opening into the cells. The steps from the guardroom entered the main passage at a right angle, and halfway down, Jeffery heard a low murmur of voices.

Keeping his shoulder close to the stone wall at his left, he descended as noiselessly as possible. Cautiously, he peered around the corner. About fifteen feet from the steps, directly in front of the cell in which Ben Partridge and he had been locked for so many months, Jeffery saw a sight which quickened him with a feeling of exaltation. It was like having fine wine flow through his veins. Scheffer had been delivered over to him.

Between them, two Kodiaks were lugging an iron specie box into Jeffery's old cell. To one side walked Scheffer, holding a lantern which he was engaged in lighting. His back to Jeffery, he had bent his head, striking flint and steel, striking again, a yellow light now forming a yellow circle around the lantern.

A third Kodiak emerged from Jeffery's old cell to help lift the box. It looked heavy and solid. Jeffery looked back toward Scheffer. He had never forgotten the worm hole which Ben Partridge and he had dug and scraped to the sea, deep down in that splitting of lava rock but he had never thought that Scheffer by enlarging it might have made a passage for escaping.

Scheffer was running off! He must have deliberately ordered his officers and Kodiaks to make a stand as long as they could while he got away. How he had managed it, by what promises or lies, Jeffery did not know. He did not care.

Very deliberately, Jeffery brought his musket to his shoulder. Hidden in the deep shadows, he watched Scheffer raise the lantern to shine light into the cell as the three Kodiaks dragged the specie box and vanished inside. Scheffer's head was shiny and pale in that dull light.

Jeffery still held his fire. His arm trembled. He did not know where Susan was or what had become of her. It was agonizing. If he shot Scheffer he might not learn in time what Scheffer had done with her.

He stepped forward, forgetting his caution. Scheffer instantly swung around, his right hand pawing at his side for the pistol thrust into his belt. He saw Jeffery come into the circle of lanternlight. His breath sucked in hard. He whistled very softly, his arms lifting little by little above his head. He said, very softly as if not to jar Jeffery by the sound of his words, "Shoot, sir. If you do, it will be the same as if you shot Miss Susan!" He never took his eyes off Jeffery's face.

"Where is she?"

"Safe by now aboard the *Otkrytie* to be used as hostage, sir, in case you lied to me that Tamehameha has offered me a maru for a safe passage. Put down your musket. I mean neither you nor her any harm."

"I've waited a long time," Jeffery said and pushed the musket barrel into Scheffer's hard belly. Jeffery held it there with the stock under his right arm, his finger curved around the trigger. With his left hand he reached carefully for Scheffer's pistol.

He remained in front of Scheffer, using him as a shield against the three Kodiaks who had leaped out from the cell and were poised there, waiting, indecisive, eyes green in the lanternlight.

Scheffer took a great breath and as he did he seemed to expand and grow bigger. His silvery eyes twinkled. "Too late, sir," he said, and whistled again.

Jeffery was knocked forward as something hurtled against him from behind. He heard his musket go off with an echoing roar within the stone walls. But Scheffer had jumped to one side. Jeffery tried to twist to get at whatever was clawing at his back, as Scheffer reached for the pistol which Jeffery had dropped.

Then in a wild moving blur, Jeffery saw Scheffer step toward him. He tried to shield his head with an upflung arm. Scheffer clubbed him with the pistol barrel. Darkness shattered and Jeffery toppled, the clawing Kodiak still clinging to his shoulder.

He only knew by what Scheffer told him later of being taken along the passage under the fort and of being hauled upwards to a sand bar covered with high, heavy-smelling rushes, where a surf would be thundering in and mist from the sea and smoke from the fort would have changed the day's brightness to a gray-reddish light. Scheffer told him he had been taken to the longboat which was waiting and the longboat was rowed through a choppy sea until the great painted stern of the *Otkrytie* loomed up before them . . .

When Jeffery came to consciousness, one whole side of his head throbbed with pain, and he was lying upon a coarse linen sheet with a fur robe pulled over him. He knew he was on board a ship which was well under way, for he could feel the shiftings and lurchings, the long deep familiar roll to one side and another, and he could hear a muttering of timbers, and the faraway crash and thunder of the sea outside.

He looked up and he had an impression of a vastness, of a shining expanse which wavered before him, retreated, separated and then took on shape and line, the not unkindly eyes regarding him. In the voice of the very best of physicians, Scheffer said, "Here, now, sir. Drink this. It won't harm you. It might ease your head."

Jeffery choked. The big hands were firm. The rim of pewter cup hurt his lip. Sweet rum went down his throat, leaving a taste of aromatics on his tongue as well as rum.

Scheffer lifted him. With a sharp knife he cut away the thongs around Jeffery's hands and legs. He stepped back, the sharp knife gleaming an instant before it was thrust inside a leather case strapped under the man's bulky left arm, hidden inside the silk jacket.

The rum drink was pungent. It burned like fire in Jeffery's stomach. He looked to the left and right of Scheffer. He saw he was in a ship's berth, a berth about twice as large as any on the Clymestre. It was fitted out richly, although the brasswork trimmings were tarnished by the sea air, and the fine mahogany panels were cracked and warped from lack of care.

"Susan?" asked Jeffery.

Scheffer chuckled, thrusting his thumbs into his jacket pockets and, turning a little, indicated the bunk opposite Jeffery's. There Jeffery saw Susan, her fine thick hair light against a linen pillow. Her cheeks were pale and her eyes were closed.

Jeffery started up—and was pushed back into his bunk by Scheffer. "Let her sleep. She is alive."

"What have you done to her?"

"Opium pills, sir. It was a choice of clapping them down her gullet or giving her a rap on her head when I decided to have Captain Radesky get her out to this ship early this morning. Give her water, if she wakes and asks for it, but no food until morning. Now, come, sir; I have little time. Are your wits enough together to understand me? I have a notion of going to China, but this ship is in perilous want of water and provisions for such a voyage. Answer me straight. Have I your assurance Tamehameha will grant me his maru if I put the young lady and you into Honoruru in exchange for supplies and a safe passage?"

Jeffery listened to that cool proposal and sat quite still for a little while. He could not help but recall what old John Young had said. Tamehameha wanted Scheffer to leave the archipelago unharmed. Scheffer's death might give the Russians an excuse to return in force with a punitive expedition. It was extremely curious to think of heathen offering mercy to their enemy. Ben and Tony and Sam were dead. All their high dreams were gone.

In that silence, while Scheffer waited for an answer, Jeffery had a confused wonderment. It was something of the same wonderment he had had last November when von Kotzebue had landed at Kailua and there was a rawness in the reality of events. Was it always this way? Was there never any real triumph? Did the enemy one way or another always escape you? It was true, Jeffery let himself finally see. He had no alternative but to accept.

He heard Scheffer ask, "Can you accommodate me or not?"

"Before I embarked for Atooie, John Young told us all you would be under Tamehameha's maru. Even if we had the chance we weren't to try to kill you."

"It went hard on you?" Scheffer asked, almost gravely.

"Very hard on us," Jeffery said.

"It's enough for me, Captain Tolamy. I believe you. I believed you when first you told me. I have no more wish than Tamehameha and Young have for my death to inflame the Czar into further action against these islands."

Scheffer laughed. Jeffery always remained undecided about that sudden burst of laughter. Perhaps in his heart Scheffer knew himself well enough to be immoderately amused at having his hopes dashed of a conquest while at the same time he was getting off with his skin whole and an iron box of gold specie. Perhaps he had laughed at Tamehameha and John Young for considering him less dangerous alive to the islands than dead. The seizure of laughter ended as abruptly as it began.

He reached into his belt and passed one of his small double-barreled pistols to Jeffery. "Take it, sir. Both barrels are charged and primed. I'm on your side now and I'll ask you not to forget it later."

Scheffer was giving him a pistol? Jeffery's hand dazedly closed on the hard little German weapon.

"What's this for?"

"To use it, sir, if you have to. Take good heed. Open the door to no one." He nodded toward Susan. Except for the faint fall and rise of breath she might have been dead. "I'll leave her with you. If you hear shots and I don't come, guard yourself and her."

"Shots? You expect trouble?"

Jeffery had thought only for Susan aboard this ship if Scheffer were expecting trouble on it.

"If you call a leaking ship trouble, we have that. Last night those savages must have swum under the hull to strip several sheets of copper from our bottom . . ." He hesitated, straddling on his solid legs. The big face was quite pale but the eyes twinkled briefly.

"Now we have got ourselves on the same side, in a manner of speaking, I see no reason not to tell you the whole of it. This morning Captain Radesky had his eyes too filled with the contents of my specie box for him to look to repairing his ship. But never fear, sir. The pumps are working. I shall get us to Honoruru."

He stepped into the passage, shutting the door. Jeffery heard the dull click of a key turning.

---

31. When Jeffery sprang from the bunk his feet crumpled under him. Unsteadily he picked himself up. As he had thought, the door was locked from the outside. A wooden door bar swung from its hinge with the motion of the ship. His next act was to throw the bar heavily into its metal clamps. That would secure the door from the inside. At least no one could take the cabin by surprise.

He bent anxiously over Susan, listening to her faint breathing. He spoke her name and spoke it more urgently but there was no response. He stood, hastily glancing toward the far end of the cabin. Through the porthole a dull light revealed a small space at the ends of the bunks with a tarnished water tank fixed on the aft wall below a tarnished circular mirror.

A battered pewter cup stood in a hole in the worn mahogany shelf under the drinking tank. Hastily Jeffery filled the cup and returned to Susan but again he failed to rouse her. With a corner of the rough linen sheet he wiped the water he had spilled, and looked down haggardly at her.

Where her heavy chestnut hair fell away in damp ringlets, one temple was revealed with a tracery of bluish veins. The closed eyelids were a pale lavender in the darkening light and had a swollen look. He felt a hard pang. The past few weeks had cost Susan all the rounded prettiness of her girlhood. Grief had hollowed her cheeks and drawn the modeling of her face into something almost unbearably poignant. He turned his eyes from her, his throat hurting rawly.

For nearly all the night Jeffery watched over Susan while the ship continued sluggishly through heavy seas. Several times his body reeled from exhaustion and slumped, but his mind would not let go. He would come awake almost instantly, with his hand clenched on the pistol.

To keep awake he made a dream for himself. All would be well. In due time the ship would arrive in Honoruru and Scheffer, the captain, and the crew would be delivered to Governor Young or Billy Pitt. The sun would be shining. The air would be soft and fresh after the rains. He would ask Captain Adams to sail Susan and himself beyond the reefs for the deep-sea wedding ceremony.

He was conscious of a feeling of infinite gratitude to Susan for loving him. He wished she were awake for him to pour out his feelings to her. How narrowly he had escaped having his own future shaped after the pattern in that heroic romance which so many months ago Rebecca had given him to read. The knight in *Polexandre* had had his victory, his triumph, rewarding himself with Princess Alcidiane at the end. But, Jeffery reflected, it was never quite that easy or simple. The story had stopped short, without explaining how the knight managed to live happily ever afterward while owing everything he had to a rich wife. It would be galling even if you had married for love and not merely for ambition. Without love, very quickly such a marriage would become intolerable. There was always something a little shamefaced and defensive in any man who had married wealth. No one, Jeffery reflected, escaped paying his dues. At the least, it would be a continuous toll on a man's pride in himself.

By having found Susan here in the Pacific he could assure himself he was saved in time from a rich bed with nettles and thorns most likely strewn over sheets of the finest silk. Even with her father dead, all lost which once her father had acquired, in herself Susan had such a store of richness that Jeffery could tell himself without a single qualm that he would not trade as much as a lock of her hair for a dozen Alcidianes and all their rich ships loaded with spices and silks. With Susan soon to be his, Jeffery had not the slightest doubt any more that the two of them would possess all of the world a man and woman ever could desire because all else would follow even to a steam-machine works.

As he waited in the blackness, the ship laboring, timbers creaking monotonously, no one yet coming into the gallery beyond the barred door, Susan's hand in his, he became a little more aware than before that there had been a victory on Atooie; that a new wind would blow across the Pacific around the world; that Ben and Sam and Tony had greatly helped to pay for it; and that by the grace of God and unsparing efforts of these same three friends he was alive and once more with Susan.

He was brought up from sleep by someone attempting to get into the cabin. It was early morning. He grasped his pistol, cocking the double hammers as his feet touched the planks. He cast a hasty glance at Susan, who now lay on her side as if only in deep sleep.

Scheffer's voice came muffled through the oak door. "Open up."

Jeffery threw up the wooden bar and stepped back, ready to fire. Scheffer entered alone, looked carelessly at Jeffery, calmly turned his back to him, and felt Susan's pulse. He placed a hand on her forehead and nodded to himself as if satisfied. He turned, regarding Jeffery for a moment, then told him good-naturedly, "You won't need that any longer, young man," and extended his large blunt hand to receive back his pistol.

"No, I'll keep it."

"As you wish," Scheffer said indifferently and nodded toward Susan. "She's beginning to come around a bit. Give her another two or three hours and she'll be as good as new."

Jeffery slowly lowered the pistol. "Are we still bound for Honolulu?"

"Why, sir, I told you last night we were."

"I'd like to see the ship's captain and have him assure me."

"I can't accommodate you on that. Captain Radesky took leave of us sometime early this morning."

"Took—leave of us?" said Jeffery rather stupidly.

"I told you I was on your side now, didn't I? I would have been down to see you sooner but it has taken me time to have the crew understand who's master." Scheffer bent a rather strange look upon Jeffery. "You see, sir, Captain Radesky wanted us to sail to New Archangel. Now, we couldn't allow that, could we?"

Jeffery felt his flesh crawl. Scheffer must have gone into the great cabin last night or somewhere above deck in the wet and windy blackness to stalk the captain and kill him. He could not help saying dryly, "You weren't willing to share your specie with him. That's why you murdered him?"

"On my oath, sir—" Scheffer appeared perplexed by Jeffery's unreasonableness. "On my oath, you should thank me for having gone to no little trouble for the three of us. The plain truth of it is, Captain Radesky refused to accommodate himself to sailing us to Honoruru. Now, sir, because I take it an honor to have you aboard as a guest, I would have ordered the cook to bring down your breakfast to you, but ten minutes ago we sighted a sail to the south. It won't surprise me if the Taamana isn't approaching to scout these waters. If you'll join me on deck, we'll have another look." He had gone toward the door, but turned, regarding Jeffery. "If it is the Taamana, I trust you'll remember I have saved Miss Susan and you this last night. I will expect you to do the same for me."

It was the Taamana. Within twenty minutes she was close enough for Scheffer to hail her. In fifteen minutes more John Young, Billy Pitt, and six aliis had come aboard. There were questions and explanations. The Taamana had cruised in these waters until Cap Adams had intercepted the canoe bearing the message Kaumuualii had sent to Kailua. Cap Adams had sailed the Taamana back to Honoruru to report to John Young of a battle about to be fought on Atooie. Two nights ago the Taamana again had sailed in the hope of bearing in close enough to Whymea either to observe what was happening or to get a man ashore to obtain intelligence.

Jeffery gave them the news of the victory on Atooie and had to break off for a little time while Billy Pitt and the aliis hugged him and lifted him up and shouted. Then Jeffery freed himself. He said both Sam Crowell and Tony Allan were dead. That cast a stillness upon the chiefs. Next, he explained a little of how King Kaumuualii had achieved the victory by locating the single weakness on the land side of the fort; he told them of how Susan had been taken and was aboard this ship; and with a glance at Scheffer, he said, now rather raggedly, that he had passed on Governor Young's promise of the king's maru to Dr. Scheffer . . .

Then Jeffery paused. He gathered his breath and seemed to gather himself, too. He told Governor Young, "Susan learned from

Kaumuualii her father died last November in the tunnel. You and Tamehameha knew he was dead before you sent her to Atooie, didn't you?"

Governor Young never flinched from the look Jeffery gave him. "Ay," he answered. "We knew."

"But you let her go?"

"Ay," said the old man, "and I will listen to w'at ye might 'ave thought to say and so will Tamehameha. 'Tis the least we could do for ye. But I must ask ye to wait till after we 'ave dealt with this ship and Scheffer."

Jeffery took another breath and all at once had to look away; for perhaps as much as a minute no one said a word. There was only the wind crying in the rigging and the sound of all the rushing water.

"About Scheffer?" he said, finally.

"We'll put w'at men we can spare from the *Taamana* aboard the *Otkrytie* to get 'er to Honoruru and see that Scheffer is protected from the natives till we're rid of 'im."

"I take that kindly, sir," Scheffer said. "Governor, you're a man of your word. I knew I was safe to trust Captain Tolamy in giving me your assurance of Tamehameha's maru."

The flaky eyes flicked toward Scheffer. Then as if Scheffer had not spoken, Governor Young said to Jeffery, "Will ye step over 'ere with me, captain?" Taking his arm, he led him a little distance along the quarter-deck to the port rail. " 'Ow's Susan? Bad off?"

"She's still unconscious. Scheffer says she'll come to in two or three hours and be as good as new. I'd like to believe him, but she needs care and attention and to be taken off this ship as soon as possible."

"I'll 'ave 'er transported to the *Taamana*, where Jade Adams can look atter 'er till she gets to Honoruru. But I must ask ye to stay aboard the *Otkrytie* and see Scheffer safely in."

"What!" Jeffery was aghast. "I'm going with Susan. I won't let her out of my sight until Cap Adams marries us and I'm not sure I'll do it afterwards until we're both safely away from the islands," he finished more calmly.

"If ye two 'ave patched up yer quarrel, I'm pleased to 'ear it. But I 'ave got to ask ye to bring Scheffer in. I can't do it because I 'ave got to get myself to Honoruru in a 'urry. I want to get word to Tamehameha the Russians are beat and for 'im to 'alt all invasion plans. I want to complete arrangements afore Scheffer arrives of 'aving 'im safely 'eld away from the natives till we can git 'im loaded aboard a ship bound for one of the continents. If I 'ad my way, I'd see Scheffer strung up now. But Tamehameha's way is better for the long view though 'tis 'ard against the grain. I want Scheffer's legs in irons and to 'ave 'im locked in one of the cabins. Ye'll be in full charge. I'll leave Billy Pitt and the aliis to bring the ship to Honoruru and watch the crew. But I want a white man aboard who knows Scheffer and who'll see 'e tries no last-minute tricks."

Jeffery did not know why he hesitated. It was true Jade Adams could take much better care of Susan than he could. He was not needed aboard the Taamana. He was needed aboard the Otkrytie. He expected Susan would think it unreasonable of him to refuse Governor Young's request. Reluctantly he agreed to remain.

Susan had not yet recovered consciousness when Jeffery carried her to the deck. It gave him a sick unsteady feeling to watch her being lowered in an olono net to the longboat below, but hands reached for her and brought her down safely. From the railing, Jeffery saw Susan taken aboard the Taamana. Cap Adams waved to him that all was well.

Before noon the Taamana had vanished to the south. The Otkrytie lagged behind with the wind steadily stiffening. The voyage was uneventful. The crew's spirit was broken. The half-castes and Kodiaks obeyed Billy Pitt without question. Men were doubled at the pumps. Scheffer had been taken to the cabin which Susan and Jeffery had occupied. His legs were clamped in irons. He was uncomplaining. He slept eighteen hours straight through before awakening, refreshed; and he ate the food placed before him with a good appetite.

Early Thursday morning the Otkrytie wallowed through heavy seas and rapidly thickening weather past the mouth of Pearl Island River and the salt flats to stand off the reefs of Honoruru Bay. Billy Pitt fired a cannon to signal for canoes.

A quarter of a league away Jeffery made out a bark flying the English colors which was also standing off the reefs, evidently waiting for pilot and canoes. As the light increased and the rain ended,

Jeffery, sighting toward the harbor, made out the *Taamana* riding at anchor with another ship on beyond.

Billy Pitt fired a second cannon. No canoes had put out, but a peleloo was launched. It sliced through the rolling sea and came in under the *Otkrytie's* leeside very neatly, receiving lines cast down to her. The kanakas in her port hull held her off with their heavy oars while Governor Young came nimbly up the ladder, followed by George Beckly.

Billy Pitt and Jeffery greeted them amidships. Jeffery's first question was about Susan. The old man looked at him coldly a moment. Then he said curtly that the *Taamana* had made port yesterday. Susan had recovered from the opium Scheffer had forced her to take. He would answer other questions after he had attended to Scheffer.

Jeffery felt that he deserved a little more consideration than this but he swallowed his annoyance and listened to Governor Young explain to Billy Pitt what had been arranged for Scheffer. The English bark, the *Santa Rosa*, was bound for China. She had come in two days ago to pick up four kanakas for her crew before sailing. Captain Deal was her master and he had consented to take Scheffer aboard and get him as far as Canton. Before daybreak this morning, Governor Young had had canoes tow the *Santa Rosa* out of the harbor to stand off the reefs and wait for the *Otkrytie*. It would save bringing Scheffer into the harbor where Governor Young feared the natives might try to kill him despite Tamehameha's maru. Scheffer was to be taken off to the *Santa Rosa* before the threatening storm broke.

Jeffery waited on deck with Governor Young while Billy Pitt and George Beckly went below for Scheffer. "Where's Susan? At the fort?"

Governor Young faced him. "She's aboard 'er ship."

"Her ship? What are you talking about?"

"The *Fair Marion*." Governor Young pointed. "Look there, and ye'll see it, near the *Taamana*."

Jeffery was stunned. Partridge had lost both his ships. Governor Young said that was the report. One ship had been lost in a typhoon but the *Fair Marion* was the other and it had arrived two days ago from Australia after a successful voyage from England. The report that she had been captured by Malay pirates was false. She had been half a year in the service of the Sultan of Mindanao, who had sailed to England, according to what Governor Young had learned from her master, with a cargo of silks and spices valued at over a third of a million dollars. The *Fair Marion* had returned by way of India and China, picking up a second cargo, and had put in at Sydney Cove for any word or instructions which might have arrived there from her owner in the islands. Upon learning that Ben Partridge was taken by the Russians, instead of sailing for New York by way of the Horn, the *Fair Marion's* master had sailed directly for the Sandwich Islands.

"Susan's sailing on 'er ship as soon as Captain Fenwick can finish provisioning the ship with food and water. And," added Governor Young, his deep voice hard and cutting, "w'at ye led me to think was wrong. She is not marrying ye."

"By God, it's not true. What has she told you?"

" 'Tis an ugly thing, captain. I think ye know w'at it is."

Jeffery knew of the ugly thing he had done, but in the pavilion by the Whymea River she had told him she still loved him and would marry him. He said, "I'd like to get to her."

"Ye 'ave done a large service to the islands, captain. If ye want to go to 'er, 'tis not me to stop ye. Take the peleloo. We'll transport Scheffer to the *Santa Rosa* by one of the *Otkrytie's* longboats. Ye'll 'ave may'ap 'alf an 'our afore the storm 'its."

Jeffery was descending the ladder to the peleloo when he heard someone crying his name. He looked up and saw Scheffer's pale broad face. A wave licked Jeffery's legs. Hands took hold of him and brought him down to the starboard hull of the peleloo. He looked across the widening gap and saw Scheffer there on the midship's deck between Young and Beckly. Scheffer had given up calling to him. Jeffery did not know what Scheffer had wanted of him at the last minute and did not care. He saw the broad face very clearly above the broad shoulders and Scheffer was waving urgently to him; and then a mist swept down. It was the very last Jeffery ever saw of Anton Scheffer.

The peleloo went surging through the passage in the reef. The wind was beginning to blow in gusts, but the steersman came under the *Fair Marion's* stern long enough for Jeffery to catch at a line. Then Jeffery went up hand over hand in a singing immensity of spray and wind and had no thought at all of doing that which would have been impossible for him a little more than a year ago. He crawled over the railing and got his feet planted on the deck.

Two or three seamen came from the forecastle, shouting angrily at him to get off the ship. But he was half across the slippery deck when the door of the great cabin opened and a tall well-made man stepped upon the deck, buckling oilskins around him as he approached Jeffery. A blistering quiet voice demanded just who Jeffery thought he was and what he meant by boarding his ship.

Jeffery stopped. "You're the captain?"

"I'm Captain Fenwick, master of this ship, and I'll have no ruffian from the beach mixing with my men."

"I'm Tolamy. Where's Miss Partridge?"

"You're Tolamy? By God, I never believed you'd have the effrontery to come aboard to see Miss Partridge. By God, sir! I could run you through or shoot you down. After her mind cleared from that damnable opium Miss Partridge told Governor Young and me of learning at last how you had run off from her father when you could have saved him!"

Jeffery clenched his fists. He was about to give a hot reply when Captain Fenwick swung around on his heels. Unnoticed by either of them, Susan had come from the great cabin. She stopped short of Jeffery with a look of loathing.

"Susan—"

"How you lied to me! Everything you ever said to me was a lie. I had to learn from Dr. Scheffer how Pa was found dead. Under a pile of wet rubble where the tunnel had caved in on him! You could have dragged him loose. But you saved yourself while he suffocated. Oh, damn you! Damn you to perdition!"

He heard himself protesting. It was not true. It was not the fact. Her father had died from a broken back. Ben had spoken to Jeffery before dying. It was monstrously untrue. Scheffer had lied to Susan.

Jeffery protested even after the seamen had seized him. He saw Susan and Captain Fenwick conferring together away from him in the rain. He shouted for them to send for Scheffer before the Santa Rosa sailed and it was too late. But Susan disappeared into the cabin, and Captain Fenwick's cold voice said the owner's orders were to throw the man overboard and rid the ship of him as quickly as possible.

———————

32. J EFFERY was cast up on a sandy beach not because he had swum in that direction but because the force of the wind sweeping over the bay had carried him there along with a broken canoe which had been torn from its moorings. He crawled a little higher on the beach and here two kanakas found him and carried him to the fort. He recognized Kala when she picked him up and he recognized the stone sleeping chamber and the Chinese-made bed upon which she laid him.

When next he opened his eyes, he saw a makaainana girl with glossy black hair, sweeping flies from him with a tufted pole. He looked to the right. Instead of seeing the row of his books which once had been along the wall, he saw Governor Young sitting upon a chair. Jeffery tried to pull his wits together. He was not even certain whether it was still today, tomorrow or perhaps yesterday.

The deep, old voice informed him it was Friday, two hours before noon; and Jeffery had slept around the clock and a little longer. Jeffery sat up. He said one word, "Susan?"

Susan was still aboard the *Fair Marion* and her ship had not sailed. Governor Young stood up from the chair and pulled something wrapped in silk from his malo. He seemed to totter a little on his legs as he approached the bed and Jeffery heard him saying something about a letter Scheffer had written after being taken aboard the *Santa Rosa* yesterday morning. After reading the letter, Governor Young had gone by longboat directly to the *Fair Marion*, where he had thought Jeff would be. The old voice was again saying "Jeff," and no longer "Captain Tolamy."

Then Jeffery was reading a note which Scheffer had penned in his large, legible writing:

Honoruru, on board the *Santa Rosa*, 16 January, 1817
My dear Miss Partridge—
Because Captain Tolamy once did me a great disservice by destroying a valuable work of mine on the language of these

islands, in which I had asked him and your father to assist, I confess to the weakness of wishing to do him a similar disservice.

With that in mind I gave you false information regarding the death of your father. Ben Partridge died of a broken back from a rock or piece of lava which fell upon him. He was not smothered to death. He was found near the opening of his cell. He must have lived several hours or longer. No one could have saved him.

When I enlarged the tunnel for my own ends, I saw where Captain Tolamy was blocked away from your father by a slide of rubble and a split of ancient tree trunk. All this may be confirmed by the kanakas who brought out your father. Unless killed during the battle for my fort, the same kanakas should be at Whymea . . .

Jeffery saw the bold signature, "Georg Anton Scheffer." After a moment he asked, "Susan's read this?"

"Ay. She gave it to me to show to ye. She would 'ave come 'erself but I promised I'd bring ye to 'er. 'Tis not good for a female to 'ave to eat crow and come to a man even if she 'as 'ad 'im thrown overboard by a mistake."

Jeffery slowly got to his feet. He studied John Young for a moment and asked, "You and I never got along any too well, did we?"

"Ye'll not want the girl ye're to marry to be kept waiting, will ye?" The governor teetered toward the door which still creaked on its pinions as it was pulled open. He halted and appeared to reflect. "I never got along with any young cock who thought 'e knew everything and 'ad to be knocked on the 'ead before 'e'd take advice. Now, come along."

Jeffery was surprised at the great crowd gathered in the compound and all along the way to the village, with a passage opening for Governor Young and himself. Governor Young said the news had been carried all over the archipelago of the Russians' defeat. There would be feasts for weeks to come. Jeffery had flowers heaped over his shoulders. His broken nose was rubbed until it began to hurt again Billy Davis, Señor Marin, Billy Pitt, everyone whom Jeffery had ever known, were all waiting for him at the stone wharf.

When Governor Young and Jeffery got into the dugout to be paddled to the *Fair Marion*, Jeffery realized hazily that this might be only a beginning of the blaze of glory he had once thought he wanted. When he returned to his homeland he could anticipate having his hand shaken by Mr. Monroe and possibly the President of the United States. His uncle would be certain to arrange a medal which would not be too insignificant. All that he had once greatly desired would be his, but now he thought of the cost which had been paid by Sam Crowell and Ben Partridge and Tony Allan for him to have it. At the fort Governor Young had spoken as if it were understood by all that Susan and Jeffery were to be married. When Jeffery had renounced Rebecca for Susan it had once seemed to him he was renouncing as well all that which Rebecca had signified to him. It now occurred to him, as he saw the *Fair Marion* looming larger, that he had made a mistake to think of Rebecca as being an Alcidiane and perhaps she had, too. In the fable made from the reality of an age-old pattern, the Princess Alcidiane lived always in the far lands. It was the knight who searched for her and brought her to his homeland in triumph.

The canoe had come alongside the *Fair Marion* and the ladder was thrown down. "Up ye go," said Governor Young's voice.

Jeffery climbed to the deck to see Susan standing there.

When Jeffery came to her he saw her color was high and there was a golden mist of freckles over her nose. He did not know how to begin. He did not want to say anything which might bring between them the image of a man with a big pale head and eyes which sometimes had become the color of silver. Quite suddenly, without forethought, he said, "Susan, will you marry me?"

She answered candidly, "I was afraid you wouldn't ask me again and I was getting up courage to—oh, Jeffery!" She protested hastily, "Not here. We can go into the wheelhouse."

In the wheelhouse he knew that if he had ever had doubts they were gone; that if he had a toll to pay in the future he would gladly pay it; and that the truth of the matter was, there was no one like Susan and never would be and he could still not quite believe he was to have her.

She pulled herself free to study his face. "You don't look the same any more with your nose all crooked."

He asked, "How soon can we get married?"

But before replying to his question she kissed his nose very lightly and said, "Jeffery," very softly and clasped him almost fiercely. Afterwards her voice was crisp. They could not be married until Sunday because the traders wouldn't finish provisioning the ship until sometime Saturday. Captain Fenwick could sail Sunday and marry them at sea. Sunday? It seemed to Jeffery that Sunday was an appalling length of time to wait. Today was only Friday. He suggested they go ashore and have Governor Young pronounce them married and Sunday they could have a second marriage—and stopped after going that far.

"Sunday," he said finally. "All right. Hell."

She merely grinned at him . . .

He remembered something and asked, "What port are we sailing for?"

"Pa's ships usually go to New York."

"Could we stop off for a day at Kailua?"

He told her of reading in Cook's Voyages how forty years ago Tamehameha had been the principal director at the first interview with white men and how he had promised himself it was time someone for once took over being the principal director at an interview with Tamehameha.

"Jeffery, you'll fail. He's too big for people."

"I think Sam might like it if I tried, don't you?"

He felt her arms tighten. "I can't talk about Sam now. Later, I want you to tell me everything, about Sam and about Pa and about Tony Allan. But wait until tomorrow—or Sunday night . . ."

Then she said, "Yes, we must see Tamehameha for the last time. I think he must like you as much as he can like anyone. He might even let you direct the interview if he knew it was what you wanted. He is the last giant, isn't he? After he goes, no one'll ever see anyone like him again."

It was true, Jeffery thought. Tamehameha was the last giant to exist upon the earth. But he was too big, too large. You could never fix him entirely in your mind. Tamehameha had used Susan. He had used everyone and everything at hand to beat the Russians. He had moved them all like pawns on a chessboard while he remained at Kailua. He was, Jeffery told Susan, like a great neutral-colored slab of lava cliff upon which the sunlight played to change the surface into all colors before night fell and changed everything to a blackness or a radiance of stars and moon.

"I suppose you'd better tell Captain Fenwick we'll sail for Kailua before he has a chance to set another course toward the Horn?" he said at last.

She glanced up at him through her lashes before replying. Her lips curved slightly at the corners. "No, Jeffery. You tell him."

It seemed all at once to Jeffery that it was necessary to phrase his reply very carefully. "It's hardly my place to, Susan. I'll be aboard only as a passenger. You're the owner."

"Jeffery," said Susan, "when you're married to me, you'll be the owner. All I have will be yours. Please tell him."

Jeffery winced. He gave a short laugh which was not really very much of a laugh because he saw he was already beginning to have everything he once had wanted. He kissed Susan and left her smiling with something secret and tender and amused in her smile; and by himself he went down to give the captain orders to sail them south Sunday morning to the old giant waiting for them at Kailua, on the island of Owhyee.

HISTORICAL NOTE

Because, like any historical novel, *The Mission of Jeffery Tolamy* is a hybrid, the reader is entitled to ask, "How much was history and how much was fiction?" My answer is that I have taken everything I have been able to gather in the past fifteen years of informing myself about the Russian adventure in the Hawaiian Islands and have tried to reveal what did happen as it might have been experienced by a single person.

Historically, the Russian adventure took place in four stages: The seizure of Honoruru and the uprising of the common natives when Scheffer's men violated the temple; the long wait during the peace season while both sides prepared for new attacks; the visit of the *Rurick* and the meeting between Captain von Kotzebue and Tamehameha; and finally the battle for the fort on the island of Atooie—or Kauai, as it is now called. I have not knowingly deviated from the facts of these four stages.

The rule I followed was to hew to the historical sequence of events as related in available accounts, using imagination only in the placing on stage of Jeffery Tolamy as the reader's means of experiencing those events. For example, Tamehameha's conversation with the Russians was not invented. What was said was taken from *A Voyage of Discovery into the South Seas and Beering Straits*, by Otto von Kotzebue, Vol. I, London, 1821. I also used the published accounts by the artist, Louis Choris, and the naturalist, Adelbert von Chamisso, for this section of the story. Tamehameha's speech at the banquet is given as reported by von Kotzebue, with the exception of the final sentence in which the Hawaiian king asks if there is to be war. Von Kotzebue's chronicle becomes fiction only in the shift of viewpoint by which everything is seen through Jeffery's eyes.

On the question of whether or not von Kotzebue arrived in the Islands when he did by chance or as part of the Russian design to capture the archipelago I find myself at odds with Harold Whitman Bradley, whose *The American Frontier in Hawaii* (Stanford University Press, 1942) is one of the two great modern histories of early Hawaii. *The Hawaiian Kingdom, 1778–1854* (University of Hawaii, 1938), by Ralph S. Kuykendall, is the other modern history of importance. Both Bradley and Kuykendall are of the opinion that von Kotzebue's voyage was solely a voyage of discovery, as von Kotzebue claimed it was; and that the *Rurick's* timely arrival was a coincidence.

However, an intensive examination of the documents pertaining to that small interval of time in Hawaii's history casts strong doubts on von Kotzebue's claim. One of the first important historians of Hawaii was James Jackson Jarves, whose *History of the Hawaiian Islands* was published in Honolulu in 1847. Jarves is as suspicious as I am of von Kotzebue's real intentions. He goes even further, implying that there was a plot to kidnap Tamehameha. One of the native historians, David Malo (*Hawaiian Antiquities*, Honolulu, 1903) shared Jarves's apprehensions. Further, we know for certain that Captain Wilcox called on von Kotzebue in Honoruru and came away from the *Rurick* convinced of a conspiracy. Finally, when the *Rurick* arrived at Kailua, Tamehameha himself was preparing against an attack.

There is one doubtful element in the Kailua sequence. The only evidence I have for a fortification above Kailua is a line in von Chamisso's journal which states that he observed fortifications above the bay. This evidence is questionable because von Chamisso wrote in German, and the German for "fortifications" could very easily have been applied to a natural ridge.

A word on the spelling of place names and of the historical characters. I have tried to spell them as Jeffery would have heard them pronounced and as the early visitors to the Islands did spell them. But because there was no uniformity in spelling by the early travelers I have had to select one version and follow it. For example Tamehameha had a Prime Minister who took the name, "Billy Pitt." Travelers who saw him and wrote about him variously spelled his name "Kalanimoko," "Karaimoko," and, simply, "Krimoko." I've used the last because it seems to me to be easier to read. William Ellis says that "Ta Mehameha" means "The Lonely One."

In our time "Tamehameha" has become "Kamehameha." Diamond Head used to be Diamond Hill. Honolulu was written "Honoruru." Prince Liholiho used to be "Riho-riho."

With the few exceptions listed at the end of this note, all the people living in the Islands in the story did exist. After his escape from Honoruru, Scheffer was allowed to sail to Canton. In 1819 he turned up in St. Petersburg where he tried to revive interest in a second campaign against the Hawaiian Islands and failed. Governor Baranov repudiated him. Believing England had taken the Islands under her protection, as von Kotzebue must have reported, Czar Alexander I refused to listen to Scheffer and even sent King Kaumuualii a gold medal, a red cloak, and a handsomely engraved sword as tokens of Russian friendship.

Young Prince George Hoomehoome finally came to Atooie (Kauai) with the first consignment of missionaries, landing in March, 1820. In 1824, George led an abortive revolt against the government of Riho-riho, whom von Chamisso had thought to be "a young monster." In his journal the Reverend C. S. Stewart wrote:

Thursday, December 23, 1824: Karaimoku . . . has been successful in putting down the insurrection. George [Hoomehoome] who has escaped death will be brought to Honoruru and kept as a prisoner at large. The rebel party proved small in number and weak in power, all avowedly pagans, with George, a professed sceptic, at their head.

Jeffery, of course, is entirely fictional, although in a short section I merged him with the young Mr. Cook whom von Kotzebue identified as being Tamehameha's interpreter. Susan, her father, and Sam Crowell were invented to give Jeffery an emotional interior and reality in his own right. Beckly had women at the fort but I have no proof he married them; and Captain Adams seems to have had a Chinese girl for a time but I doubt if there was a ceremony. All the others did live at the time, even to the unhappy queen at Kailua who cried bitterly when told Captain Vancouver had been dead for so many years.

Darwin Teilhet
Los Altos, California